THE
ASSASSINATION
OF THE
PRIME
MINISTER

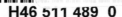

THE
ASSASSINATION
OF THE
PRIME
MINISTER

JOHN BELLINGHAM
AND THE MURDER OF
SPENCER PERCEVAL

DAVID C. HANRAHAN

The
History
Press

Cover illustration: Painting by H. Warren, engraved by J. Rogers
(Mary Evans Picture Library)

First published 2008
This paperback edition published 2012

The History Press
The Mill, Brimscombe Port
Stroud, Gloucestershire, GL5 2QG
www.thehistorypress.co.uk

British Library Cataloguing in Publication Data.
A catalogue record for this book is available from the British Library.

ISBN 978 0 7509 4401 4

Typesetting and origination by The History Press
Printed in Great Britain

CONTENTS

List of Illustrations

ACKNOWLEDGEMENTS

As with my other books, this effort would not have been possible without the help of a great number of people and institutions. I wish to thank the following: the Hardiman Library, National University of Ireland, Galway and in particular Special Collections and Inter-Library Loans; The National Archives, Kew; the British Library; the Bodleian Library, Oxford; the National Portrait Gallery, London; my friends and colleagues at the Education Department, NUI, Galway; all at The History Press. I would also like to thank my agent Robert Dudley and remember my former agent the late David O'Leary. A special word of thanks and love goes to all my family: my wonderfully supportive wife, Margaret; my daughter, Aisling, and my son, Michael, for their photographic and computer know-how, and much else besides; my mother, Mary; my brothers and their families.

I wish to note that where I have quoted from contemporary accounts, in the interest of simplicity and when it does not alter the meaning, I have, at times, modernised the spelling, capitalisation and punctuation.

Chapter 1

ASSASSINATION

On Monday 11 May 1812, an unremarkable, anonymous man, just over 40 years of age, made his way to the Palace of Westminster, the seat of government in the United Kingdom of Great Britain and Ireland. No one could have known that on the inside left of his overcoat he had a specially designed, 9-inch-deep pocket in which was hidden a loaded pistol, and elsewhere on his person he carried a second pistol. The man's thin, angular face should have been familiar to some of those within the Houses of Parliament that day, as over the past few weeks he had become a frequent visitor there, sitting in the gallery of the House of Commons and carefully examining the various members of the government through his opera glasses. No one had taken any particular notice of this quiet man nor sensed the deadly intent in his presence. At 5.00 pm on this day he walked to the lobby leading to the House of Commons and sat near the fireplace.

The business of Parliament that evening was a committee of the whole house inquiring into the Orders in Council that had placed embargoes upon French trade but that, as a result of the discomfort they were causing at home, many now wanted repealed. The place was not very busy, with only around 60 of the 658 members present. The House of Commons was in committee examining witnesses to find out whether, and if so by how much, people were suffering as a result of the Orders in Council. Mr Spencer Perceval, the Tory who held the positions of Prime Minister, or First Lord of The Treasury, and also Chancellor of the Exchequer, had not yet arrived, a fact that annoyed Henry Brougham, the member who had first brought forward the motion that had led to this Inquiry. Brougham was one of those arguing for the repeal of the Orders.

As he prepared to speak, he complained that this was the second occasion on which Mr Perceval had failed to arrive at the appointed time of 4.30 pm. He informed the Secretary of the Treasury that he would begin anyway and conclude his examination of the first witness, Mr Robert Hamilton, a potter from Stoke-on-Trent, who was arguing that the Orders in Council were ruining his trade and should be repealed.

Spencer Perceval had gained the respect of most of his colleagues at Westminster. 'His character is completely established in the House of Commons; he has acquired an authority there beyond any minister in my recollection, except Mr Pitt,' was what one future Prime Minister, Liverpool, wrote of him to another, Wellington.[1] 'The country can never be under the direction of a more honourable and virtuous man,' wrote another contemporary.[2]

By five o'clock, those members present in the House of Commons were listening to the Member of Parliament for Grinstead, Mr James Stephen, cross-examining the witness, Mr Hamilton. In the House of Lords the peers were finishing off other business before also proceeding to discuss the Orders in Council. By now the Prime Minister was on his way. It was a fine, sunny, May evening, and he had decided to dismiss his carriage and travel on foot from No. 10 Downing Street to the Palace of Westminster. As he walked along Parliament Street he was met by a messenger from the Secretary of the Treasury reminding him of the Inquiry proceeding in the House of Commons and informing him of Mr Brougham's complaint about his late arrival. On being told this, the Prime Minister quickened his walking pace. Around 5.15 pm he arrived at the Houses of Parliament.

He entered the building and walked down the corridor towards the lobby entrance to the House of Commons. He handed his coat to the officer positioned outside the doors to the lobby. William Jerdan, a journalist, was just about to enter the lobby. He pushed the right-hand panel of the high folding doors, knowing that the left-hand panel was usually locked in place. Behind him he noticed the Prime Minister approaching with his 'light and lithesome step'.[3] He greeted him and received a typically gracious greeting and smile in reply. Jerdan stood aside to allow Mr Perceval to enter.

As Perceval entered the lobby a number of people were gathered around.[4] Most turned to look at him as he came through the doorway. No one noticed as the quiet man stood up from his place beside the fireplace and removed the concealed pistol from his inner pocket. Neither did they notice as he walked calmly towards the Prime Minister. When he was close enough, he fired his pistol directly at Mr Perceval's chest. There was a moment of shocked silence around the lobby in response to the bright flash, the intense sound and the odour of gun powder. The Prime Minister staggered forward before falling to the ground, calling out as he did: 'I am murdered!'[5]

William Smith, the MP for Norwich, who had not seen the Prime Minister enter, turned around on hearing the sound of the shot and, at first, did not know who this man was who had fallen face down on the ground in front of him. It was only when he and Mr Francis Phillips, from Longsight Hall near Manchester, turned the victim over onto his back that Smith recognised the face of the Prime Minister.

Those inside the chamber of the House of Commons had also heard the loud shot ring out, followed by the sound of a disturbance. Some members left the chamber immediately and ran in the direction of the commotion, while others attempted to continue stoically with their business. Eventually the shocking news began to filter back to the chamber that someone had been shot. The confusion mounted until there was no option but to suspend the business of the House.

The sound of the shot also disturbed the business of the House of Lords, situated on the other side of the lobby. After the shot, the Peers heard a chilling shout come from outside the chamber: 'Mr Perceval is shot.' An official ran in to inform them of what had happened. Many of them crowded around the man to listen to his account. On hearing the news, everyone but Lord Chancellor Eldon and three bishops rushed out into the lobby to see for themselves.

Mr Smith and Mr Phillips, assisted by a number of others, carried Mr Perceval into the Speaker's apartments, where they placed him in a sitting position on a table, supporting him on either side. He had not uttered a single word since falling on the floor of the lobby, and the only noises to have emanated from him since had been 'a few convulsive sobs'. After a short time Mr Smith, on failing to find any perceptible sign of a pulse, came to the terrible conclusion that the Prime Minister was dead.

Mr William Lynn, a surgeon from No. 15 Great George Street, arrived on the scene and soon confirmed that Smith was correct. The surgeon noted that there was blood all over the Prime Minister's coat and white waistcoat. He examined the body and found 'a wound of skin about over the fourth rib on the left side near the breastbone'. It was obvious that this was where the large pistol ball had entered. He probed an instrument into the wound and found that 'it had passed obliquely downwards and inwards in the direction of the heart'.[6] The wound was more than 3 inches deep, and he was in no doubt but that it had caused Mr Perceval's death. The Prime Minister was not yet 50 years of age and left behind his wife, Jane, and twelve children.

Chapter 2

'I ADMIT THE FACT'

In the aftermath of the shooting, as chaos erupted in the lobby and people rushed to the scene, the assassin had not attempted to escape but had instead returned to his place near the fire and sat down. People eventually regained their senses enough to start shouting out: 'Who did it?' William Jerdan, the journalist who had entered the lobby directly behind the Prime Minister, noticed Mr Eastaff, a clerk of the Vote Office, pointing to a man beside the fire and saying: 'That is the murderer.' Henry Burgess, a solicitor from Mayfair, also heard the same claim and approached the man. Jerdan grabbed him by the collar while Burgess took the pistol. The weapon in question was described as 'a small pocket pistol, about six inches long, the barrel rather better than two inches in length, with the cock on the top, and a stop to the trigger. The calibre . . . nearly half an inch in diameter, and the barrel very strong.'[1]

As they disarmed the man, they met with no resistance. Jerdan noticed large drops of sweat running down the suspect's pallid face. His chest heaved as if in a strained effort to breathe, causing him to strike it with his hand a number of times in an attempt to get relief.[2] By this time he was surrounded by a group of angry and very agitated men. When Burgess asked him why he had done such a thing, he answered simply: 'Want of redress of grievances.' General Isaac Gascoyne grabbed him so violently that the man called out: 'You need not press me. I submit myself to justice.' The man then identified himself: 'I am the unfortunate man – I wish I were in Mr Perceval's place. My name is John Bellingham. It is a private injury – I know what I have done. It was a denial of justice on the part of Government.'[3]

The man who had identified himself as John Bellingham also freely admitted that he had another loaded pistol concealed on his person. This weapon, which was primed and loaded with one ball, was confiscated by the journalist Vincent Dowling. At 27 years of age, Dowling realised that he was witnessing the story of the century. As he looked at John Bellingham's face, Dowling now realised that he had seen this man many times before in the visitors' gallery of the House of Commons. He remembered that the assassin had, on a number of occasions, asked him the names of various members of the Cabinet as they contributed to debates. He remembered, in particular, one occasion when Bellingham had asked him to point out Mr Ryder, the Home Secretary: 'Bellingham looked at him through a glass, with great attention; and afterwards on Mr Ryder's sitting down, desired Mr D[owling] to point him out again, which he also did, when Bellingham said, "Now I cannot mistake him when we meet."'[4]

Among the assortment of objects found in his pockets were a small penknife, a bunch of keys, a pencil, a guinea in gold and his opera glasses. He also had in his possession a bundle of papers bound with red tape. These papers were obviously very important to him as, at first, he did not want to hand them over. He held them high above his head in an attempt to protect them. They were taken from him, and Joseph Hume wrapped them in paper upon which he placed his own seal before they were sent to the Foreign Secretary, Lord Castlereagh.

Bellingham was then marched into the Chamber of the House of Commons and up to the bar to face the Speaker. However, it was decided that he could not be questioned there, as he was not yet formally in legal custody. The Speaker ordered that he be brought instead to the Prison Room of the Serjeant-at-Arms, where he could be legally questioned by any Members of Parliament who were Middlesex magistrates. It was agreed that, in order to avoid the danger of the prisoner being rescued by some of his accomplices, he would not be brought back through the lobby but would instead be transported 'through the private avenues round the House'.[5] Such was the fear of an attempted escape that Mr Whitbread, Mr Long and Mr Bootle were sent ahead to make sure that the way was clear of insurgents.[6] The House of Commons was then duly adjourned.

The House of Lords reassembled and the Lord Chancellor addressed the House with the words:

> I am not certain, my lords, whether what I am now about to suggest is in exact conformity with the orders of your lordships' House; but there may be occasions when a rigid adherence to orders, established for the convenience of ordinary business, may lead to the greatest disorder. I have just been informed of a most melancholy and atrocious event, which has happened in the lobby of the other House. In this situation, I feel it my duty to apprise your lordships, that I shall take care to give the proper directions to the officers, that none go out of the doors of this House of Parliament till we have been fully satisfied that they have not the means of doing farther mischief.7

The Duke of Cumberland put it on the record that he had seen the Right Hon. Spencer Perceval wounded and lying dead in the Speaker's chamber, with a surgeon and several other persons standing around him. Richard Taylor, senior doorkeeper of the House of Commons and witness to the terrible event, was questioned for the record. He established that he had seen the pistol, heard the shot and saw the Prime Minister fall. Before the Lords adjourned they agreed an address to be presented forthwith to the Prince Regent regarding the events of the day:

> the House had heard with horror of the attack made upon, and the assassination of the right hon. Spencer Perceval, one of his Majesty's most honourable privy council, and praying that his Royal Highness would be graciously pleased to direct such steps to be taken as he should deem expedient for the apprehension of the offender or offenders.8

Bellingham was brought, without a struggle, to the Prison Room for his examination. The room soon became so overcrowded that the door had to be locked, which left a large and disgruntled crowd outside. The chair for the examination was taken by Harvey Christian Combe MP from London, assisted by Michael Angelo Taylor MP and William Watson, Serjeant-at-Arms of the House of

Lords. Witnesses began to give their evidence, including a number of people who had been in the lobby at the time of the shooting: Mr Henry Burgess from Mayfair, Mr Michael Sexton of No. 12, China Row, Lambeth, Mr Francis Romilly, a clerk working at 56 Gower Street. Meanwhile, a Bow Street Officer was dispatched to search John Bellingham's lodgings at 9 New Millman Street. Sir John Coxe Hippisley MP warned Bellingham 'not to say anything to criminate himself'.

The suspect listened calmly to the evidence being presented and seemed to agree with most of it apart from qualifying a number of small points of detail. He contradicted Burgess's evidence by saying: 'Perhaps Mr Burgess was less agitated than I was, but I think he took the pistol from my hand, and not from the bench under me.'[9] Of the force used by General Gascoyne in restraining him, he said that he had feared his arm would be broken. Gascoyne in his evidence stated that he was acquainted with the suspect. He said that he had seen him often and 'had received many petitions and memorials from him respecting some claims upon government . . .'. For the most part Bellingham remained calm and unemotional throughout the examination. The only time he was seen to shed tears was when Francis Phillips made the comment: 'I supported Mr Perceval into the secretary's room, and in a few minutes he died in my arms.'[10]

The Bow Street Officer returned from Bellingham's lodgings, with a package of things he had found tied up in a handkerchief. This was given to Lord Castlereagh to be produced later at Bellingham's trial. Bellingham defended his action with the words:

I have admitted the fact – I admit the fact, but wish, with permission, to state something in my justification. I have been denied the redress of my grievances by Government; I have been illtreated. They all know who I am, and what I am, through the Secretary of State and Mr Beckett, with whom I have had frequent communications. They knew of this fact six weeks ago, through the Magistrates of Bow Street . . . I . . . have sought redress in vain. I am a most unfortunate man and feel here . . . sufficient justification for what I have done.[11]

He was informed by Lord Castlereagh that this was not the time for a defence of his actions, but merely for a contradiction of the accusation of murder, if one was merited. In reply, Bellingham said: 'Since it seems best to you that I should not now explain the causes of my conduct, I will leave it until the day of my trial, when my country will have an opportunity of judging whether I am right or wrong.'[12]

When the examination was concluded, two Bow Street Officers handcuffed him. He asked that his money be returned to him, but, since Burgess had already left with it, he was promised that it would be returned in the morning. This he accepted.

As the news of this terrible occurrence began to spread, there was a growing sense of fear. Many people believed that John Bellingham's heinous act represented only the initial blow in a more widespread outbreak of anarchic violence and rebellion to come. There had already been evidence that the lower classes in society were ready to rise up in violent revolt. It was well recognised that the poor state of the economy, the war with France and the hardship caused by the Orders in Council, among other issues, were leading to unrest in the country. In Lord Holland's words: 'All expressed horror; some few seemed to ponder on the changes likely to ensue, and more were manifesting apprehension that the crime was connected with extensive designs, and the result of conspiracies which the state of the country rendered by no means improbable.'[13]

The sheriffs went to the Mansion House, where they had an urgent meeting with the Lord Mayor and a number of magistrates regarding 'the steps necessary to be taken for the tranquillity of the city'.[14] Consequently, the mail coaches were delayed so that instructions could be prepared for dispatch to numerous authorities around the country; the Foot Guards, the City Militia and the Horse Guards were all called out to maintain order; the doors of Westminster were locked and guarded.

To add to these fears of insurrection, around eight o'clock, when a coach arrived at the iron gates in Lower Palace Yard to transport the assassin to Newgate Prison, a large and noisy mob had assembled. It soon became evident that this crowd was interested not in attacking the assassin, but actually in freeing him.

A number of people climbed onto the coach and tried to open the door, mistakenly thinking that the assassin was already inside. They cheered for him, many thinking that he was the radical Member of Parliament Sir Francis Burdett. In the end, things grew so heated that the coach had to be sent away and the mob forced back by a party of Life Guards.

It was around midnight before Bellingham could finally be taken out, handcuffed, through the Speaker's Court and on to Newgate Prison by means of a coach well guarded by Dragoon Guards. He was accompanied by Lord Clive, whose coach was used for the transportation, Michael Angelo Taylor who had committed him, Stephen Lavender the Chief Constable of Police and a King's Messenger called Mr Ross.[15]

At Newgate Prison John Bellingham was received by the Keeper, or Head Gaoler, John Addison Newman. He was put in irons, and placed in the cell beside the chapel.[16] The cell had a stone floor and was doubled ironed; its door was guarded throughout the night by two keepers and the principal turnkey. Their newest prisoner was quiet and not in the least troublesome. He took refreshment and went to bed. It was noticed, with some surprise, that he fell asleep promptly. He was able to do so clear in his mind that his actions had been justified and that he would soon be found not guilty of any crime.

Chapter 3

'LITTLE P'

King George III's Prime Minister, Spencer Perceval, a man of firm religious principles and reactionary politics, now lay dead at Westminster. Perceval had been born into Hanoverian Britain on 1 November 1762 at Audley Square, London. The Perceval family was one with a long and distinguished lineage. An ancestor, Richard Perceval, born in 1550, is credited with deciphering the dispatches that gave Queen Elizabeth I vital intelligence about the imminent threat from the Spanish Armada. Richard began the family's long association with Ireland by acquiring large estates there.[1] His son, Philip, added to this by acquiring another 100,000 acres of land in Ireland during the reign of Charles I.

Spencer Perceval was not the first member of his family to die a violent death. On 5 June 1677 an ancestor of Perceval's fell victim to a murderer's knife. This young man, Robert Perceval, who was around 20 years of age, was in London studying law under his uncle, Sir Robert Southwell. Ironically, he had told his uncle some days earlier about a bloody premonition of his death that he had experienced during his sleep. Robert was, it seems, not averse to conflict, as he had already been involved in, and survived, nineteen duels. On the night of his murder Robert noticed that he was being followed from place to place as he went around town on his night's entertainment. At each establishment he visited, he saw the same man waiting in the porch for him to emerge. He decided to approach the stranger and ask him what he wanted, only to be told by the man that he was attending to his own business. When Robert informed his friends about this, they wanted to send a footman to accompany him, but he refused the offer.

The trouble began at eleven o'clock, when, as he was entering a tavern in the Strand, he was attacked and injured by a number of men. He survived this attack with only slight wounds. He walked into the tavern, ordered a glass of brandy, wiped some blood from his sword and tied his handkerchief around a bleeding wound on his leg. He told his friends that his attackers were 'persons who bore him an old grudge'.[2] He told them that he had dealt with the villains and once again refused to accept any protection. Later that night Robert's dead body was found under the May pole in the Strand by the watchman. It was believed that he had been killed elsewhere and his body moved to its final location. It was hoped that a hat sporting a bunch of ribbons, which had been found beside the body, would point to the identity of the murderers. In the end, however, despite all investigations, no shortage of enemies who could have been responsible, and a proclamation by the King, the crime went unsolved.

The nephew of the murdered Robert Perceval was Spencer Perceval's grandfather, Sir John Perceval, born in Cork, Ireland, in 1683. He was created 1st Earl of Egmont in the peerage of Ireland in 1733. He served as a Member of Parliament and became a Privy Counsellor at the time of Queen Anne. He played a significant part in founding the colony of Georgia in America and became its first President in 1732.

Spencer Perceval's father, John Perceval, was born in 1711. Having served in the Irish Parliament as a very young man, he was elected to the House of Commons in 1741, as a representative of the Borough of Westminster. In 1748 he succeeded to the Earldom of Egmont on the death of his father. He was created Lord Lovel and Holland in the peerage of England in 1762 and took his seat in the House of Lords.[3] He served as First Lord of the Admiralty in 1763-6. Following on from the influence of his father in the American colonies, he acquired 10,000 acres of land in Florida. His influence in the colonies is attested to by the naming in his honour of Egmont Island and Egmont Key in Florida and also Port Egmont in the Falkland Islands. His promotion of Captain Cook's endeavours was recognised when Cook renamed Taranaki mountain in New Zealand for him as Mount Egmont in 1770.

Perceval's father married twice. The 2nd Earl's first wife was Lady Catherine Cecil, daughter of the 5th Earl of Salisbury, whom he married in 1737. They went on to have five sons and two daughters. Lady Catherine died in 1752, and in 1756 the Earl married his second wife, Catherine Compton, third daughter of the Hon. Charles Compton. Catherine had been born near Lisbon in Portugal in 1731. She was created Baroness Arden of Lohort Castle in County Cork in Ireland in 1770.[4]

They had three sons and six daughters. Perceval was the second son born of this union. He was christened Spencer after his mother's brother and his uncle, Spencer Compton, who was later the 8th Earl of Northampton.

Perceval's half-brother from his father's first marriage, John James Perceval, later succeeded to the titles of Earl of Egmont and Lord Lovel and Holland, while his elder full biological brother, Charles George, inherited the title Lord Arden of Lohort from their mother. Spencer himself, at 1 year and 10 months, was granted the second reversion to the sinecure of Registrar of the High Court of the Admiralty. He would not, however, inherit a title and one day would have to earn a living.

During his early years the young Perceval lived a comfortable life with his family in the village of Charlton, Kent. His father had taken Charlton House, to be in close proximity to the dockyards in his capacity as First Lord of the Admiralty. The house, built during the reign of James I, was Gothic in style, with a spacious courtyard circled by a row of old Cypress trees, in which the children loved to play. In December 1770 the secure world of the 8-year-old Spencer Perceval was shattered, when his father died suddenly while staying at his town house in Pall Mall. The 2nd Earl of Egmont was only 59 years of age. Two years later this loss was added to by the deaths of his siblings Henry and Ann, both of whom were said to have succumbed to sore throats.

In 1774 'Little P', as Perceval was called by Lord Eldon because of his small, thin stature, was sent to Harrow School, where he proved to be a diligent student, winning many prizes and becoming a school monitor.[5] After leaving Harrow in 1779, he went up to Trinity College, Cambridge, where he won the College Declamation Prize for English. His sense of duty and justice, which characterised his life, is demonstrated by the anecdote that once, when he forgot to cast a vote for a candidate in an election as he had promised, he insisted on paying the candidate the salary he would have earned from the office.[6] It was during his time at Cambridge that he became an evangelical Christian. He was awarded his MA in 1782.

It was now time for Perceval to settle on a career. As his chosen field was the law, he went to Lincoln's Inn to become a student at the Inns of Court. It was during his period there that personal tragedy struck once again when his mother, Baroness Arden, developed a bad cough and died in June 1784.[7] While attending to his legal studies, Perceval became an active member of the debating society known as the 'Crown and Rolls'. Here he gained the kind of valuable experience that honed those oratorical skills he would later require in the House of Commons.

Called to the Bar in 1786, he began to practise law on the midland circuit using his brother's old chambers at No. 20 Field Gate Court and Kitchen Garden Row. At first the financial situation was not easy for him, and he had to live a frugal existence taking account of every penny.[8] He seems to have been liked by his colleagues, with Samuel Romilly praising 'his excellent temper, his engaging manners, and his sprightly conversation' and William Windham writing that 'Perceval is a young lawyer, and from his quickness and acuteness likely, I should think, to be some time or other a distinguished man'.[9]

Perceval and his brother Charles fell in love with a pair of sisters, the daughters of Sir Thomas Spencer-Wilson, Member of Parliament for Sussex, who held the Lordship of the Manor of Charlton. With his superior prospects and wealth as the future Lord Arden, Charles was able to wed the elder sister, Margaretta Elizabeth, in 1787. But Perceval's interest in Jane Wilson, with his meagre income and prospects, was not welcomed by her family with the same enthusiasm. Undeterred, the lovers waited until Jane reached the age of 21 in 1790 and got married secretly while she was on a visit to relatives in East Grinstead in Sussex. Perceval was 28 years of age. The bride presented herself at the wedding ceremony wearing her riding attire.[10] If it is true that the father knew nothing of the marriage in advance, he soon came to accept it. Perceval himself wrote of their first reunion following the nuptials:

Mrs P. and myself have been to Charlton, on Sir T[homas]'s invitation, and were received with all the kindness and warmth that a very affectionate parent (as he certainly is) could bestow on his daughter. He also has told me that he will make up her fortune, just what it would have been had she married with his consent, and was not satisfied till he made us repeatedly assure him that we were convinced we had his full forgiveness . . . In short everything that I could have wished and much more than I could have expected, has concurred to make the step I have just taken the happiest and most prosperous event of my life.[11]

The marriage was to prove a happy one and would later produce six sons and six daughters, to whom Perceval was devoted. But in these early years the young couple had to face financial difficulties and they were forced to take relatively humble lodgings over a carpet shop in Bedford Row, London.

Their financial situation did improve slowly. Perceval had been appointed Deputy Recorder of Northampton around 1790 with the assistance of his grandfather, Lord Northampton. He was also appointed a commissioner of bankrupts and in 1791 obtained two sinecures in the Mint: Surveyor of the Meltings and Clerk of the Irons. This brought him £123 per annum.[12] In addition, more legal work was coming in all the time. As a junior counsel he was involved in the trials of Tom Paine in 1792 and Horne Tooke in 1794. In 1794, with the help of his brother Charles, Perceval was appointed counsel to the Board of Admiralty.

Perceval's publication in 1791 of a pamphlet on the constitutional issues surrounding the impeachment of Warren Hastings had brought him to the attention of the politicians, most notably the Prime Minister, William Pitt the Younger. In January 1796 Pitt formally offered him the position of Chief Secretary for Ireland:

Mr Pelham's declining to return to Ireland has produced a vacancy in the situation of the Secretary to the Lord Lieutenant. You will easily believe how important an object it is to us to find a successor whom we think qualified for the post; and, on the fullest consideration, the Duke of Portland and Lord Camden, as well as myself, are fully satisfied that such an object cannot be more completely obtained than if you can be prevailed upon to undertake the task. I do not know how far you may have formed a determination to adhere to your professional pursuits, or whether there may be any other considerations to prevent your listening to this proposal. But, if that should not be the case, I can with great sincerity assure you that your acceptance would, in all our opinions, contribute very essentially to the public service, as well as to the personal satisfaction of all those with whom you would have to act . . .[13]

On the grounds of financial necessity Perceval decided to decline the offer. 'If I had no interests to consider but my own,' he said in his reply, 'I should not from any private motive hesitate to accept it.'[14] He was concerned about supporting his young family and, consequently, felt he could not abandon his developing legal career. By 1796 he had three daughters and two sons to support. They had, by now, moved from the rather cramped conditions over the carpet shop to purchase a house at No. 59 Lincoln's Inn Fields for £4,500.[15] Instead of accepting the position in Ireland, he asked Pitt for permission to approach Lord Loughborough, the Lord Chancellor, about furthering his claim to be made a King's Counsel.[16] He achieved this in February 1796, when he was elected a Bencher of the Inn at the age of 34. But, notwithstanding his love of the law, the allure of politics would not evade him for long.

Chapter 4

ENTRY INTO POLITICS

In 1796 Perceval's first cousin, Lord Crompton, succeeded to the Earldom of Northampton and vacated his seat in the House of Commons. In May, at the ensuing by-election, Perceval was selected as MP in his place and that result was reaffirmed at the general election that followed shortly afterwards. It was the beginning of a career that would see him returned to the House of Commons without a contest at the general elections of 1802, 1806 and 1807 and also when he had to seek re-election after being appointed to an office in the government on three occasions. He continued to pursue his legal career alongside his duties in Parliament. The Percevals now had the funds to rent a country residence, Belsize House in Hampstead. This property did not work out too well for them, however, as, although the house was large and inexpensive, it was in poor condition and Perceval came to regard it as 'a miserable hole'.[1]

Perceval was entering Parliament at a momentous time in British history, as the kingdom was involved in what was to be a long and difficult war against the French. Britain became one of the countries involved in the so-called First Coalition in the war against France. By 1799 France's greatest general, Napoleon Bonaparte, had seized power, and Britain was at war as part of the Second Coalition, which it had been instrumental in bringing together. Perceval was a strong supporter of the war. It was to continue throughout his time in Parliament. Indeed, at times, it would challenge the very survival of the country itself.[2]

The figure of the small, thin man with a pale complexion, usually dressed in black, would soon become familiar to those around the corridors of Westminster. He was described in a rather derogatory manner, by Sydney Smith, as 'the Sallow Surveyor of the Mints' and the 'Sepulchral Spencer Perceval'.[3] His slight figure would lead Sheridan to refer to him in verse:

> I, the chance poet of an idle hour,
> With thee in verse will battle, when ...
> Spencer Perceval shall challenge Cribb.[4]

This would be recognisable to contemporaries as a humorous reference to Perceval's small size and slight build, as Tom Cribb was the bareknuckle boxing champion of England.

By political temperament Perceval was conservative: 'I am sorry to say that we live at a time when to be unprecedented and paradoxical is to have no mean title . . . when men adopt opinions as they choose their dresses, according to the mode of the hour; when nothing is followed but what is fashionable and nothing esteemed fashionable but what is new ...'.[5]

His religion was very important to him, informing his philosophy of life and his actions. He was an evangelical Anglican and genuine in the observance of his Christian duties, praying daily with his family. One writer even went as far as describing him as 'Christianity personified'.[6] He gave generously to charity and disliked pursuits such as gambling and hunting, seeing them as a waste of time and money that could be more honourably used in helping the needy.[7] It was his opinion that adultery should be considered a crime. His record, however, shows little done to alleviate the suffering of the disadvantaged in society, such as the children forced to work long gruelling hours in factories. But he did advocate and support the abolition of the slave trade.[8]

He was a great admirer and supporter of the Tory Prime Minister, William Pitt the Younger. Pitt, whose father had also served as Prime Minister, had become Britain's youngest ever to hold the position at the age of 24 in 1783. He was the pre-eminent statesman of his era. He, like Perceval, had studied at Cambridge, was the younger son of a peer and a lawyer by profession. He was not abstemious like Perceval, however, having been prescribed a bottle of port a day as a cure for gout at the age of 14; he continued the habit right throughout his life.

Perceval supported Pitt in his determination to continue the war against France and also in his desire to forge a political union with Ireland, but he could never support the Prime Minister in trying to introduce Catholic emancipation. Catholics at the time were excluded, by law, from a whole range of rights and privileges, including a seat in Parliament, the office of Lord Lieutenant and many other military and legal positions. Perceval's political attitudes, especially those regarding Ireland and his opposition to Catholicism, were informed by his fervent evangelical support for the Church of England. In the aftermath of the French Revolution many feared that there would be a move towards a similar event in Britain. It was particularly felt that the ideas of the revolution would take root in Ireland and that the country would be used as the base for a wider insurrection. It was true that the war against France had led to a hope among Irish revolutionaries that France would be willing to send an army to Ireland.[9] These fears were realised when an expedition led by General Hoche headed for Ireland in 1796, only to be prevented from landing by a fierce storm off the coast. Another expedition, led by General Humbert, which was defeated by government forces in County Mayo in 1798, was supposed to support a countrywide insurrection organised by the group called the 'United Irishmen'. In the end the insurrection managed to make any serious impression only in County Wexford.

While Perceval was a dedicated opponent of Catholic emancipation, he claimed to be a supporter of religious toleration.[10] His religious stance has, however, led to accusations of bigotry being laid against him. For example, the *Edinburgh Review* would later write of him: 'His religious feelings were mingled with so much bigotry that he was quite incapable of viewing the claims of the Catholics with the eye of a statesman.'[11] He consistently opposed all attempts to increase funding to the college for Catholic priests in Maynooth, Ireland.

Notwithstanding his difference of opinion with Pitt on the Catholic question, Perceval soon began to play an important role in Parliament, becoming an effective opponent of Pitt's greatest rival in the House of Commons, Charles James Fox. Fox, educated at Eton and Oxford, wealthy and charismatic, a speaker of several languages, a skilful orator, was one of the most impressive politicians of the time. Yet, for all his ability, his life is often viewed as one of wasted talent. He could not have been more different from Perceval, noted as he was for his drinking, gambling, agnosticism and neglectful attitude towards mundane, everyday work. When presenting an argument in the House, he was frequently forced to use his oratorical brilliance to cover up for his lack of preparation. Fox was to spend most of his political life in opposition. He had been a vocal supporter of the revolution in France and was totally opposed to the war.

Perceval soon began to build his political reputation through his speeches in the House of Commons. His performance in a speech given in the summer of 1797, supporting a bill of Mr Pitt's concerning 'sedition and mutiny in his Majesty's service', was widely praised:

> The speaker's figure was not commanding, but graceful; his delivery not dignified, but easy; and the clearness and melody of his voice, the unaffected placidity of his manners, and the benevolent nature of the sentiments he expressed, gained upon the ear and the heart of all parties. If he did not enforce, he won conviction; the propriety of his suggestions was admitted, and the beneficial amendments which he proposed, were adopted.[12]

A speech of his made early in 1798, in support of the Assessed Tax Bill of Mr Pitt, was described by Sheridan, who was an opponent of the Bill, as 'of great talent, ingenuity, and considerable force'.[13] Even Fox, whose arguments were the main target of Perceval's speech, said it was 'very ingenious'. It was a performance that had not escaped the Prime Minister either, who wrote: 'Our last debate (to my great joy) produced a speech from Perceval which was in all respects the best I ever heard; and was an attack upon Fox pointed and galling enough to have drawn forth one of Grattan's warmest encomiums. It certainly sent him home very sick to this supper...'.[14]

Such was his growing reputation that, when Prime Minister Pitt, in 1798, on his way to take part in a duel, was asked, rather indelicately, whom he though capable of taking over from him should he not survive the event, his answer, which surprised many, was Spencer Perceval.[15] As it happened, Pitt survived the duel, and that year Perceval was appointed both Solicitor General to the Queen and Solicitor to the Board of Ordinance. All this meant an increase in income. By 1800 he was earning £2,600, £1,800 of which came from his legal work.[16] With the increase in their family, they now had seven children, the Percevals decided to buy No. 60 Lincoln's Inn Fields to add to the house in which they already lived, No. 59.

In 1801 practically the only issue on which Perceval and Pitt disagreed, Catholic emancipation, caused an upheaval at the highest levels of government and led to the resignation of Prime Minister Pitt. Pitt had promised emancipation for the Catholics if the Act of Union between Britain and Ireland was passed. The Act had been passed by the Parliaments of both Ireland and Britain in 1800. It abolished the Parliament in Ireland, moved the Irish political representation to Westminster and created the United Kingdom of Great Britain and Ireland. However, the King refused to approve Pitt's Bill for Catholic emancipation, under which Catholics would be permitted to sit in Parliament and hold other public offices. Although George III was absolutely opposed to the Bill, he did not wish Pitt to resign. Pitt felt that in all conscience he could do nothing else.

The new Prime Minister was Henry Addington, a supporter of the Act of Union but an opponent of Catholic emancipation. Addington, a childhood friend of Pitt's, had been first elected to the House of Commons in 1783 and made Speaker, at Pitt's instigation, in 1789. Although a popular figure, in the aftermath of the recent controversy, he found it no easy matter to put together a government. Two major figures, Lord Castlereagh and George Canning, had resigned with Pitt, although Castlereagh later agreed to serve as President of the Board of Control. Castlereagh had been born in Ireland and educated there and at Cambridge. He had been Chief Secretary of Ireland and had been integral to the passing of the Act of Union between Britain and Ireland. He was, like Pitt, a supporter of Catholic emancipation. Although a man of great energy, directness and courage, he was also intensely disliked by many people. Shelley wrote of him:

> I met murder on the way –
> He had a mask like Castlereagh –
> Very smooth he looked, yet grim,

Lord Byron was even more disparaging:

> Here lie the bones of Castlereagh,
> Stop traveller, and piss.

Castlereagh was disliked by no one more passionately than George Canning. Canning was a tough, intense and hard-working politician. His was a character forged on the events of childhood; his father had died when he was a child of 1 year old, and his mother did her best to support him and his siblings. He was fortunate to have been helped by an uncle who sent him to Eton and Oxford. He entered Parliament in 1794 and was appointed Under-Secretary of State by Pitt in 1796. He was clever, resourceful and witty, but could also be touchy and hard to handle. He was a loyal supporter of Pitt and very critical of those who decided to serve under Addington. The antagonism between Canning and Castlereagh would soon be revealed for all to see.

Perceval decided that he would serve under Addington. After all, he agreed with the contention that Catholic emancipation should not be introduced. He had made his attitude to Catholics clear in a speech made in June 1800, when he said that 'they could not obtain for us a greater blessing than to make Catholics of us all'.[17] Addington appointed him to his first ministerial position as Solicitor General in the new administration. The King always insisted that his law officers receive a knighthood, but Perceval, as the son of an earl and therefore already of a higher rank, was permitted to decline the honour.[18] The following year he was appointed to one of the most important legal offices in the land, that of Attorney General.

Addington was among those who had had enough of the war with France. It began to look to many as if the war could not be won and it was placing crippling demands upon the economy of the country. It was during the Addington administration, therefore, in March 1802, that France and Britain agreed peace terms under the Treaty of Amiens, and brought the so-called Second Coalition to an end. It was later that same year that Napoleon had himself appointed First Consul of the French Republic for life. Although he was now the legal adviser to the government, Perceval was not one of those who agreed with the peace.

Chapter 5

PERCEVAL THE CROWN PROSECUTOR

The early years of the century were busy ones for Perceval. Because of his growing political work he decided to move his legal practice from King's Bench to Chancery. By 1804 he was earning nearly £10,000 per annum. Now appointed to the prestigious legal position of Attorney General, Perceval became involved in a number of high-profile cases for the government. In 1803 he conducted the prosecution of Colonel Edward Marcus Despard for high treason. Despard was an Irish-born colonel of the British navy whose early career had been exemplary. After a military victory over the Spanish, he added to his duties taking charge of a new British enclave in the Bay of Honduras, later called Belize, and enforcing the terms of a newly signed treaty under which the British living on the Mosquito Shore were required to resettle there. Colonel Despard was to oversee the allocation of the new settlers' accommodation and plots of land. A problem seems to have arisen because he did so without any regard to race, allocating equally to black, white and mixed race. This policy did not endear him to the already established white settlers living in the area.

The ensuing controversy meant that Despard was suspended by the then Home Secretary, Lord Grenville, and in 1790 recalled to England. He returned to England with his black wife, Catherine. Lawsuits were brought against him by enemies in the Bay of Honduras, and his fall from grace was completed by his committal to the King's Bench Prison for debtors in 1792. Although released in 1794, he was understandably embittered by the experience. He was rearrested in 1798, accused of involvement with the Irish rebellion of that year, and held without trial until 1801.

Despard was charged in 1802 of having, with others, plotted the seizure of the Tower of London and the Bank of England as well as the assassination of George III, as the monarch made his way to the opening of Parliament. At his trial, Lord Nelson, who had served with Colonel Despard and held him in high regard, appeared as a witness for the defence. The prosecution was conducted successfully by Perceval and the jury found Despard guilty of high treason. He was sentenced to be hung, drawn and quartered, but, because of the fear of unrest among the people, the sentence was later commuted to hanging and beheading. On 21 February 1803 Colonel Despard was executed on the roof of Horsemonger Lane Prison, as an estimated 20,000 people looked on.

During the Peace of Amiens, Perceval was called upon to prosecute another case that captured the public interest. This was the case against Jean Peltier. Peltier was the editor of a French language journal, L'Ambigu, printed in London, who was being tried for committing a libel on Napoleon Bonaparte. Peltier's paper had called for Napoleon's assassination. At the time the British authorities did not want any such publications to damage the fragile peace that was in existence with France. Peltier was a French royalist in exile from his country who for a long time had been writing about the injustices in his home land. He was defended by Sir James Mackintosh. It is ironic that it was Perceval, a most ardent supporter of the war against Napoleon, who was called upon to prosecute a libel against the French leader. He managed to carry out his duties with detached professionalism. 'I am standing here for the honour of the English law, and of the English nation,' he told the court. 'I state this to be a crime, and as such have brought it before an English jury.'[1] He denounced Peltier's publication:

The offence here charged to have been committed by the defendant is this: that his publication is a direct incitement and exhortation to the people of the French Republic to rise up in arms against their First Consul and Chief Magistrate, to wrest the power from the hands in which, de facto, it is placed, and to take away the life of the man who presides over them. Is it possible we can have any difficulty in supporting the proposition that such a publication is an offence against the law of this country?[2]

It is somewhat ironic that, while prosecuting the case, Perceval made the following comment about assassination: 'There is something so base and disgraceful, there is something so contrary to everything that belongs to the character of an Englishman, there is something so immoral in the idea of assassination, that the exhortation to assassinate this or any other Chief Magistrate would be a crime against the honourable feelings of the English law.'[3]

Peltier was found guilty. However, in May 1803, before sentence could be passed on him, the peace collapsed and hostilities with France were resumed. This meant that sentence was never passed on Peltier, and, in fact, with the resumption of war, it once again became a free-for-all for anyone to write anything they liked about Napoleon Bonaparte.

In May 1804 Perceval conducted the prosecution of William Cobbett for libel. Cobbett was the publisher of the *Political Register*. A self-educated farmer's son, born in Surrey, Cobbett had spent the previous few years in America, where he had produced a number of well-known publications, including the *Porcupine's Gazette*. On his return to England he was, at first, the darling of the Tory side of the political divide, but soon this relationship broke down as he became more and more critical of their policies. He became a fierce critic of Perceval. On this occasion Cobbett had printed a number of letters by an anonymous author in which were attacked some leading members of the Irish government, including the Lord Chancellor of Ireland, Lord Redesdale, who was Perceval's brother-in-law. During the trial Perceval gave his opinion of Cobbett:

He seems to imagine himself a species of censor, who, elevated to the solemn seat of judgement, is to deal out his decisions for the instruction of mankind. He casts his eye downward, like the character represented by the poet of nature, from Dover cliff, and looks upon the inferior world below as pigmies beneath him. Perhaps in the proud contemplation of his own abilities, he supposes he is not to submit to the laws and institutions adapted to the vulgar herd of society. But, gentlemen, whatever may be our inclination to forgive what comes from such a censor, I am afraid we must be content to consider him in this court as a common being, and to subject him to the restrictions which he will admit to be accommodated only to our inferior capacities.[4]

Cobbett was found guilty and fined. Perceval also success-fully prosecuted the author of the letters in question, Mr Justice Johnson, although this decision was later overturned when a *nolle prosequi* was entered against it by a subsequent Attorney General, Sir Arthur Pigott.

Meanwhile, outside the courtroom, political life was forging ahead. In 1804 Napoleon declared France an empire and crowned himself Emperor. Hostilities with France were soon reignited, and with the restart of the war there was a genuine fear among the British people that Napoleon would invade the country. It was a fear shared by many of those in Parliament, and many of them showed that they were willing to be involved in defending the coun-try in a practical way. Perceval showed his willingness by being a member of the Light Horse Volunteers. Addington, who proved himself lacking in leadership when war was resumed, began to lose his grip on power. When he was attacked in Parliament by Fox, Pitt, Windham, Canning and others, Perceval did his best to defend him. Eventually, though, Addington was forced to give way, and Pitt once again became Prime Minister.

As Perceval was Attorney General, on the death of Lord Alvanley he was offered the position of Chief Justice of the Common Pleas and a peerage. It was an offer he decided to decline, presumably feeling that he had much more to offer in the House of Commons and that the opportunity to take up such a position would be available to him later in life. At least this is what Lord Redesdale believed:

I think you have done right. At a later period of your life, the Common pleas would have been a highly respectable retreat, and the peerage of little consequence to you personally. At present it would have thrown you out of your habits into an uncomfortable line of life, and a society you would scarcely have relished.[5]

When James Mansfield was appointed to the position of Chief Justice of the Commons Pleas, Perceval did seem to show some interest in Mansfield's old position as Chief Judge of Chester.[6] But, in any event, Pitt was very keen that he should serve in the new government. A friend of Perceval's from Harrow, Dudley Ryder, now Lord Harrowby, was asked to mediate. Perceval's main conditions for his participation in government were that there would be no recriminations made regarding the Addington administration, that Fox would not be at the Cabinet table and that there would be no movement on the granting of Catholic emancipation. He was as determined as ever on the Catholic question and, in fact, if anything, his stance on this issue had hardened over the years, perhaps influenced by his correspondence with his brother-in-law, Redesdale, the Lord Chancellor of Ireland.[7] Redesdale told him that the Catholics of Ireland would be satisfied at nothing but repeal of the union and a separate legislation based on the French Revolution. Pitt, through Harrowby, was able to reassure Perceval that all his conditions could be easily met, and in the new government he retained his position as Attorney General. George Canning was appointed Treasurer of the Navy and Castlereagh Secretary of State for War. Fox assumed the role of one of the major opponents of this new administration.

In October 1805 Napoleon's navy lost to Nelson in the famous battle at Trafalgar, but the same day the nation lost Nelson to an enemy shot. The battle dealt a fatal blow to Napoleon's ambitions for an invasion of Britain, but his victory at the battle of Austerlitz later that same year reaffirmed his military strength on land. It was still a long way from Napoleon's final defeat at Waterloo in 1815.

In January 1806, the Prime Minister, William Pitt the Younger, probably the person most admired by Perceval, died. Pitt had played a significant role not only in the history of his country but also in Perceval's life. He was one of the first to have recognised the young Perceval's abilities and to have promoted him accordingly. For all his political abilities, the late Prime Minister's personal life was rather sad, as he had no family and very few close friends. He died leaving behind great debts. Perceval offered £1,000 pounds that he could ill afford to help pay off those debts, a gesture described by Wilberforce, who was collecting the money, as 'warm and generous'.[8]

Understandably, the Tories were in disarray following the death of an influential and charismatic figure like Pitt. Perceval knew that it would be impossible for them to form a government in the short term:

> In my humble opinion the state of parties renders the attempt
> of forming a government out of the remains of the present
> totally impracticable; and therefore the true wisdom seems to
> me to point out the necessity of the King's immediately sending
> for whatever person in the Opposition he may think unexcep-
> tionable, and making the best arrangements which he can by
> means of him.[9]

In the absence of Pitt, his former Foreign Secretary and first cousin, Lord Grenville, became Prime Minister with the Whig administration that became known as 'the Ministry of all the Talents'. Grenville's father had served as Prime Minister in the 1760s. Grenville was a firm supporter of the war with France and had opposed the Peace of Amiens. He supported Pitt in his efforts to achieve Catholic emancipation. In his early years in politics Grenville had been a loyal supporter of his cousin, William Pitt, but, following the removal of the Pitt administration from office in 1801, he began to move more towards the politics of Fox and Charles Grey. So much so that he refused to accept office from Pitt in 1804 without Fox being included. Fox was appointed Secretary of State in Grenville's new administration and was, in effect, joint leader. Grey became First Lord of the Admiralty. Perceval was also offered a place in government but declined. Among other things, he disliked Grenville's tolerant attitude towards Catholic emanci-pation and his policies towards Ireland in general.

Instead Perceval became a member of the group in opposition comprising former supporters of Pitt, known as 'Pitt's friends.' He felt it was his duty to try to keep this group unified in opposition. However, in actuality, in the wake of Pitt's death, they found it dif-ficult to find any sense of unity or to identify an effective leader. Some wanted to become an effective opposition while others were willing to go into coalition with Grenville. They eventually found a nominal leader in the now ageing Duke of Portland. Perceval's

time in opposition was not unproductive. He became a very effective critic of the government in the House, speaking on at least
sixty-nine occasions in the session of 1806.[10] He was also involved
in his legal work and, in particular, two very high-profile cases.

Chapter 6

THE DELICATE INVESTIGATION

The wayward Prince of Wales and the evangelical and sober Spencer Perceval were never going to be close friends. But their relationship went through a particularly difficult period during the years 1806 and 1807. The Prince of Wales was now 44 years of age, and his relationship with his father was a combative one. It had not always been so; when the Prince was a child, the King doted on him and, in many ways, indulged him. He was intelligent and, with the other royal children, was exposed to a rigid programme of education. He developed into a tall, good-looking adolescent. But, as he matured, he became a morally bankrupt young man with little care for the feelings of others. He had romantic affairs from the age of 16 and developed a fondness for the habits of drinking and gambling. By his forties he was very overweight. He was no supporter of the politics of Perceval, instead being of Whig tendencies. The Prince's marriage to Caroline, the daughter of the Duke of Brunswick and of the King's sister Augusta, in April 1795, was not his first. Some years earlier he had become besotted with a Catholic widow and commoner, Maria Fitzherbert, whom he got to marry him after he had staged an attempted suicide.[1] That marriage was eventually declared null and void.

During his time in opposition during the Grenville's 'Ministry of all the Talents', Perceval got involved in two noteworthy and controversial legal cases, both of which concerned the Prince of Wales. The first of these was the case concerning Miss Minney Seymour. When Minney was orphaned in 1799 she was in the care of Mrs Fitzherbert, the Princes of Wales's lover and former wife. After some time the executors of her father's will and the guardians of the children, Lord Euston and Lord Seymour, grew unhappy about Minney's situation. In particular, they disliked the fact that Mrs Fitzherbert was a Catholic, and they wanted Minney removed from her care. Mrs Fitzherbert, supported by the Prince of Wales, did not want to lose Minney and was prepared to fight to hold onto her. A legal battle ensued. The guardians brought their case to the Court of Chancery in 1804 and were successful. Mrs Fitzherbert and the Prince of Wales then brought the case before the Court of Appeal, where the first ruling was upheld.

In June 1806 the Seymour case was considered by the highest court of appeal, the House of Lords, and Perceval was one of those retained as counsel by the guardians. The Prince used all his influence to sway as many peers as possible to his and Miss Fitzherbert's side of the argument and he was ultimately successful. The Lords decided that the child's uncle Lord Hertford should be declared her guardian, and, under the influence of the Prince, he declared himself satisfied that Mrs Fitzherbert remain as Minney's carer. Naturally the Seymour side was extremely unhappy about the decision. During all this, when the Prince heard that Perceval had effectively referred to him as a liar and a bankrupt, he was infuriated and ranted that 'he could jump on him [Perceval] and stamp out his life with his feet'.[2]

The Prince of Wales's dislike of Perceval was intensified that same year as a result of a commission that was set up to inquire into allegations of misconduct on the part of his wife, the Princess of Wales. This is the episode that became known as the 'Delicate Investigation'. The Prince's marriage to Caroline had never been a happy one. He had not liked her from their first meeting and was rumoured to have been drunk at their wedding ceremony.[3] He was unfaithful to her from the beginning. Caroline's behaviour was no better. She proved herself to be uncouth and lacking in character. Her outrageous behaviour scandalised polite society. There were stories of numerous affairs linking her with people such as George Canning and Rear Admiral Sir Sidney Smith. Among many faults she was criticised for being vulgar in her conversation and for having too much of a liking for ale. Even though their daughter, Princess Charlotte, was born nine months after the wedding, the

Prince and Princess were soon living apart and the Prince of Wales sought a formal separation, which the King refused.

Caroline was very fond of children and adopted several, many of whom were rumoured to be her own. The question of whether or not she had conceived illegitimately in 1802 became the subject of the so-called Delicate Investigation. Perceval, by becoming the Princess's chief legal adviser, found himself once again on the opposing side to the Prince, who hoped that the investigation would damage his wife. The roots of this scandal are to be found in an argument that occurred between Princess Caroline and Lady Charlotte Douglas. The two women had been very close friends until a bitter falling-out. As a result Caroline evicted Lord and Lady Douglas from a house in Greenwich Park on which they had spent a lot of money. The Douglases then made the startling and scandalous claim that Princess Caroline had become pregnant in 1802, as the result of an illicit relationship, and that she had subsequently given birth to a boy whom she was now bringing up in her household.

Princess Caroline's version of events was very different. She said that for some time she had been allowed to see her daughter only weekly and she felt the need to have a baby around the house. She asked her servants to look out for some needy person who would be willing to allow her to adopt her baby. So it happened, in 1802, that arrangements were made for a woman named Sophia Austin to give her infant male child to the Princess as soon as he had been weaned from his mother's milk. She claimed that that was the child to whom the Douglases referred. Lord and Lady Douglas denied the veracity of the Princess's story and continued to claim that this child, named Willy Austin, was in fact the Princess's own flesh and blood.

All this was brought to the attention of the Prince of Wales and resulted in much 'behind-the-scenes' activity. The Prince had Samuel Romilly, the Whig lawyer, investigate the matter initially. Lady Douglas, her servants and others were interviewed. The Princes of Wales's brothers 'fronted' this initial inquiry so that the heir to the throne could maintain a dignified distance from it. Romilly's findings were reported to the King, who, in May 1806, set up the secret commission of Cabinet ministers to carry out the Delicate Investigation. Given the responsibility of investigating this matter were Lords Grenville, Erskine, Ellenborough and Spencer, with Romilly appointed as their legal adviser. They considered the evidence from Lord and Lady Douglas, the Princess's servants, her physician and other witnesses. They heard Lady Douglas tell the story of how she had been privy to the fact of the pregnancy from the beginning and that she believed the father to be Sir Sidney Smith. Robert Bidgood, a former page of the Princess, gave evidence that he had often seen Sir Sidney at the Princess's house. Reports of various infidelities began to come out, including those with a Captain Manby. On the other hand, throughout all this, Sophia Austin was adamant that the child in question was hers. She told the investigators that she still visited him regularly. The commission was able to confirm from the Brownlow Hospital that Mrs Austin had indeed given birth to a male child in July 1802, as she claimed.

On 14 July 1806 the commission reported its findings. It concluded that there was no foundation for believing that the child in question was the son of Princess Caroline or, in fact, that she was delivered of any child in 1802 or was ever pregnant in that year. However, they did conclude that reports of her adulterous activities, especially with Captain Manby, must be given credit until some contrary evidence was forthcoming. They concluded that she had acted frivolously.

So now, although she had been cleared of giving birth to Willy Austin, Caroline stood accused of the serious charge of adultery. The King received a copy of the report and, as a result of the charge, decided that from then on Princess Caroline, whom he liked a lot, would no longer be treated as an intimate but only with 'outward marks of civility'.[4] The Prince of Wales, who desperately wanted grounds for a divorce, was disappointed with the conclusion of the commission, regarding it as too lenient towards his wife.

The Princess was receiving the advice of a number of Tory politicians, most noticeably Perceval, who as a principled evangelical politician was an odd ally for the uncouth, flirty Princess. He seems to have been persuaded by the justice of her case and the degree to which she was being persecuted. Perceval assisted the Princess by writing a response to the King on the charge made by the secret commission. This letter, sent in August, declared that the Princess was innocent and pointed out that it was unjust that all the evidence had been taken behind her back, without her being afforded any opportunity to contradict the statements made or to defend herself. It requested copies of all the documents used as evidence in the investigation, which were duly supplied. Perceval then set about writing a more considered response, a long detailed document, which was presented to the King on 2 October. This response and body of evidence became known as 'The Book'. It was variously referred to as 'a model of acute argument and eloquent composition', 'one of the finest specimens of epistolary writing which the English language can produce' and of 'great art and ability'.[5]

The King decided to refer the matter back to the Cabinet, and on 23 December 1806 it gave its verdict. Out of its twelve members, all but one, William Windham, agreed with the conclusions of the secret commission. This, of course, was no surprise, since all four members of the commission were also members of the Cabinet. The Cabinet stated that the findings did 'not warrant their advising that any further step should be taken'. The King was not satisfied with this response and pressed them for a more 'explicit answer'. Finally, this answer came in the form of a Cabinet minute dated 25 January 1807, which reiterated the former statement and advised King George III that it was no longer necessary for him to bar Princess Caroline from his presence.

This was a great result for the Princess. The Prince of Wales, however, was infuriated by the outcome. He wanted his divorce, and the commission had not helped his cause by failing to find the Princess guilty of any specific crime. He decided to try and prove her guilty of adultery and advised his law officers accordingly. This led the King to delay receiving the Princess into his presence until the outcome of his son's action was known. The Princess was left once again in a purgatorial no man's land, not condemned and not exonerated. Once again, in February, Perceval composed a letter on the Princess's behalf complaining of the treatment she was receiving. He also threatened publication of all the evidence pertaining to the secret commission by alluding to the fact that this might be the only way to 'efface . . . the inferences drawn in the public mind'. The printing of copies of 'The Book' began for such a purpose.

In the end the matter came to a conclusion in early 1807 when Grenville's 'Ministry of All the Talents' fell, and in March the Duke of Portland was invited to form a government. Perceval and his colleagues were now in power. The Delicate Investigation had raised his personal profile significantly, and he was appointed Chancellor of the Exchequer in Portland's new government.[6] The new administration decided that it was best that 'The Book' not be published after all. Those copies that had already been printed had to be destroyed. Perceval was reportedly seen burning copies of it himself in a bonfire at Lincoln's Inn Fields.[7] However, copies had already begun to stray out to the general public. The task of trying to retrieve these copies began. The authorities wanted all copies of the publication back so badly that they were prepared to pay handsomely for them. A rather unseemly buying-back of copies began, costing thousands of pounds.[8] An advertisement was placed in *The Times* newspaper in March 1807:

> The Book – Any person having in their possession a CERTAIN BOOK, printed by MR Edwards, in 1807, but never published, with W. Lindsell's name as the seller of the same on the title page, and will bring it to W. Lindsell, Bookseller, Wimpole Street, will receive a handsome gratuity.

The King accepted the Cabinet's advice that Princess Caroline should be received by him once again. He also gave her apartments at Kensington Palace. Perceval had defended Princess Caroline diligently and had also managed to facilitate her reconciliation with the King. As a mark of her gratitude the Princess attended the House of Commons personally to hear him make his maiden speech as Chancellor of the Exchequer. He used his new position to push through some necessary repairs on her Kensington apartments, saving her the bother of having to wait for the customary treasury warrants. In 1809 he arranged for the settlement of her debts and she acted as godmother to his youngest son, Ernest Augustus. However, with the differences apparent in their personalities, it is no surprise that their friendship did not last. She continued her outrageous behaviour in society, began to align herself more and more with the Whig opposition, and declared that Perceval was 'entirely governed by that silly woman his wife'.[9] She eventually commented publicly that she regarded him unfit to be Prime Minister. Perceval had also made an enemy of the man who would one day be king. At this stage it was not known whether that would have any effect on his political career.

Chapter 7

PERCEVAL AND THE
PORTLAND ADMINISTRATION

The Grenville administration had fallen. The death of Fox in September 1806 had been a big loss. He had found out in his last few months that, when he finally had the power and the opportunity to make peace with France, Napoleon was unwilling to cooperate. After his death, tentative feelers had been put out to see if Perceval would now be interested in joining the government, but these were rejected. He still objected to their policies on Ireland and America and also, now, had bad memories of Grenville's handling of the Delicate Investigation. Grey, now Lord Howick, moved from the Admiralty to replace Fox as Foreign Secretary and also became leader of the Whigs. When Grenville had Parliament dissolved, Perceval was returned unopposed to his seat.

The issue that had brought about the fall of the 'Ministry of All the Talents' was the question of Catholic emancipation, which by 1807 had once again become critical. In February of that year the Lord Lieutenant of Ireland, Bedford, had warned the government that the Catholics of Ireland were growing very agitated about the issue and should be conciliated in some way. Grenville and his colleagues decided to introduce a Bill allowing Catholics to hold commissions in the armed forces. Perceval was vehemently opposed to the move, calling it 'most important and dangerous'.[1] His response was reported:

> Lord Howick, in 1807, brought forward the Catholic Petition, and a Bill was proposed to remove the political disabilities of which the members of that sect complain, Mr Perceval really

alarmed for the safety of the Protestant Church, rose in its defence . . . his speech may be considered as having inflicted the death-blow to an already tottering Administration, whose existence only survived it a few days.[2]

Perceval also wrote anonymous letters to the press opposing the legislation. He played a significant part in the downfall of the government.

In March the King told the Prime Minister of his opposition to the move, and the disintegration of the government began. Grenville and his colleagues had to drop the idea. Then the King, in response to a minute in which the ministers stated that they could not be restrained from introducing a similar measure in the future, demanded a formal pledge that the Catholic question would never be reopened. The government refused this, and, consequently, the King sent for the opposition to form a new government. There was much residual animosity regarding the controversy:

They were required to pledge themselves that they would not hereafter agitate the question; but as to this they would not consent, they were dismissed, and in a great measure rendered ridiculous to their opponents and the country at large.[3]

On one side it was contended that the King could do no wrong; and on the other, the ex-ministers insinuated that the King had done wrong, in demanding a pledge from them which their honour and their oaths as privy counsellors forbade them to give.[4]

Probably the biggest legacy of Grenville's administration was the passing of the legislation providing for the abolition of the slave trade. The famous anti-slavery campaigner, William Wilberforce, in return for his support of the new government, got an assurance from Perceval that the implementation of the legislation would proceed unopposed.[5]

In 1807 the Tory, William Bentinck, the Duke of Portland, took up the honour of the office of Prime Minister for the second time in his life. He had enjoyed a long and distinguished career. Earlier in his life he had been a leading Whig, serving twice under

Rockingham. After the death of Rockingham he resigned from the administration of Shelburne. He became Prime Minister in 1783 of the so-called Fox–North coalition. He was leader of the Whigs in opposition when Pitt became Prime Minister. He altered his views, however, after the French Revolution and decided to turn away from Fox and his colleagues, instead joining Pitt in coalition in 1794. Thereafter he remained a Tory. Like Perceval, Portland was an opponent of Catholic emancipation. By now, however, he was an old man, infirm and ineffectual, and he contributed little or nothing to the work of Parliament during this term. George Canning was appointed as the new Foreign Secretary, Castlereagh as Secretary of State for war again and Lord Eldon as Lord Chancellor. At first, Perceval was reluctant to accept the offer of Chancellor of the Exchequer in Portland's government. He was aware that such an important portfolio would require his full-time attention and would, therefore, result in a considerable decrease in his earnings from his legal practice. With a large family to support, he expressed a willingness instead to take on the less onerous and more lucrative positions at the Home Office or as Attorney-General again. He was finally persuaded to accept the position of Chancellor of the Exchequer, along with the Chancellorship of the Duchy of Lancaster for life, which came with an additional salary of £4,000 a year. However, when this plan of granting him the Duchy of Lancaster for life was opposed and defeated in Parliament, he decided to take on the position of Chancellor of the Exchequer anyway. He also took on the role of Leader of the House.

It was a period in office that he began with no little sense of trepidation: 'I shudder as you do at the financial and other labours,' he wrote to his brother, Lord Arden.[6] Others shared his unease about his ability to do the job. Sheridan said that the new Chancellor of the Exchequer, 'though a very frequent speaker in the House, had never, to his knowledge, uttered one word on the subject of finance in this life'.[7]

Soon after getting into office, in an effort to increase the majority, the Cabinet decided to ask the King to dissolve Parliament. The major issue of the election that followed became the so-called No Popery theme, reflecting the great fear of many Protestants about

Catholic emancipation. Perceval was seen, correctly, as a staunch opponent of Catholic emancipation. He told his constituents 'that he was called upon to give up his profession, to make a stand for the religious establishment of the country'.[8] He criticised the policy of the former government: 'A measure had been proposed to Parliament by the late Administration, which, opening to the Roman Catholics the highest commands in the army and navy, appeared to me in itself highly objectionable and alarming.'[9] He was returned once again unopposed in an election that he and his colleagues won decisively.

In 1808 the Percevals decided to relinquish the rented Belsize house and bought a new country residence called Elm Grove in Ealing at a price of £7,500, with an expected £4,000 cost for repairs. Along with the house went thirty-six acres of land. Perceval borrowed the money from the trustees of Jane's dowry.[10] Perceval, as Chancellor of the Exchequer, would now move with his family to Downing Street.

The major problem facing the new government would be the war against Napoleon's France, which was still raging on the Continent. Britain had become part of the Third Coalition in 1805, and the Fourth in 1806. In 1807 George Canning came into possession of intelligence indicating that Napoleon intended to take and use the Danish fleet, and so Canning decided to seize it first in order to prevent this. In the House of Commons Perceval commented that the action 'was both wise and politic, as we could not entirely prevent the execution of his plan, at least to endeavour to render it abortive, by disarming those powers of their means of hostility'.[11] In 1808 that crucial period of the war known as the Peninsula campaign, fought on the Iberian peninsula, commenced. It also saw the first period of command by Sir Arthur Wellesley, the future Duke of Wellington, as a commander of the British forces in the peninsula. He won a victory over the French army at Vimeiro, but the effect of this was damaged when his superior officers did not allow him to rout the enemy and instead agreed, under the Convention of Cintra, to allow the French to leave Portugal with their plunder. The enemy was even carried away to safety on British ships.[12] These events negated any motivational or propaganda advantages that had come from Wellesley's victory, and caused much political embarrassment to the government at home.

In early 1809 there was more trouble when a House of Commons Committee was established to investigate a scandal that had erupted regarding the Duke of York and the selling of military appointments. It came to light that the Duke's mistress, Mrs Clarke, had accepted money from army officers who were then promoted. Mrs Clarke, in her evidence, claimed that the Duke was not only aware of this illegal practice, but was involved. The Duke wrote to Perceval denying that he was involved or that he even knew it was going on. During the investigation, Perceval, along with the Attorney General, was rebuked by Mr Wilberforce for browbeating witnesses in the House.[13] Perceval himself got drawn into the investigation as a witness as a result of a controversy regarding a written note. Some time earlier William Adam MP had brought to Perceval's attention the information that a Captain Sandon was claiming to have in his possession a note written by the Duke of York, which proved the royal's involvement in the corrupt practices. Adam and Perceval sent a message to Captain Sandon telling him to preserve the note until he was asked to appear before the Bar of the House to give evidence. They also informed the Duke of York of the alleged existence of the note. Captain Sandon then claimed to have destroyed the note before receiving their instructions. Perceval and Adam were criticised by some because they had not informed the House of this information immediately, but had remained silent about the note until the case against the Duke had been presented. Perceval explained his motives to the House:

When the communication was made to me, I thought at the first it was a very extraordinary circumstance; and when I found that the note was . . . destroyed, coupled with the direct assertion of the royal Duke, that this note was a forgery, I thought it to be a forgery, and I determined to act upon the supposition of its being such, and upon that impression, and with a view the better to detect it, if it were so, I thought it better that all the witnesses that could in any degree have been concerned in that transaction, should have told their own tale to the Committee, before they were in any degree informed, by me at least, or by the course that we took, of our being in possession of any fact, or inclined to make use of the information we had of any fact; it might break in upon their own plan of narrating it to the Committee . . .[14]

On 8 March the House began to debate the evidence. Late that night Perceval began his contribution to the debate, which he concluded the following morning. His speech was widely praised. His daughter Fanny became aware of its merits, writing: 'You may have read Papa's speech. Don't you think it excellent? Everybody thinks so, even some of the Oppositionists.'[15] Perceval's resolution that the Duke of York was innocent was passed on 17 March. But the small majority, only 278 votes to 196, and the scandal caused by Mrs Clarke's evidence meant that the Duke had to resign as Commander-in-Chief anyway, and Sir David Dundas was appointed in his place.

The Duke probably did not feel altogether satisfied that a majority of eighty-two members of the House of Commons had acquitted him of *connivance* in Mrs Clarke's business, and he might probably think that the two hundred members who had voted him guilty, although a minority in the House of Commons, spoke the unequivocal sense of a very great majority of the people out of doors.[16]

In May 1809 Perceval became involved in another controversy, this time concerning the issue of parliamentary reform, when William Madocks MP proposed a motion in the House of Commons charging him and Lord Castlereagh of corrupt practices regarding the influence of the Treasury in the election of Members to Parliament. A famous quote of Perceval's was made during the ensuing debate when he said that he would make no reply 'to the nothing that had been said'.[17] In the end, Madock's motion, and the attempt he made to proceed with it again a few days later, came to nothing. It was, however, part of the inexorable move towards the reform of the electoral system that was to come.

Tensions between two leading members of the Portland administration reached a dramatic climax in the autumn of 1809. Castlereagh, the War Minister, and Canning, the Foreign Minister, had not agreed with each other for some time, differing over matters of policy such as the Convention of Cintra and the scandal concerning the Duke of York. In March 1809 Canning had written to the Prime Minister complaining about the inadequacies of the government as it was constituted at that time and threatening to resign.[18] In the discussions that followed he made it clear that he wanted changes, primarily the removal of Castlereagh from the Ministry of War. Portland brought these concerns to the King, and it was agreed that Castlereagh would be ousted from his ministerial position after the next prorogation of Parliament. Canning was dissatisfied but, for now, went along with this arrangement. Castlereagh knew nothing about it.

Perceval found out about this secret arrangement to oust Castlereagh only as Parliament was prorogued in the summer. The Cabinet was in the process of planning a major military expedition, known as the Walcheren expedition, and he felt it was the wrong time to remove the War Minister. The King agreed, and Castlereagh's removal was thus postponed. Frantic covert negotiations continued in an attempt to find a way to remove Castlereagh without causing a split in the government. Yet the principal player was still kept in the dark.

By this time the Duke of Portland's health was failing, and when he suffered a stroke, it became very obvious to all that the government ought to consider the question of who would eventually replace him. There was a delicate balance between the various members of the Cabinet at the time, with no one apparently head and shoulders above the rest. Perceval, for his part, recognised how difficult a group it would be to lead and, at this point, was saying that he did not want the position.[19] Eventually, he was persuaded to change his mind, and the leadership question came down to a choice between him and George Canning. The main contenders discussed the matter between them in what was, outwardly at least, an amicable fashion, but came to no agreement over which of them was to become Prime Minister and which of them was to step aside.[20]

The Walcheren Expedition did not go well, and news of its failure reflected badly on Castlereagh as Minister for War. Canning once again called for him to be replaced. By now Castlereagh had found out about what was going on behind his back, and, infuriated, he resigned. Some days later he challenged Canning to a duel. Canning answered Castlereagh's demand for satisfaction, and they met on Putney Heath on the morning of 21 September. Perceval had tried in vain to prevent the duel by showing Castlereagh some letters that Canning had written to him, in which it was clear that Canning had not wanted to keep Castlereagh in ignorance of what had been going on.[21] But his efforts came to nothing, and the duel went ahead. Both men missed with their first shots, but on the second attempt Castlereagh managed to wound Canning in the upper thigh.[22]

Portland, now a very ill man, was persuaded to offer his resignation in September 1809, but the King asked him to remain in office until his successor was decided upon. Canning, damaged by his actions in the dispute with Castlereagh, began to lose ground, and Perceval became the only serious contender for the leadership of the Tories and the position of First Lord of the Treasury or Prime Minister. He had, after all, played a significant role in running the administration for some time and had a good record both as Attorney-General and Chancellor of the Exchequer.

Chapter 8

PRIME MINISTER PERCEVAL

On 4 October 1809, at 46 years of age, Spencer Perceval became First Lord of the Treasury or Prime Minister of the United Kingdom of Great Britain and Ireland. King George III described him as 'the most straightforward man he . . . [had] . . . almost ever known'.[1] Within a few weeks the former Prime Minister, the Duke of Portland, died. Canning, whose attempt to become Prime Minister had failed, now refused to serve in Perceval's administration. As Perceval failed to find anyone willing to accept the position of Chancellor of the Exchequer, although he offered it to at least five people, he was forced to retain that post as well. On a point of honour he felt that it would be wrong to accept the additional salary of £2,800 for the position. The fact that he declined the Chancellor's salary was something he said nothing about either in Parliament or to the press, and it became known only six months later, when he was accused in Parliament of being a 'placehunter' or covetous of Cabinet positions.[2] Perceval's new government included Lord Wellesley as Foreign Secretary, Lord Liverpool at the Colonial Office and Richard Ryder at the Home Office. Many believed that this new government would not last long. It had many problems to face, not least, of course, the fact that the country was still in the throes of the difficult Peninsular campaign of the war against France.

Nor were the members of Cabinet permitted to find their feet. When Parliament opened in January 1810, they were bombarded by opposition criticisms regarding the conduct of the war, and, in particular, the ill-fated Walcheren expedition. The country was, at that time, part of the Fifth Coalition formed in 1809. The aim of the Walcheren expedition had been to attack the French naval base at Antwerp, but when the British captured and stationed themselves on the swampy Island of Walcheren they soon found themselves suffering from thousands of cases of Malaria. To make matters worse their medical provisions proved to be wholly inadequate to cope with the crisis. In the end the expedition had to be abandoned, the government lost millions of pounds on the debacle, and thousands of men had died or were seriously ill. As a result of all this the government suffered a number of defeats in the House. In March the findings of an inquiry into the Walcheren expedition were debated and the government only narrowly managed to win the subsequent vote. The reputation of the Commander of the Walcheren expedition, the Earl of Chatham, was fatally damaged by the whole affair and he later resigned.

Perceval's government was not only under attack from the opposition benches but also from a radical element in wider society. One contentious issue became ignited in February when Charles Yorke enforced a standing order requiring the removal of all strangers from the House during the Committee of Inquiry into the Walcheren expedition. This was followed by a speech from William Windham in which he attacked the press. These events raised the hackles of those who supported the concept of the freedom of the press, and one group in particular, the British Forum, began to agitate by placing placards in Westminster and holding a public debate on the issue. Yorke then put forward a motion that led to the Secretary of the British Forum, John Gale Jones, being summoned to the Bar of the House to answer for his group's activities. Jones found himself dispatched to Newgate Prison.[3] This, in turn, drew the firebrand MP, Sir Francis Burdett, into the fray in March. He made a strong speech on the issue and wrote a letter, published in Cobbett's *Political Register*, in which he supported the rights of the people and the press to watch and report on the proceedings of the House of Commons. In April it was decided by the House that Burdett should be sent to Tower of London for his comments, a move strongly supported by Perceval: 'Mr Perceval . . . was for punishing, what he called one of the grossest attacks ever made upon the character and privileges of the House.'[4]

By this time a mob was already beginning to gather and constables had been forced to disperse a number of people who had collected in the lobbies and Palace Yard. Rioting began in the city. It was not long before the windows had been smashed in a number of houses, including those belonging to Yorke, Castlereagh and Perceval. Anyone brave enough to pass through Piccadilly without calling out 'Burdett for ever' was pelted with mud. Foot and Horse Guards had to be mobilised to seal up Piccadilly, most shops had to shut and the Riot Act was read. Meanwhile, after a number of failed attempts to apprehend Sir Burdett, accompanied by much legal wrangling, he was finally arrested on 9 April. After this the situation on the street calmed somewhat. On 17 April a motion in the House of Commons for the release of Gale Jones was carried. Burdett was eventually released in June after Parliament had been prorogued.

That same month the trial took place of William Cobbett, the famous publisher and writer of the *Political Register*, against whom Perceval, as Attorney General, had earlier won a conviction for libel. Cobbett had been a vocal critic of the government for some time, and the authorities were waiting for an opportunity to quieten him. On this occasion he had written an article criticising the putting-down of a mutiny of English militiamen by having them flogged by mercenary Hanoverian soldiers. The article resulted in a conviction for libel and a two-year prison sentence for William Cobbett. He also received a £1,000 fine, and the court declared that on his release he would be bound over on a £3,000 bond with two sureties in the amount of £1,000 to ensure that he kept the peace for seven years. Undaunted, Cobbett continued to write his powerful political pieces from Newgate Prison.

One of Perceval's biggest political challenges came in October 1810 when King George III, faced with the terminal illness of his daughter Amelia, began to show signs of the mental illness that had struck him before in 1788, 1801 and 1804.[5] All through October his psychological health continued to deteriorate until his doctors felt it necessary to constrain him in a straitjacket. The Princess died on 2 November and was buried on the 14th. Four days before her death Perceval had an audience with the King and afterwards described his Majesty's conversation as 'hurried' and 'diffuse, explicit and indiscreet'.[6] Following a number of adjournments of Parliament, Perceval was forced to come to the conclusion that the King was gravely ill, and this time likely never to recover his sanity.

This created a situation that was to bring Perceval once more into conflict with the heir to the throne. In December 1810 he advised the Prince of Wales that the Cabinet planned to introduce a Regency Bill, by which he would effectively take his father's place, but with several restrictions on power. William Pitt the Younger had faced this situation before, and the restrictions proposed by Perceval had been devised by Pitt in the late 1780s. These restrictions would be in place for one year and they stipulated that the Prince Regent would not be permitted to create peers or to grant offices or pensions except under clearly defined circumstances. All the King's property would be vested in trustees and his care entrusted to the Queen and a council appointed by Parliament.

Perceval and his supporters thought the restrictions necessary because of the frivolous, wayward and profligate nature of the Prince of Wales. The Prince, understandably, was furious. He was not well disposed towards Perceval anyway and he objected strongly to any restrictions being placed upon his rule. In response he brought together all the male branches of the royal family, his six brothers and his cousin, and had a protest document drawn up and signed by them all, which was forwarded to Perceval. The Prime Minister replied, telling the Prince firmly that the proposals had the support of a majority of the House of Commons and the House of Lords. The Whig opposition fought against the Bill in Parliament with every hope that the government would fall on the issue. Perceval, however, was determined to face down any opposition on the Bill, including that coming from the Prince of Wales. After some serious parliamentary confrontation, Perceval's oratory and doggedness won the day, and the Regency Bill passed into law. The Prime Minister's skilful handling of this delicate issue was widely recognised:

> Perceval had succeeded in steering the Regency Bill through troubled waters in practically its original state. Handicapped from the commencement, he brought the Bill single-handed through the House of Commons with a determination and pluck that won the admiration of both sides.[7]

Although he won great praise from both sides of the house for his performance, Perceval was, according to Plumer Ward, modest about his victory:

> I told him, with unfeigned regard and pleasure, the various things said of him by all parties, and congratulated him on the spreading of his fame. I said . . . I might do this without any gross flattery. I mentioned (what my City friends enabled me to know) the high opinion of him there entertained, as a worthy successor of Mr Pitt. He replied, in all that unaffected simplicity of heart and manner that belongs so peculiarly to him, that, though he could not fail being pleased with all that his friends told him, he really could not help wondering that anything he had done should be thought so praiseworthy; that what he had to do was the merest plain-sailing in the world . . .[8]

Many now felt sure, especially the Whigs, that, once the Prince of Wales had become Regent, he would not delay in removing Perceval and his colleagues from office. After all, he had waited some time to vent his anger on Perceval, the man who had been involved in the Seymour case and had been counsel to the Princess of Wales during the Delicate Investigation. He had now placed restrictions on the Prince's ability to rule. Many were of the opinion that Perceval was the old King's man and that the Regent would insist on change. The truth of these sentiments seemed to be confirmed, only the month before, when the Prince had made the statement that 'By God, they shall not remain one hour!'[9] But then, on 1 February, the Queen wrote to the Prince warning him that to hear of a change in government might do the King's health no good at all. The Prince also knew that there was a possibility that the King might make a good recovery, which at times looked highly possible. If that turned out to be the case, then there was little point in the Prince making sweeping changes in government. The Whigs believed that this idea of the King's recovery was being used to put pressure on the Prince. Lord Grey regarded the letter from the Queen, in which she told the Prince how attentive the King had been to the Prime Minister's report on business in Parliament, as nothing more than a plan on the part of Perceval to retain power:

The letter is evidently written in concert with Perceval, appears indeed to be of his dictation, and is evidently part of a plan . . . to intimidate the Prince by the expectation of the King's immediate recovery, from changing the Administration. So bare-faced a plot . . . ought to have a directly contrary effect. But I believe it will be successful.[10]

But there was the fact that, by now, the Prince Regent's opinions regarding a number of serious political matters was closer to those held by Perceval and the Tories than to those held by the Whigs. He was in favour of the continuation of the war against Napoleon and was opposed to the introduction of Catholic emancipation. He also wanted to reinstate the Duke of York as Commander-in-Chief, and the Whigs were very uneasy about that. Neither could they countenance an alliance with George Canning and his supporters, which the Prince suggested. None the less, the Whigs felt hopeful enough to draw up a list of possible Cabinet members, which included Grenville as Prime Minister and Grey as Foreign Secretary. However, they soon began to suspect that things were not going their way. Lord Grey was worried: 'I do not believe he will have the nerves to take the manly and decisive measures which alone can enable him to conduct the Government with effect, and I am persuaded, if the present reports of the King's improved state continue, that he will not dare to make any change in the Administration.'[11]

Finally the news came; following a long discussion with the Duke of York, the Prince announced that he had decided against making any change of government for now. He wrote to Perceval on 4 February telling him so and explaining why:

The Prince feels it incumbent on him, at this precise juncture, to communicate to Mr Perceval his intention not to remove from their stations those whom he finds there as His Majesty's official servants. At the same time the Prince owes it to the truth and sincerity of his character, which he trusts will appear in every action of his life, in whatever station placed, explicitly to declare that the irresistible impulse of filial duty and affection, to his beloved and afflicted father, leads him to dread that any act of the Regent might in the smallest degree have the effect of interfering with the progress of the Sovereign's recovery.

This consideration alone dictates the decision now communicated to Mr Perceval.[12]

The Prince Regent was sworn in on 6 February 1811 at Carlton House. During the ceremony the Privy Counsellors approached the Regent one by one, knelt and kissed his hand. Although he had decided to keep Perceval in office, his continuing unease about the situation was believed by some to be demonstrated by the fact that when the Prime Minister took his hand the Prince turned his face away.

The Regent's speech that was read at the official opening of Parliament on 12 February 1811 was written by Perceval and 'could not be better', according to the Prince.[13] Indeed, over time, a good working relationship developed between the two men. The Whig Tomas Creevey was struck by this as he noticed dinner being prepared for the Prince at Downing Street one evening:

I passed Perceval's kitchen just now, and saw four men cooks and twice as many maids preparing dinner for the Prince of Wales and Regent, – he whose wife Perceval set up against him in open battle, who, at the age of fifty, could not be trusted by the said Perceval with the unrestrained government of these realms during his father's incapacity . . .[14]

With the question of the regency resolved for now, Perceval could turn his attention back to the many other problems facing the country.

Chapter 9

FINAL DAYS

The Prime Minister had a number of difficult issues to face in the coming months such as the campaign for Catholic emancipation, which he opposed, the depressed state of the economy and, as ever, the conduct of the continuing war with France. What was to become a major problem in the country emerged at the end of 1811 in the East Midlands when the skilled framework-knitters began to smash up the machines that had been developed to allow unskilled labourers to produce inferior quality stockings, which they regarded as a threat to their livelihoods. This practice, which became known as Luddism, soon began to spread. The government responded by making the breaking of machines in this way a capital offence, despite the opposition of Lord Byron and others.

As for the war, the Opposition still railed against it and used every military failure to score political points. After the low point of the Walcheren expedition, Arthur Wellesley, later Duke of Wellington, went back into action to assume chief command of the British Forces in Portugal and began to enjoy a number of military successes. In April 1809 he defeated the French troops at Porto. He won the Battle of Talavera de la Reina, for which he was created Viscount Wellington of Talavera and of Wellington. In 1810 Wellington managed to slow down the invading French army in Portugal and prevented them from taking Lisbon by constructing an earthwork at Torres Vedras. He eventually managed to drive them out of Portugal, the enemy making their last stand at a garrison in Almeida, which he placed under siege and took. His successes continued in 1811 and in May of that year he was promoted to the rank of general. Wellington himself was pleased with the progress being made. He wrote to Liverpool in February 1811:

'We are becoming a more efficient army every day.' These successes reflected well on Perceval's leadership. The good news from
the war continued in January 1812 when Wellington captured
Cuidad Rodrigo, which he achieved by attacking while the French
were moving into their winter quarters. Wellington's military successes were a great encouragement to those like Perceval and the
Prince Regent who believed that it was the right policy to continue
the war to its end. The Prince expressed his pleasure: 'Instead of
suffering any loss of her possessions by the gigantic force which
has been employed against them, Great Britain has added most
important acquisitions to her Empire.'[1]

The Regency restrictions were due to terminate in February
1812, and the Whigs had hoped that this would mark the end of
Perceval's period as Prime Minister. But Wellington's recent successes in the war had made that less likely. The Whigs damaged
their cause even more when, in January, they introduced a motion
in the House of Lords, and afterwards in the House of Commons,
concerning the question of Catholic emancipation. They were
defeated in the vote, and it did them no good with the Prince. All
in all, the Prince was happy with the way things were progress-
ing. Just days before the end of the restricted Regency he wrote:
'I cannot but reflect with satisfaction on the events which have
distinguished the short period of my restricted Regency.'[2] The
most he felt he could offer the Whigs at this time was an invitation
for a group of their leading members to join Perceval's ministry.
Grenville and Grey refused the offer on behalf of the Whig party
saying that the 'differences of opinion' between them and the present government were 'too many and too important'.[3] The Whigs
felt sorely betrayed by the Prince. Their one-time ardent supporter,
and the almost fanatical admirer of the late Charles Fox, had let
them down. Perceval remained in power.

At the end of April 1812 news reached London that Wellington
had been successful yet again and had taken the Spanish Fortress
of Badojoz. But, at home, there was a growing sense of discon-
tent. Now only was there the problem of the Luddites, but also, by
1812, the Orders in Council were causing a lot of anger among
the general population. Since 1806 there had been an economic
dimension to the war with France. Both sides were attempting

to hinder and damage the trade of the other. Under the Berlin and Milan Decrees Napoleon had banned all neutral trade with Britain. The French were seizing and confiscating British goods and attempting to intimidate neutral countries from trading with Britain. It is doubtful to what extent this policy had been success-ful for them. The introduction of a series of Orders in Council represented the British side of this struggle, the intention being to blockade French ports and search and seize neutral ships sus-pected of carrying French goods. The effect of these Orders on trade, however, was now creating unrest. They were being blamed for creating difficult economic conditions for many industries at home in Britain, such as cotton manufacturing in the north. Moreover, the problem was not just felt at home, as there was also a negative impact on American trade. In response the American Congress passed the Embargo Act and later the Non-Intercourse Act. Protracted negotiations were held between Washington and London in an effort to settle their differences on the issue, with little success. In Parliament the Opposition was fighting hard for the repeal of the Orders. Mr Brougham MP called for a commit-tee to look into the matter: 'The object of this committee will be, to enquire into the effects of the Orders in Council, to enquire whether they have counteracted or assisted the policy of the enemy, what is the nature, the cause, and the extent of the dis-tress felt throughout the country, and what is the most advisable remedy to be applied . . .'[4]

Perceval rose in the House to speak against the motion. He objected to it, he said, not 'from any apprehension that he enter-tained of enquiry, confident as he was that the distresses of the merchants and manufacturers, which had been so strongly alluded to on the other side, did not all arise from the Orders in Council; but he objected to the inquiry because it was not calcu-lated to produce any possible benefit'.[5]

He gave the background to the implementation of the Orders as he saw it:

What was the occasion that led to the Orders in Council? France had declared that Great Britain should not have any trade with any nation upon earth; the British government, in return, said,

'You (France) shall have no trade but with us.' The object of government was to protect and to force the trade of this country, which had been assailed in such an unprecedented manner by the French Decrees. If the Orders in Council had not been issued, France would have a free colonial trade by means of neutrals, and we should have been shut out of the continent . . .[6]

Petitions began to come in from all parts of the country objecting to the Orders and in April the government eventually assented to a committee of the whole House to look at the issue.

Throughout the early days of May 1812 the work of this committee continued. Members were engaged in the examination of witnesses. On Thursday 7 May Brougham proposed that the committee should sit on the following Saturday from three o'clock to five o'clock. This was objected to by Perceval. If the Saturday sitting could not be agreed upon, Brougham urged that they meet on Monday so that they could conclude with the work as quickly as possible. This was agreed.[7] On Friday 8 May Perceval made what was to be his last contribution to debate in the House of Commons. The House was debating Mr Brand's motion respecting reform in Parliament and an alteration in the representation there. Perceval spoke against Brand's motion, which was defeated.

With business in the House of Commons concluded for the week, Perceval spent the weekend with his family, which was something that always gave him pleasure. The responsibilities of being Prime Minister did not make for an easy family life. His brother Lord Arden would later allude to 'the labour, fatigue and anxiety of his situation'.[8] No. 10 Downing Street was split in two, with the living quarters above and the Prime Minister's working area on the ground floor. He rose early every morning and had his breakfast alone. His days were filled with work and after a solitary dinner he would continue to labour, usually late into the night. Even when Parliament was in recess and the family moved to their country residence at Elm Grove, Ealing, he would still travel to Downing Street regularly.

Still, Perceval did all he could to find time for his family. His eldest son, Spencer, would, in a few days time, take part in the Speech Day activities at Harrow, the school that he himself had attended. Before the boy had been sent to the school, Perceval had employed John Carey, who had worked previously for Thomas Jefferson in America, at half-a-guinea a time to prepare him for the academic work ahead. Perceval himself composed a set of rhyming rules for Latin versification for him. As he neared the end of his time at Harrow, Perceval sent him an edition of Bell's *Edition of the Poets* and told his son that study of such things would:

> improve and enrich your knowledge of the English language which, at least, is the language which you will have most occasion in life to employ, and which perhaps is generally too little attended to in schools. Not that I would have you attend to that in preference to the learned languages, but neither should be neglected. Remember this is the last year of your schooling and that I have always told you more may be done in the last year than in any of the five years which have preceded it.[9]

The father, like many another before him, worried about the boy's interest in other activities and gently scolded him with the words: 'I fear that football is upon the whole a more favourite pursuit with you than your books.'[10] Of the other boys, Frederick, the second son, was not healthy and attended a special school, while Henry and Dudley Montague also attended Harrow.

On the previous Sunday, at St Martin's Church, Perceval had seen his elder, gregarious and lively daughters confirmed by the Bishop of London.[11] Fanny had recently decided to add Eleanor to her name to become Frances Eleanor Perceval, which she felt was more becoming to the daughter of the Prime Minister. Most of the Perceval children, John, Isobella, Louisa, Frederica and Ernest were still very young.

Sundays always began with a trip to the church at Ealing, or St Margaret's, Westminster, for religious services. On this particular Sunday morning, 10 May 1812, the Prime Minister enjoyed the pleasure of being with his family, away from the bustle of political life. When his valet informed him that he was to have no guests for dinner that evening, he commented: 'Then I am happy, for I shall have a pleasure I very seldom enjoy, of dining with my family alone.'[12] Once prayers had been said and they had read from the Bible, he asked his wife Jane to allow the children to stay up for a little longer. When the time came for them to go to bed, they all gathered around their father and kissed him good night. He blessed each one of them. Perceval believed that the happiness of children was 'as great as anything . . . this world can produce'.[13]

He spent Monday morning, 11 May 1812, working at home. He said goodbye to his wife around lunchtime as she went on a visit to Frederica Ryder, the wife of the Home Secretary. It was later that day, on his way to take part in the continuing inquiry into the Orders in Council, that Spencer Perceval was assassinated by John Bellingham.

Chapter 10

THE ASSASSIN

John Bellingham was born around 1770 and spent most of his infant years at St Neots, Huntingdon.[1] His father, also called John Bellingham, was a land surveyor and painter of miniatures who may have exhibited in the 1760s in the Great Room of the Spring Garden as part of the Annual Exhibition of the Society of Artists of Great Britain.[2] His mother was Elizabeth Scarbrow, the daughter of a well-to-do family from St Neots.[3] Bellingham's parents were married on 12 May 1767 in the parish church of St Dunstan-in-the-West, Fleet Street.[4] He had an elder sister, Mary, who in adult life became a dressmaker.

By 1779 the Bellinghams were living in London at No. 8 Great Titchfield Street, close to Oxford Market, in a house that had previously been owned by the diplomat Caleb Whitefoord. Around 1780 Bellingham's father began to show signs of mental illness. Although he was committed to St Luke's Assylum, they could do nothing for him and after a year he returned home, where he died. At this point the Bellingham family could have become destitute except for the fact that his mother's brother in law, William Daw, came to their assistance. Mr Daw was the clerk of the King's silver in the Court of Common Pleas and a barrister.[5] He was good to them, even though Elizabeth's family had never wanted her to marry John Bellingham senior in the first place.

The young John Bellingham seems to have developed into a troublesome and somewhat stubborn youth. At the age of 14 he was sent as an apprentice to a jeweller, Mr Love in Whitechapel, from where he ran away and went to sea. Mr Daw seems to have helped out again when, in 1787, he took advantage of the boy's interest in maritime matters and got him a place on the East

Indiaman *Hartwell*, a 900-ton ship sailing from Gravesend to China. This was the maiden voyage of the ship and, unfortunately, did not proceed uneventfully. The crew mutinied and had only just been brought under control by the officers and the captain when the ship hit a reef near the Cape de Verd Islands and sank. As it happened the entire crew, including young John Bellingham, managed to make it to land.[6]

Perhaps having had enough of the perils of sailing and mutinous crews for a while, Bellingham decided to find work in London, where he took a position as a clerk. He was later sent on his first visit to Archangel in Russian as a representative of a London commercial house. After a time he began operating on his own behalf as a merchant broker in Liverpool. His work consisted of acting as an agent for importers and exporters in both Russian and Irish trade, and arranging for the insurance cover of shipping with London insurance companies.

In 1803 Bellingham married Mary Neville, who came from a family of Quakers. Her father was a ship's broker, merchant and auctioneer from Newry in Ireland and it was probably through his business connections with Mr Neville that Bellingham first became acquainted with Mary. Her family had gone through difficult financial times, with her father being declared bankrupt twice, in 1797 and 1804, after which they moved to Dublin. She was under 20 years of age when she married John Bellingham.

When Bellingham sailed on business from Liverpool to Archangel in Russia during the summer of 1804, he brought with him his young wife Mary and their infant son. Archangel was at that time Russia's most important port in the north, and Britain, especially in commodities such as timber and iron, was its principal trading partner. The port was built on the banks of the Dvina river. Because of the harshness of its climate it was open for shipping only during the summer months. Bellingham did not know it yet, but events were conspiring in Archangel that would lead to his downfall. In 1803 a ship called the *Sojus* had sunk in the White Sea.[7] This ship was owned by the wealthy Russian merchants Solomon van Brienen and Vassiley Popoff, the Mayor of Archangel. Although the ship was insured by Lloyds of London, the insurance company refused to compensate the owners on the basis of an anonymous letter they had received in which it was claimed that the ship had been sabotaged by themselves for fraudulent purposes. Van Brienen believed that John Bellingham had sent that letter.

By November 1804 Bellingham had concluded his business in Archangel. He was preparing, with his wife and child, to travel home through St Petersburg, as the severe winter weather had, as usual, closed up the port of Archangel. Van Brienen and Popoff were planning their revenge, however, and they did not want Bellingham to leave until they had proved their case regarding the anonymous letter sent to Lloyds. They arranged to have him accused of non-payment of an outstanding debt. Bellingham was accused of owing money for a consignment of iron, to a Mr Conrad Dorbecker, a bankrupt for whom van Brienen and Popoff were assignees. At first it was claimed that he owed as much as 38,000 roubles but this was eventually reduced to 4,890 roubles.[8]

Without warning, the police arrived at Bellingham's lodgings and deprived him of his legally obtained travelling pass, his *Petrosnick*, until the matter of this outstanding debt could be settled. Bellingham was shocked and denied vehemently that he owed any money to these people. He told the authorities that he had already paid in full for all the iron he had received from Mr Dorbecker; furthermore, he was emphatic that, if the assignees could supply him with an account of any monies owing, and if their claim was found to be valid, he would willingly pay any outstanding bill.[9] Nevertheless he was prevented from leaving Archangel, and for the next three months was kept under the surveillance of the authorities. He later described the turn of events in his own words:

> I arrived at Archangel from Liverpool in a vessel chartered by myself for mercantile purposes in the summer of 1804, and was illegally prevented from returning to England by the said ship as was my intention, and also was so much injured as to be deprived of the opportunity of loading my own goods on board of her and for which she was expressly chartered, which detention and prevention occasioned me very serious losses.

> . . . I took out a travelling pass or petrovnick for St Petersburg
> . . . the said petrovnick was forcibly taken from me by the police
> Master without any cause whatever, and soldiers and police
> officers were placed on [my] person day and night to prevent
> [my] quitting the place . . .[10]

Bellingham believed that the real intention of van Brienen and Popoff was to hold him in Russia until they could prove that it was he who had informed the insurance company that their ship had been sabotaged by themselves: 'Had the supposition . . . proved true, this masked intention was intended to be dropped, and he was to have been prosecuted for the amount of the insurance on the *Sojus*, which the Underwriters at Lloyds refused to pay.'[11] Bellingham was adamant throughout the whole affair that he had not informed the insurance company of anything to do with the *Sojus*, and his accusers never managed to prove that he had.

Meanwhile, it was decided that Bellingham's wife and young child should travel on to St Petersburg, where they could wait until the matter was resolved and he could join them. Bellingham continued to deny that he owed any money to Drobecker. The Governor-General of Archangel, Furster, received almost daily letters from him in January and February of 1805 in which he complained of the unjust treatment he was suffering and requested a new travel pass. Finally, in February, the matter seemed to be resolved when an examination of the books appeared to show that Drobecker had, in fact, treated Bellingham badly and that, therefore, there were no monies outstanding. Bellingham got his travel pass and finally set off to join his wife and child.

But then, on 3 March, as he was leaving the province, events took a turn for the worse once again. He was seized by the authorities and forcibly brought back to Archangel to face the *Duma*. This time his papers were seized as well. It seems that the powerful van Brienen had got the Governor-General to change his mind and Bellingham was now declared a prisoner. Two days later he was sent to the guardhouse. He once again appealed to the Governor-General for justice in his case:

I have nothing more to do with the Assignees in any shape.
So the affair hangs, and the matter remains with you and the
policy Master to determine whether I am indebted or not . . . I
both hope and expect an immediate order for my liberation after
this notice, or request the favour of your reason in writing why
you suffer my detention.[12]

A hearing was held at which Bellingham only made his situation
worse by becoming infuriated. He was exasperated by the obvious
'U-turn' of the Governor General, who, only a short time earlier,
had admitted that he had no case to answer. He stated this to the
official directly:

In a conversation with your Excellency at the time the pass
was given to me, you acknowledged that the Assignees had all
along acted beyond the law, and if I thought proper could seek
redress. Afterwards, when the Assignees accompanied by three
gentlemen came together before you, this conversation was
introduced by me – which, however you were pleased to deny,
and before them said quite the contrary, and was astonished I
could have the assurance to assert it to your face . . . Mr Brienen
and you supported each other in denying it.
     These are truths which your own conscience must confirm,
and though disacknowledged, yet the facts remain.[13]

Bellingham was also trying to get help from the British authorities.
He wrote a number of letters to the British embassy. When he was
contacted by Bellingham, the British Consul, Sir Stephen Shairp,
wrote to the Russian authorities seeking information about the
case, but was told bluntly that Bellingham's detention was legal
and that, furthermore, the prisoner's behaviour had been 'highly
indecorous'. Bellingham soon grew very dissatisfied with the level
of interest his case was receiving from the British officials. His dis-
satisfaction was not alleviated by a letter he received from Lord
Granville Leveson Gower, the British Ambassador Extraordinary
at St Petersburg, dated 6 May 1805:

Sir,

I have received your several letters to the 31st March inclusive, with the copies of your correspondence enclosed therein.

I am sorry to find that you are involved in so unpleasant a dispute at Archangel, but however desirous I may be of assisting you, it is not in my power to forward any application for permission for you to come to St Petersburg on your sole representation of the circumstances of the transaction in question, particularly as I find this statement contradicted by the letter of the Governor General of Archangel to Mr Shairp.

At the same time, however, that I say this, I wish you to understand, that provided you can furnish me with such evidence of your having been unjustly used, as will authorize my interference on this subject, I shall very readily take such steps in your behalf as the occasion may appear to me to require.

> I am, Sir,
> Your most obedient
> Humble servant,
> Granville Leveson Gower.[14]

At last things seemed to be improving for Bellingham when the Procureur of Archangel, Ivan Fedorisch Makcemove, sent a report to the Minister for Justice, Prince Lapuchin, in which he commented that Bellingham was 'extremely ill used and illegally detained'. Bellingham later claimed that it appeared that Stephen Shairp had also read that report but had taken 'no notice' of it.[15] Finally in September, having spent six months in prison, Bellingham was released but was still not free to leave Archangel.

In October he set about composing a long handwritten petition to the *Graschdanskaja Palata* or State Court in which he appealed, using sixteen arguments, against the resolution of the *Duma* from 9 March, which he had heard about only on 5 October. Under this resolution the verdict had been awarded to the assignees. He once again stated clearly in this document, dated 9 October 1805, that, if the assignees could furnish him with an account proving that he owed any additional money for the iron he received from Mr Dorbecker, he would gladly pay the amount. They could not do this, he claimed, because their accusation was fraudulent.

However, before he could even send his petition, he received a communication from the *Duma* telling him that, since he had not yet made any objection to their decision, he had 'consequently forfeited the right of appellation'. Understandably, he was shocked and angered at this new development. He replied by adding an additional piece to his petition, dated 11 October, in which he informed them that he had been 'perpetually complaining which is a complete refutation of the assertion'.[16] When a new Civil Governor, Baron Asch, was appointed to Archangel and Bellingham brought the case to his attention, finally there was some action. Bellingham wrote:

To him I stated the cruel circumstances under which I was detained. He very candidly said that I was either innocent or guilty: if innocent I ought to be discharged, and if guilty I ought to be tried. He took up my cause, for I had no friends besides: I was surrounded by enemies; but he generously stepped forward, and bringing the matter into a Court of Justice, I obtained judgement against the whole party, including the Military Governor who had injured me.[17]

Bellingham's travel pass was returned and he got ready, once again, to leave Archangel. Just to underline the fact he wrote to the police on 18 October 1805, informing them of the situation:

The Assignees of Mr Dorbecker not having established their claim as required by law after a complete investigation of the affair in the Dooma – the obligation I gave on the 6th Sepr is entirely done away – and moreover the Procureur has reported that I have been illegally detained. Therefore this is to give notice that I purpose parting for St Petersburg in a few days unless legal cause is shown to the contrary in writing, notice of which have also been given to His Excellency the General Governor & Procureur.[18]

Finally, Bellingham set off to meet his wife and son in St Petersburg. This, however, was not the end of the affair.

Chapter 11

FREE FOR NOW

Bellingham arrived in St Petersburg in November 1805. Finally he was free and reunited with Mary and his young son. He could move around, without restriction, and enjoy the delights of that great city. He could, at this point, have returned home to England. But, instead, he chose to attempt an impeachment of General Furster, the Governor General of Archangel, to the Imperial Senate, citing three grounds:

1. For having sanctioned Mr Solomon van Brienen in an improper oath, knowing it to be so.
2. For having written an untrue account of the affair to Sir Stephen Shairp, his Majesty's Consul, for the purpose of preventing justice.
3. For causing him to be thrown into a loathsome military prison, for the purpose of extorting from him a sum of money, with a view to colour the transaction, and thereby pave the way to a justification of his own conduct, and that of others.[1]

His case for impeachment was presented to Count Kotzebue, the Minister of Justice, who had it investigated through the Chief Government Court at Archangel. According to Bellingham, that court found all his allegations to be valid and Count Kotzebue referred him to the Senate with a document 'for the purpose of obtaining an indemnification for his sufferings, according to law'.[2]

However, events did not proceed as Bellingham expected and on 5 June 1806, his arrest was ordered once again on charges of having left Archangel 'in a clandestine manner' and owing an outstanding debt of 2,000 roubles to some persons there. He was arrested on 11 June and held in custody first in the High Court of Justice, and then in the town prison. Inquiries were made to establish if he was in possession of a legal travel pass, as he claimed. It took the authorities forty days to establish this fact before he was released. But on 20 July he was rearrested for the debt of 2,000 roubles and sent once again to the town prison. At some stage during all this Mary Bellingham, pregnant with their second son, decided that she and their child ought to return home to England. She was helped by an anonymous English gentleman and made the voyage while eight months pregnant. She went with their son to live with her uncle, James Neville, in Wigan, Lancashire.

Back in St Petersburg, on 27 August, Bellingham appeared before the High Criminal Court. On the issue of the debt he made the same argument as before: 'if [they] will have the goodness to produce a proper document on which it is demanded', he told the court, he 'would settle that instant'. The only effect of his argument, however, was that he was sent back to prison and put on bread and water for three days. He was to spend seventy-two days suffering the horrendous conditions of overcrowding, dampness and rat infestation in a variety of Russian prisons. He was subjected to the ignoble experience of being marched through the streets of St Petersburg with the other prisoners. The fact that he was marched in such a degrading manner past the residence of the British Ambassador, whom he felt had done nothing to help him, became deeply imprinted upon his mind and would influence his later actions.

On 1 October things became somewhat easier for him when he was transferred to the custody of the College of Commerce, where he was to remain for the next two and a half years. The college, established under the terms of a treaty between Britain and Russia, had jurisdiction in the area of commercial matters relating to British subjects. It was decided that he should remain in custody there until the matter of the debt was settled. By 1807, however, the terms of his confinement had been relaxed somewhat and he was permitted to go into the streets every now and again in the company of a guard.

Throughout these years he continually solicited the help of the British authorities. During his time as ambassador there the Marquis of Douglas made representations on his behalf but these came to nothing. With Lord Gower back for a new term as ambassador, Bellingham wrote to him on 27 May 1807 with a full account of what had happened to him thus far. He swore to the accuracy of the document before the Revd Benjamin Beresford, acting officiating Minister in St Petersburg for the British congregation. The document began:

> In presence of the Revd Mr Beresford Minister to the English Church of St Petersburg I, John Bellingham, British subject and a Merchant of Liverpool at present under arrest in the College of Commerce St Petersburg, finding my health considerably damaged by an illegal detention in prison, in justice to myself and family have thought it prudent for many reasons to make the following solemn declaration upon oath.[3]

The document went on to lay out the details of his case. On 1 June, on behalf of his brother Stephen, the British Consul-General, Alexander Shairp attached his seal to this document and testified in writing to the identity of the Revd Beresford and the genuineness of the clergyman's signature.

One day in July 1807 Bellingham's actions became more daring when he managed to evade his guard while out on a walk and run into the British Embassy for help. Lord Gower later wrote of the incident: '[He] came running into my house one evening, and solicited me to allow him to remain all night, in order to avoid being retaken into custody by the police, from whom he had escaped. I complied with the request, though I could not, upon any ground, assume to myself the power of protecting him from legal arrest.' He penned a hastily written note to Bellingham explaining his position and asking him to leave:

> Sir,
> I cannot think myself justified under the circumstances of your case in exerting the privilege of the House of the Ambassador to protect you from the custody of the police officer who escorted

you here. I must therefore request you to give yourself up again into his custody, but shall think it my duty to make representations to the Government upon your affair, & shall be happy to use any means in my power towards forwarding an arrangement of the Business in which you are involved.

I am Sir, etc.

G.L. Gower.[4]

Lord Gower later claimed that he had had a conversation with the Russian Minister for Foreign Affairs in which he asked that Bellingham be released on condition that he return to England immediately.[5] This, however, did not come about.

Perhaps in an attempt to resolve the matter, in July 1807 the Senate and the College of Commerce moved to have Bellingham declared a bankrupt. They claimed that all his money and effects were in England and he was, therefore, unable to pay any money owed by him. Bellingham opposed this development vehemently saying that he had never claimed non-payment because his money was in England. Neither would he countenance paying some token amount just to end the matter. He was convinced that, if he did so, it would vindicate the actions taken by the authorities all along, those same authorities against whom, he claimed, he had already won a legal decision. He felt sure that, if he agreed to use the bankruptcy strategy, they would then sue him for bringing false charges against them and he would be sent to Siberia.

In the following November, 1807, Russia cut off political relations with Britain, which added to the difficulty of Bellingham's situation and made the possibility of political intervention in his case more remote. It was not until October 1808 that the Russian authorities, perhaps failing to find any other solution, decided to release him without a pass. This left him in a rather strange legal situation, since he had still not been cleared of the charges against him. To exist in St Petersburg at the time without a pass was difficult and would subject one to harassment from the police. Perhaps they hoped that he would slip secretly and silently out of the country and the problem would disappear. But this was not John Bellingham's way. When there was no sign of a pass being issued to him, he decided that he had no option but to petition the Czar,

His Most Imperial Majesty Alexander Pavlovitch, directly, which he did in December 1808:

> The petitioner has been detained in the Empire of Russia near five years – the last two years and half, he has been under criminal and civil arrest in St Petersburg . . . the College of Commerce proceeded to final judgement on the charge on the 3d June last (1808) and in consequence thereof referred to the Liquidation Commission to bring the affair to a final arrangement, and furnish the necessary clearance that he might obtain his pass for his departure, but notwithstanding this reference and his repeated solicitations so to do, the said commission positively refuses to espouse his cause.
>
> Therefore he most humbly implores your Imperial Majesty will most graciously order said Commission to furnish him with the necessary clearance and at the same time remunerate him for the loss of time occasioned to his prejudice by such long detention . . .[6]

Once again, no immediate answer or help seemed to be forthcoming. But then, ten months later, in October 1809, five years after this terrible episode had first begun, John Bellingham received his discharge from confinement, a travel pass and 'an order to quit the Russian dominions'. All this he regarded as a vindication of his reputation. He left Russia, arriving home in England in December 1809. In his own mind, however, complete justice had not yet been served.

Chapter 12

HOME AGAIN

John Bellingham had spent five years struggling to prove his innocence in Russia. He had been held captive in awful conditions and treated as a common criminal. He had been forced to fight his way alone through the intricate layers of Russian bureaucracy. In addition to all this, in his absence, his business interests back home had fallen into neglect and he was facing financial ruin. It is not surprising to discover that he arrived home to England in December 1809 with intense feelings of bitterness not only towards the Russians, but more importantly towards the British officials and, in particular, Lord Granville Leveson Gower, the British Ambassador, who, in his opinion, had done little or nothing to help him.

He found out that his wife, Mary, and his two sons were living in Liverpool. As it happened, Mary had managed to look after herself and the children very well. After her return to England from Russia, she had spent three months living with her uncle James. She had gone from there to her father's house, but that arrangement had not worked out. She got to know a Miss Mary Stevens, through an aunt of Miss Stevens, and eventually the two women set up a millinery and dressmaking business at No. 46 Duke Street, Liverpool. Mary received some financial help from Uncle James to help establish the enterprise. Surprisingly, Bellingham did not rush to see his family immediately. He chose instead to go to London, where he could pursue his quest for justice.

In London he stayed first with his cousin, the widow Mrs Billett, formerly Ann Scarbrow, and later took lodgings at No. 53 Theobalds Road. It was around Christmas 1809 that Mary received a letter from Mrs Billett telling her of her husband's arrival back in England. Later Bellingham wrote to her himself.[1] It was at this point that he experienced, what was for him at this time, a rare occurrence of good luck. He inherited an amount of money, perhaps up to £400, from his deceased mother, who had been bequeathed it by her sister, Elizabeth Daw.[2] But even this stroke of good fortune did not lessen the deep and bitter desire for justice that was burning within him. He was determined to pursue financial compensation from his own government for its refusal to assist him, with much the same stubborn determination that he had demonstrated while refusing to submit to the authorities in Russia. In his own mind he was sure that he would receive the compensation from the government to which he believed he was entitled. His confidence on this matter worried Mrs Billett. He even told her that he was going to buy an estate in the country and a house in London. When she asked him how, 'he said he had not got the money, but it was the same as if he had; for that he had gained his cause in Russia, and our government must make it good to him'.[3]

Almost immediately Bellingham began to lobby the authorities in London to achieve satisfaction. On 27 December 1809 he petitioned the Marquis of Wellesley, the Foreign Secretary, giving him the background to the case:

> The affair arose from an attempt to obtain an improper insurance out of Lloyds in the year 1804 on the ship *Sojus* of which Mayor Popoff and van Brienen were owners and mistakenly fancied they should be able to recoup the money if they could detain me at Archangel. Van Brienen made [an] affidavit of debt totally devoid of truth or possibility . . .[4]

The letter of rejection he received was dated 31 January 1810 and signed by Charles Culling Smith:

> Sir, – I am directed by the Marquis Wellesley to transmit to you the papers which you sent to this office, accompanied by your letter of the 27th of last month.
>
> And I am to inform you that his Majesty's government is precluded from interfering in the support of your case, in some

measure, by the circumstances of the case itself, and entirely so
at the present moment, by the suspension of intercourse with
the Court of St Petersburg

I am Sir, etc.[5]

On 16 February he wrote to the Lords Commissioners of His
Majesty's Treasury and received a reply from George Harrison at
the Treasury Chambers dated 24 February:

Sir, – Having laid before the Lords Commissioners of his
Majesty's Treasury your Petition of the 16th instant, submit-
ting a statement of losses sustained by you in Russia, and
praying relief, I am commanded by their Lordships to return you
the documents transmitted therewith, and to acquaint you that
my Lords are not able to afford you any relief . . .[6]

Undaunted, Bellingham then tried the Privy Council and received
a similar negative response dated 16 May 1810:

Sir, – I am directed, by the Lords of the Council, to acquaint
you, that their Lordships having taken into consideration your
Petition on the subject of your arrest in Russia, do not find that it
is a matter in which their Lordships can, in any manner, interfere.
I am, Sir, your most obedient humble servant,
W. Fawkener.[7]

One of the places from where he sought compensation was the
office of the Chancellor of the Exchequer and Prime Minister,
Spencer Perceval. He presented a petition dated 22 May 1810 to
Downing Street in person and then followed it up with a letter.[8] A
reply, dated 27 May 1810, came from Perceval's private secretary,
Mr Thomas Brooksbank:

Sir, – I am desired by Mr Perceval to state to you, in reply to your
letter of yesterday . . . that Mr Perceval cannot encourage you
to expect his sanction in introducing into the House a petition,
which Mr Perceval thinks is not of a nature for the consideration of Parliament.[9]

His wife, Mary, who came to London to see him, and his cousin Ann became very worried about his continuing obsession for justice. After so many rejections they felt that it would be better for him to give up on the issue entirely and carry on with his life. They attempted to persuade him thus, but with very little success. In order to convince them about the wisdom of his actions, he persuaded them to visit the Office of the Secretary of State with him. They agreed, but found the meeting far from convincing. A Mr Smith agreed to meet him only because of the presence of the ladies. During the course of the meeting Bellingham, in a reference to Mary and Ann, asked him: 'Sir, my friends say that I am out of my senses, is it your opinion, Mr Smith, that I am so?' Mr Smith answered politely yet clearly: 'It is a very delicate question for me to answer, I only know you upon this business, and I can assure you, that you will never have what you are pursuing after.'

Mary and Ann may have hoped, as they left the Secretary of State's office that day, that he would now be convinced of the futility of his quest, but, to the contrary, on the way home he commented to Mary: 'Now I hope, my dear, you are well convinced all will happen well, and as I wished.'

Mary now decided that it was time, for his own good, to issue her husband with an ultimatum. She had been considering whether there was any point in continuing with their relationship at all in the present situation. After all, she had moved on with her life, she had a business, and she was, effectively, raising the boys on her own in Liverpool. Her Uncle James was one of those whom she asked for advice, and he would later regret urging her to return to her husband, whom she had married 'for better or for worse'.[10] Mary decided that she would live with John again only if he 'made a Solemn promise to give up wrong thoughts of his wild goose schemes and expectations'.[11] He was now faced with a choice of losing his wife and children, or of giving up his perceived fight for justice.

Chapter 13

A LIFE OF DOMESTICITY
AND BUSINESS

I t was only for the love of his wife that Bellingham agreed to accede to her wishes and, for a time, he gave up on his obsessive quest for compensation from the government. He does seem to have made an effort at this point to move on with his life. He moved into No. 46 Duke Street, Liverpool, where he lived with Mary, the children and Miss Stevens. He did all he could to return to a normal life of commerce, opening a warehouse in Park Lane and travelling to Ireland to re-establish his business connections there.[1] For eighteen months all looked well for the Bellingham family. Mary and Miss Stevens were running the millinery business from the house, while Bellingham was once again beginning to build his reputation in business and enjoying some success as a ship's broker. In addition, Mary gave birth to another baby, named Henry, in the summer of 1811. In reality, however, all was not as it seemed. There was no possibility that Bellingham could forget what had happened to him in Russia. He could not abandon his campaign for compensation. He had decided to keep quiet about his real feelings and was keeping up a façade of normality.

In December 1811 Bellingham prepared for what he said was a business trip to London. Mary had decided to give up her interest in the millinery business, and the stated intention of the trip to London was to make arrangements with various suppliers for the transfer of the business to Mary Stevens. The fact that Mary was unaware of Bellingham's real intentions is clear from a letter she sent to him in London, dated Sunday 18 January 1812, in which she interwove matters of family and business:

My dear John,

Your letter I received in course and I am glad to relieve your anxiety regarding darling Henry who is wonderfully recovered and has cut two teeth. I feel most obliged by your attention in regard to our business, but must request you call again at Phillips and Davisons as it is their travellers' mistake and not any fault of ours . . .

She had, however, become worried about the length of time his trip to London was taking:

I feel very much surprised at your not mentioning any time for your return, you will be three weeks gone on Thursday . . . I request you to write by return of post. The children send dear Papa . . . an affect[ionate] . . . kiss, with one from Mamma . . .

She added:

Pray let me know when you intend to return, Miss Stevens desires to be remembered.[2]

But Bellingham had never planned his stay in London to be a short one. He had found lodgings at No. 9 New Millman Street, in the house of Rebecca Robarts, and he soon got back to work on his obsessive quest for justice and compensation from the government. He prepared and sent to the Prince Regent a petition in which he outlined all the particulars of his case and the treatment he had received from the Russians. It seems that this petition was somehow lost and he had to send the document a second time.[3] Once again it outlines the story of his experiences in Russia:

your petitioner [was] arrested and imprisoned on various erroneous allegations, the erroneousness of which their own Courts were afterwards obliged to furnish official testimony; after having tortured your Petitioner for a series of years, sometimes by closely confining him in a loathsome prison, at others condemned to a dungeon, to be kept on bread and water, often marched publicly through the city, with gangs of felons and

criminals of the worst description, and even then by the house
of his Majesty's resident: at best he was never suffered to go
out but like a person under serious criminal arrest, and was
the object of attention, not only of all the Foreign Ministers
resident at the Court, but of the public at large, to the great
disparagement of his Majesty's Crown, and the heart-rending
humiliation of himself.

Through the whole course of these proceedings your
Petitioner made innumerable applications to the Consul and
Ambassador for an appeal to the Emperor on such a national
disgrace, and was not only uniformly rejected, but the Consul
went so far as to assert the proceedings to be right.

Thus, without having offended any law, either civil or criminal, and without having injured any individual in this manner,
was your Petitioner bandied from one prison to another,
through the various ministrations of Lord Granville Gower,
Mr Stuart, the Marquis of Douglas, and Lord Leveson Gower's
second Embassy, and two year subsequent thereto.

In this document he refers to the case of another British subject
in Russia who, it seems, was treated in a much more favourable
manner:

during this period a dispute happened betwixt a Captain
Gardener, of Hull, and the Captain of the guard-ship, on a
squabble of only two roubles for pilotage, which trifling affair
was carried to the Emperor no less than four times, by his
Majesty's Minister, within the space of two months, while
your Petitioner's case was sedulously suppressed, although the
honour of both countries was materially concerned in the issue.

He explains how differently he was treated by the British authorities:

previous to Lord Gower quitting St Petersburg the last time,
your Petitioner waited upon his Lordship, and also upon Sir
Stephen Shairp, urging the nationality of the case, and praying
for an appeal to the Emperor, as both law and justice required,
when your Petitioner was, for the last time, positively denied,

through Mr Rick, his Lordship's Secretary, who said his Lordship could not do it. Thus both the Consul and Ambassador left St Petersburg, leaving your Petitioner the object of persecution, without any aid whatsoever. At length the Senate, being tired of its own proceedings, your Petitioner was furnished with a pass to quit Russia in October 1809, which act was a declared judgement in your Petitioner's favour . . .

He also describes the significant effects the whole affair had had upon him:

your Petitioner, by this long-continued series of cruelty and oppression, has not only had his health and reputation materially injured, with the loss of his business, but his whole property has been absorbed in supporting the expenses, and making good the consequences of the proceedings, leaving him at present considerably involved.

He makes it clear that he wants to be compensated:

That your Petitioner pledges himself to prove, at the Bar of your Honourable House, the facts stated in this his humble Petition, if he shall be permitted so to do.

Your Petitioner humbly conceives that, having undergone such a series of persecution . . . the Consul and Ambassador have neglected and declined interfering in his behalf with the Emperor, which your Petitioner is of opinion they ought to have done, your Petitioner therefore humbly thinks that in justice he is entitled to satisfaction for the damage he has sustained from the Government of this Country . . .[4]

At first, correspondence he received from the Under-Secretary, John Beckett, dated 18 February 1812, seemed to hold out some hope:

Sir,
I am directed by Mr Secretary Ryder, to acquaint you that your Petition to his Royal Highness the Prince Regent has been referred,

by the command of his Royal Highness, for the consideration of
the Lords of His Majesty's Most Honourable Privy Council.

I am, Sir,

Your most obedient,

Humble Servant,

J. Beckett.[5]

But the next letter from Mr Beckett, on behalf of the Home
Secretary, Richard Ryder, dated 9 March 1812, dashed his hopes
for a speedy resolution:

Whitehall, March 9, 1812.

Sir,

I am directed by Mr Secretary Ryder to acquaint you that your
Petition to his Royal Highness the Prince Regent, praying that
he would be pleased to order your Memorial therein enclosed,
addressed to the House of Commons to be brought before
Parliament, has been laid before his Royal Highness, and that he
was not pleased to signify any commands thereupon.

Your memorial to the House of Commons is accordingly
herewith returned.

I am, sir,

Your most obedient,

Humble Servant,

J. Beckett.[6]

On the advice of General Gascoyne MP, Bellingham decided to
endeavour to get individual Members of Parliament interested
in representing his case. He sent the following circular, dated
17 March 1812, to all members, with the letters referred to
above attached:

Sir, – having suffered in a most unprecedented manner, for a
period of six years in Russia – on my return, two years ago, I
made a representation of the case to the various departments
of his Majesty's Government, and in January last I applied for
redress, by Petition, to his Royal Highness the Prince Regent,
who was graciously pleased to refer the affair to his Majesty's

Most Honourable Privy Council . . . The council declined to act in the business; upon which I requested an official copy of their Lordships' decision – and was answered by the Clerk of the Council, it could not be complied with. In consequence, I renewed my application to his Royal Highness the Prince Regent, accompanied by the enclosed Petition to the House of Commons, praying his Royal Highness that, as the affair is purely national, he would be graciously pleased to direct my complaint to be brought before Parliament . . .

Having borne the weight of this unhappy affair abroad for a series of years, in a manifold way – on my return home I had the mortification to find my affairs gone to ruin – my property sold up – my family distracted, and suffering in the most severe manner by the inevitable ruinous consequences of my detention – and for the preceding two years they had not been able to ascertain whether I was alive or dead. Since my return I have not only been bereaved of a farther property (bequeathed in my absence), to make good the consequences of this business, but am now considerably involved – so fatal has it proved. Thus circumstanced, I trust I shall be pardoned in addressing the House of Commons, individually, in the hope that, on the behalf of national justice, some Member will do me the favour to bring forward my said just Petition – as common justice is all I solicit, and what everyone will agree I ought to have, more especially as my sufferings for the last eight years have been almost too great for human nature to sustain.

In soliciting your kind aid, I beg to be understood that it is far from my intention, by this Address, to complain of any party whatever, being convinced that in no country upon earth is justice so purely administered as in this; and justice I am sure I shall have, so soon as the affair is known to the Tribunal where alone it can be taken proper cognisance of.

With assurance that my sole wish is to obtain what is right, without prejudice to any individual, I have the honour to be, Sir, your very humble and obedient servant,

John Bellingham.

No. 9, New Millman Street, March 17, 1812.[7]

Thus, he circularised every member of the House of Commons. The bill for the production of copies of the relevant documents, from A. Macpherson Printers in Covent Garden, came to £9 15s 0d.[8] His hopes, however, of making progress were fatally damaged by a letter from Mr Beckett dated 20 March 1812:

Sir, – I am directed by Mr Secretary Ryder to acknowledge the receipt of your letter of the 17th instant, requesting permission, on the part of his Majesty's ministers, to present your petition to the House of Commons; and in reply I am to acquaint you, that you should address your application to the Right Hon. the Chancellor of the Exchequer.[9]

Of course, Bellingham had already tried to bring his case to Mr Perceval, the Right Hon. Chancellor of the Exchequer and Prime Minister, and this notion of referring him back there once again was particularly disheartening. It confirmed in his own mind that he was going round in circles and achieving very little. He made similar unproductive approaches to the Clerks of the Privy Council, Mr Buller and Lord Chetwynd, and the Solicitor for the Treasury, Mr Litchfield. It was with a growing sense of futility that he wrote to the Police Magistrates of the Public Office in Bow Street on 23 March 1812:

Sirs, – I much regret its being my lot to have to apply to your Worships under most peculiar and novel circumstances – For the particulars of the case, I refer to the enclosed letter from Mr Secretary Ryder, the notification from Mr Perceval, and my petition to Parliament, together with the printed papers herewith. The affair requires no further remark than that I consider his Majesty's government to have endeavoured to close the door of justice, in declining to have, or even to permit, my grievances to be brought before Parliament for redress, which privilege is the birthright of every individual.

The purport of the present is, therefore, once more to solicit his Majesty's ministers, through your medium, to let what is right and proper be done in my instance, which is all I require.

The letter also contains what, with hindsight, represents an ominous threat, but which understandably went unnoticed by the police magistrates:

> Should this reasonable request be finally denied, I shall then feel justified in executing justice myself – in which case I shall be ready to argue the merits of so reluctant a measure with his Majesty's Attorney General, wherever and whenever I may be called upon so to do. – In the hopes of averting so abhorrent but compulsive an alternative,
>
> I have the honour to be, Sirs,
>
> Your very humble and obedient Servant . . .[10]

Bellingham visited Bow Street a few days after sending this letter in order to request a reply. To his great disappointment all he received was 'a little memorandum' written by Mr Justice Read, informing him that the contents of his correspondence had been communicated to the Secretary of State.[11] He then wrote again to the Home Secretary, Richard Ryder, in early April and received a reply dated 18 April. There is no doubt that Mr Ryder and Mr Beckett had, by now, become somewhat irked by Bellingham's persistence and had decided that he should be convinced of the futility of his enterprise once and for all. The letter, with a palpable sense of impatience, reads:

> Whitehall, April 18, 1812.
>
> Sir, – I am directed by Mr Secretary Ryder to acknowledge the receipt of your letter of the 12th instant, requesting to be informed 'in what state your claim on his Majesty's government for criminal detention in Russia now is'. In reply, I am to refer you to my several letters of the 18th February, 9th and 20th March, by which you have been already informed that your first petition to his Royal Highness the Prince Regent, praying for remuneration, had been referred to the consideration of the Lords of Council. That upon your second Memorial, praying his Royal Highness to give orders that the subject should be brought before Parliament, his Royal Highness had not been pleased to signify any commands. And, lastly, in

answer to your application to Mr Ryder, requesting permission
on the part of his Majesty's ministers to present your Petition
to the House of Commons, you were informed that your application should be addressed to the Right Hon. the Chancellor of
the Exchequer.

> I am, Sir, Your most obedient humble Servant,
> J. Beckett.[12]

Bellingham described this letter as 'a final and direct answer,
which at once convinced me that I had no reason to expect any
adjustment whatever of those claims which I had on His Majesty's
Government, for my criminal detention in Russia'.[13] During the
month of April he spent around an hour in private conversation
with General Gascoyne, the MP for Liverpool, in the politician's
residence.[14] But, once again, he left having gained no satisfaction.
He now resolved that he had no option but to take drastic and violent action so that his claim could finally be heard. Such was his
desire to do everything in a correct and orderly manner that he
decided to go in person to the Office of the Secretary of State and
inform the officials directly that he now felt he had to take the law
into his own hands. He informed a Mr Hill of this fact, who seemed
to take no special notice of the threat and, in fact, told him that he
should do as he thought proper.

On 16 April Bellingham wrote a letter to Mary, again discussing
some family issues and reassuring her that he was attending to her
business in London:

My dear Mary,
Yours dated the 12th did not reach my hands till yesterday
evening – you have acted right in following my instructions,
and the rest leave to my solicitude, as can assure you it is not
forgotten. I could have wished you had mentioned where and
with whom Henry is and to let me know how the dear boy goes
on. Herewith a few lines for Miss S[tevens] – for her government
in the Business – and which you may consider as the remainder
of your letter.

He then addressed the rest of the letter to Miss Stevens:

My dear Miss Stevens,

As my affairs in London are terminating according to wish, you may easily imagine it's my desire for Mrs B[ellingham] to quit the business as soon as possible, and for you to come into full possession of it. The money that has been put in I do not look to, my family having had the benefit of a maintenance and the outstanding debts I am willing to take upon me. Therefore, when you come to town, I will accompany you to the respective trades people for the arrangements . . . Bring the books and confide in me to do what is right and proper. You will not be deceived . . .[15]

By now, Mary was worried. She had found a number of suspicious papers at home regarding the affair in Russia, including a draft of her husband's petition to the Prince Regent. She replied to his letter immediately, telling him that she now intended giving her share of the business to a person called Eliza. In a veiled allusion to his tendency not to be focused upon the business in hand she told him:

Dear John,

If I could think that the prospects held out in your letter received yesterday were to be realised I would be the happiest creature existing, but I have been so often disappointed that I am hard of belief. With regard to Miss Stevens going to London . . . be certain you can make good your intentions, for should you not ultimately be enabled to fulfil them we would be sunk in ruin from not having sufficient means to meet the trades people.

At this point her annoyance becomes obvious, probably driven by the fact that she had found the documents and was fearful that he was about to return once again to his fight for justice. Her anger is displayed as a form of jealousy towards his mode of addressing Miss Stevens:

I cannot help remarking that in writing to Miss Stevens you address her in the same manner as me. Oh my dear Miss Stevens & yours truly John Bellingham. Now I cannot help feeling hurt that there is no distinction made between an indifferent person and an affectionate wife who has suffered so much for you and your children – it appears as if I was no more to you than any woman that you were obliged to write a letter to. I can confess to a delicate and feeling mind . . . these are insults, more particularly as my indisposition seems to have been forgotten . . . the change in my appearance will convince you that I have been very ill, as I am now as thin as I ever was . . . If I was to follow your example, six lines might fill my letter but perhaps I am not worthy of more. I shall expect your answer by return of post, say Thursday, by that time I hope something will be concluded about your affair.

Yours truly, Mary Bellingham.[16]

As outwardly he appeared to be carrying on this apparently normal correspondence with his wife and Miss Stevens regarding business and family matters, in another part of his mind Bellingham was preparing for the implementation of his deadly plan of assassination. His latest correspondence to the Treasury Office passed through a few hands until a letter to him was drafted in early May 1812 in which his request for a hearing was once again denied. It was lying on a desk waiting for the signature of one of the Secretaries of the Treasury when the need for it to be signed and posted was made redundant by Bellingham's act in the lobby of the House of Commons on 11 May.

Chapter 14

FINAL PREPARATIONS

Taking no notice of his wife's growing frustrations in Liverpool, Bellingham, now believing that he had no other option left open to him, began his final preparations for the assassination. He planned every small detail and, where necessary, rehearsed. He began visiting the House of Commons regularly so that he could become familiar with the faces of those in power. Back on 5 March 1812 he had patronised the business premises of the aptly named tailor, James Taylor, of No. 11 North Place, Gray's Inn Lane, where he bought a pair of pantaloons and a waistcoat. On 25 April he met Taylor again on Guilford Street and invited him to his lodgings to discuss a rather important job. Taylor thought their meeting on the street to be serendipitous, but, considering the fastidious preparations being undertaken by Bellingham, it may not have been. He informed Taylor that he needed an urgent job undertaken. He asked the craftsman to sew an inside pocket, to the length of a piece of paper supplied by him, which was about 9 inches long, on to the inside left of a dark coloured overcoat. He said that he wanted a pocket that he could get at conveniently. The coat was to be returned, finished, that evening. Also in April he went to the gunsmith, W. Beckwith, at No. 58 Skinner Street, Snow Hill, where he bought a pair of half-inch calibre, steel pistols for four guineas. These were around 6 or 7 inches long with a barrel of only 2 inches. He immediately began to practise shooting these weapons on Hampstead Heath.

On Wednesday 6 May, Mary Stevens arrived in London, as arranged, to conclude their business. But when she and Bellingham met the following Friday at her lodgings in Kirby Street, Miss Stevens made it known to him that both she and his wife now knew the principal reason for his presence in London and were very much hurt by his deception.[1] She tried to make him see sense, reminding him of the needs of his wife and family, but, as ever, he would not be dissuaded. 'You know Miss Stevens,' he told her, 'it is always a matter of dissension between me and Mrs Bellingham.' He said that they 'never should be happy until it was settled' and 'he was determined to have justice done him and he should be undeserving the name of a parent if he did not endeavour to make some provision for his children'.[2]

He returned to her lodgings the following day, Saturday, to examine some ledgers pertaining to the millinery business, which Miss Stevens had brought with her from Liverpool, and, on this occasion, she asked him if he had made any progress with his petition. He said he had not as yet, but was 'determined to set about it vigorously on Monday'.[3] Mary Stevens could not have known the terrible plan that he had in mind. That day Bellingham, Miss Stevens and Mrs Barker, in whose home Mary Stevens was staying while in London, went to Spring Garden to attend 'The Eighth Annual Exhibition of the Society of Painters in Water-Colours'. Afterwards he returned to Mrs Barker's with them and took away the business ledgers to study that night.

On Sunday morning, 10 May, Bellingham attended a religious service in the Chapel of the Foundling Hospital on Guildford Street with his landlady, Rebecca Robarts, and her son. That evening, although it was raining, he walked there once again with Mrs Robarts and attended the evening service.

On the morning of that faithful day, Monday 11 May 1812, Bellingham became annoyed at the shilling charged by his washerwoman to wash a dressing gown. He told her that he would have washed it himself if he had known that it would cost more than eight pence.[4] He then sat down to write some letters. A letter dated that day, reputedly written by Bellingham, later appeared in the press. It dealt with a number of business matters before concluding with the words:

> I wish my affairs were come to a conclusion; – everything, in
> point of law, is in my favour; but Mr Perceval and the Ministry
> have shown themselves more inclined to favour Lord Gower,

> than to do justice to me; however, as I am resolved on having
> justice . . . I will very shortly play a court card to compel them to
> finish the game. I am Yours sincerely . . .[5]

At eleven o'clock that morning he called on Mary Stevens at her
lodgings and gave her the letters he had written to deliver to his
wife and their solicitor. Before they parted, probably out of sympathy for his wife and family, Miss Stevens decided to try once
more to get him to give up on what she perceived to be his vain
quest for justice:

> '. . . would you not be better to relinquish it than to oppose the
> powerful so much?' she suggested.
> 'I will not,' he answered. 'If ministers refuse to do me justice I
> will do it myself.' He laid his hand upon his heart before continu-
> ing: 'You do not know, Miss Stevens, what I have endured the
> last six months; I would rather commit suicide.'
> 'God forbid that you should commit such an act but your coun-
> tenance shows what you must have suffered,' said Miss Stevens.

Indeed, it was true, she did notice how much his appearance had
changed for the worse since she had last seen him in Liverpool.

> 'But how are you to obtain this?' she inquired.
> 'I will bring it into a criminal court . . .' was his determined
> answer.

Miss Stevens, though not believing that he was in any way
deranged, would later remember how 'when speaking of his application to Government he was very violent'.[6]

Bellingham then returned to his lodgings, carefully loaded his
pistols and placed them into his pockets. He then calmly, and with
the pistols in his possession, walked with Rebecca Robarts and her
son the 2 miles to King Street, St James's, to visit an exhibition at
the European Museum. They viewed the display there and then set
off on the walk home in the fine weather. But when they reached
Sydney's Alley, between Coventry Street and Leicester Square, he
told Mrs Robarts that he had some business to attend to and parted

with her and her son. As they walked towards home, Bellingham set off in the direction of Westminster. It was just before five o'clock. It was some time between six and seven o'clock that evening when Rebecca Robarts was visited by two Bow Street Officers, Vickery and Adkins, who told her the terrible and incredible news of what her kind, polite lodger, John Bellingham, had done to the Prime Minister.

Chapter 15

INQUEST

In the aftermath of the shooting, once he had been pronounced dead, the body of the Prime Minister was removed from the table in the Speaker's Secretary's room and laid on a sofa in the Speaker's drawing room. Mr Perceval's brother Lord Arden came in and, in a poignant scene witnessed by others, laid his hand gently upon the body and said to himself: 'he is gone to that happiness which he merited, but his children – his dear children, what will become of them!'[1] A number of newspapers reported the equally sad and unfortunate story that one of the Prime Minister's sons had also arrived on the scene. *The Day* reported that 'a fine boy of about thirteen years of age, happened accidentally to come down a few moments after the assassination took place . . . The unhappy child's distress is beyond description.' Other papers had similar reports: 'We heard that a son of Mr Perceval's was in town with his father, and saw a boy in the House, under the gallery, in great affliction, whom we suppose to be the unfortunate youth placed in the midst of these unhappy circumstances.'[2] This boy may have been the 9-year-old John Perceval.[3]

Lord Redesdale, as the late Prime Minister's brother-in-law, was given the unenviable task of informing Jane Perceval about her husband's assassination. She heard the terrible news on her return from her visit to Mrs Frederica Ryder, the wife of the Home Secretary, in Great George Street, Westminster. Redesdale later described her as being 'as well as can be expected'.[4] The truth was that she was too shocked to respond. It was around one o'clock on the morning of Tuesday 12 May, by the time her husband's body was taken home to No. 10 Downing Street accompanied by his

brother Lord Arden and the Speaker of the House, Charles Abbot.
As the entourage pulled up outside No. 10, Jane was observed,
watching from behind the window blinds, still in a state of unemotional shock. The body was placed in the Prime Minister's dressing
room, where it was surrounded respectfully by an array of can-
dles. Jane remained in that state of inexpressive shock in which
she had been since being told the dreadful news:

> she neither wept nor spoke, nor appeared to be sensible of any
> thing that was afterwards said to her. She remained in that
> state from six o'clock on Monday evening 'til eleven o'clock
> on Tuesday morning:– during that interval, her relations and
> friends endeavoured to rouse her, and, if possible, to excite her
> to tears by mentioning the circumstances of Mr Perceval's
> death to her, but in vain.[5]

It was only when the widow was brought in to see her husband's
body in the morning that she finally broke down in tearful,
uncontrollable grief. Lady Redesdale, who also saw the body
of her deceased brother, described the look on his face as 'calm
and undisturbed'.[6]

The inquest into the Prime Minister's death took place at
eleven o'clock that morning, Tuesday 12 May 1812, at the Rose
and Crown public house in Downing Street.[7] The Coroner for
Westminster, Anthony Gell, brought all twenty-one jurors to
No. 10 to see the body. After ten minutes they returned the short
distance to the public house, where they heard evidence from a
number of witnesses to the killing.[8] Henry Burgess, who gave his
address as Curzon-Street, Mayfair, and his profession as solicitor,
gave evidence that he heard the shot and saw the Prime Minister
fall to the ground. He also told how he took a warm pistol from near
or under Mr Bellingham's hand and how he had asked him why
he had done such a thing. He told the inquest that Bellingham's
reply was '"want of redress of grievance, and a refusal by government" or words to that effect'. Burgess also told of taking a
number of items from Bellingham's pockets and how someone else
confiscated the second pistol from him. He told of Bellingham's
subsequent examination:

In the course of the afternoon, I believe, I was the first person examined; and when my evidence was read to me, in the presence of the prisoner, on his being asked if he had any remarks to make, or words to that effect, he replied, 'I think Mr Burgess's statement is correct; only I wish to observe that, instead of my hand being upon, or near the pistol, I think he took it out of my hand,' or words to that effect. When I first saw the prisoner he was greatly agitated; but by the time I was examined, that agitation had subsided, and he appeared to be perfectly calm.

General Isaac Gascoyne, MP for Liverpool, giving his address as Hertford Street, Mayfair, stated:

About a quarter after five o'clock yesterday I was writing a letter in the committee-room; I heard the report of a pistol-shot, and jumped up, exclaiming that it was the report of a pistol; I went downstairs; I saw a number of people standing about and a person pointed out a man to me sitting on the bench by the fire-side; the person saying that is the man who fired the pistol: I sprung upon him, and grasped him by the breast and neck; I perceived him raising his left hand with a pistol in it; I let go my hold, and seized his wrist with both hands, and twisted his arm round with all my force; he seemed to have little hold of the pistol; I desired a person standing by to take the pistol from his hand, which was done. I took papers from his pocket, and tied them up; he appeared to be dragging from my hold, but I kept him fast. I delivered the paper to Mr Hume, and then told the prisoner it was impossible he could escape: he replied, 'I am the person who shot Mr Perceval, and I surrender myself.' I took him to the body of the House of Commons, and delivered him into the custody of the messengers. I saw him lodged in the prison-room before I . . . lost sight of him.

Gascoyne also informed the inquest that the prisoner had called upon him about three weeks before the assassination to discuss his grievances. He testified that 'during this conversation, he was as calm and as collected as any man could be, and had not the least appearance of a person insane'.

Joseph Hume, MP for Weymouth, also gave his version of events:

> I was sitting in the House of Commons yesterday evening, a few minutes after five, when I heard the report of a pistol, and an immediate bustle or noise; I left the House; and went into the lobby; pushed immediately towards the fire-place, where the crowd was; I saw a man sitting on the bench, who has since, in my presence, declared his name to be John Bellingham; he appeared to be forcibly pulled, on every side, by the bystanders; appeared to suffer considerably from the force used by such bystanders; appeared considerably agitated, and in the act of disengaging his hand from the person who grasped it severely. I seized his left arm at the moment that General Gascoyne was pulling from the person of the prisoner a bundle of papers; one of the General's hands being occupied grasping the prisoner, I seized hold of the papers from the General's right hand, informing him that I would take care of them; I still retained hold of the prisoner, and saw a person in the act of pulling about the waist of the prisoner a small pocket steel pistol, which he immediately examined, and found primed; I desired that person to take care of it, and, on subsequent examination, I found that same pistol to contain a ball and powder. I held the prisoner, and assisted to conduct him to the bar of the House of Commons, where I quitted my hold, leaving him in the custody of two servants of the House, as directed by the Speaker. The Speaker having directed the prisoner to be conducted to the prison-room, and all members who had witnessed any part of the transaction to follow, I accompanied them, and attended the examination of witnesses for about one hour; the agitation under which the prisoner seemed, at first, appeared to me gradually to subside; and by the time the first deposition was taken, he was able to answer, and to speak distinctly and calmly . . . On the whole, I do consider that he was perfectly sane, making a little allowance for the agitation of the moment.

William Smith MP told the inquest of his efforts to assist the injured Mr Perceval:

Yesterday afternoon, about quarter past five o'clock, passing through the lobby to go to the House of Commons, I stopped to speak to a gentleman about the centre of the lobby, and while in conversation with him, I heard the report of a pistol. I immediately turned my head, and observed some conversation at the end of the room. Several voices called out to shut the door to prevent any person escaping. There might have been present in the lobby from thirty to forty persons. In an instant I observed a person rush from the cluster of people who were standing about the door, and come staggering towards me; he reached about the spot where I was first standing, and then fell flat on his face on the floor. I walked round him, not immediately recognising his person; and not supposing he was mortally wounded, but observing he did not stir, I stooped down to assist him, and on raising his head perceived him to be Mr Perceval. I then requested the assistance of a gentleman who was standing close to the body, and we carried him between us into the Speaker's secretary's room. We set him on a table, he resting on our arms. I think he was not only speechless, but perfectly senseless, and blood came from his mouth. His pulse in a few minutes ceased, and he soon died. I think he was quite dead when Mr Lynn, the surgeon, came. He died in less than a quarter of an hour. The body was afterwards deposited in the Speaker's drawing-room.

Mr Smith testified that he was unable to give any evidence about 'the person who committed this horrid murder'. The physician who had arrived on the scene and pronounced the Prime Minister to be dead, Mr William Lynn, also gave evidence. With the weight of evidence it is no wonder that the Coroner's Court returned a verdict of 'wilful murder' against John Bellingham.

Back in Westminster the members of the House of Commons and the peers of the House of Lord were struggling to come to terms with what had happened to one of their own colleagues. On Tuesday, in the House of Lords, a reply from the Prince Regent to their Lordships' address regarding the assassination was presented by the Duke of York. It expressed the Prince's indignation and regret at what had happened and assured their Lordships that 'no steps should be wanting on the part of his Royal Highness, to

bring the offender or offenders to condign and exemplary punishment'.[9] Another message from the Prince Regent respecting the
family of Mr Perceval was presented by the Earl of Liverpool to the
Lord Chancellor to be read to the House. The Lord Chancellor was
so overcome by reading the message that he was unable to finish
it, and it had to be concluded by a clerk. It expressed the Prince's
desire that the deceased Prime Minister's wife and family be provided for. Lord Liverpool used the opportunity to say of the late
Prime Minister that 'few men ever existed, who were endowed
with more virtues; and that no man whatever had fewer faults'.[10]

A similar message regarding the family of the late Prime
Minister was presented by Lord Castlereagh in the House of
Commons and read by the Speaker. Castlereagh had been brought
back into the Cabinet by Perceval as Foreign Secretary after the
resignation of Lord Wellesley in February 1812. He reminded the
house that 'everyone must be sensible of the peculiar situation of
the family of his right hon. friend, from the circumstance of his
having so disinterestedly devoted himself to the public service'. He
went on to say that 'never had man more friends and fewer enemies – nay, a single enemy was not to be found in the circle of those
who personally knew him'.[11] Mr Ponsonby stated for the record
that he had known Mr Perceval in his early years and that he 'had
never known a man of greater worth. As a husband, as a father, as
a friend, no man was more to be admired.'[12]

There was a widespread notion that this particular issue was
too sensitive for anyone to play politics, so there was very little dissension to be heard from a packed House of Commons. An address
to the Prince Regent was agreed in which was stated the members'
desire 'to make such provision for the Widow and Family of the
Right honourable Spencer Perceval, as may be consistent with the
justice and the liberality of Parliament'.[13] It was also agreed that
the address should be presented to the Prince Regent by the whole
House at a suitable time.[14]

By now, as details of Bellingham's very personal motivation
began to leak out, the initial fears of a widespread revolution
began to lessen. The *Morning Chronicle* tried to allay the fears: 'It
indeed afforded some relief to the agitated feelings of the commu-
nity to find that the assassin was neither a Roman Catholic nor

a Manufacturer – that he had nothing to do with the Orders in Council – and was not a Reformer of Political Abuses'.[15] A number of Members in Parliament also expressed relief at the knowledge that the assassination had been the work of one man working alone and not the vanguard of a more widespread rebellion. None the less, the fear that the assassination would inspire a wide-scale eruption of violence was still very real.

The papers described the very worrying events in Nottingham as the news of the assassination reached there:

> No sooner had the news of Mr Perceval's murder been received in this town than the most enthusiastic demonstrations of joy of the most horrible description were evinced. The bells were rung, bonfires were lighted up, and a tumultuous crowd of people assembled in front of the guard room with drums beating, flags flying, etc., etc. Here they stood shouting and huzzaing and expressing their savage joy by their gestures. In this perturbed and threatening state of the town, the military drums beat to arms, and, the troops being assembled, the Riot Act was read, and the most energetic measures were adopted by the General, to preserve the public peace . . .[16]

The *Nottingham Journal* was highly critical of the rioters: 'We could not have believed that an Englishman (naturally humane) could be found whose mind was so poisoned by the gangrene of prejudice, as to openly applaud a deed so dark, so foul, the very contemplation of which makes humanity shudder!'[17]

Nottingham was not the only place to witness jubilation at the news of the Prime Minister's assassination. It was reported that the people in Leicester were feasting and singing, while in Sheffield 'there were sheep roasted whole'.[18] Placards were even placed on the House of Commons stating that 'Mr Perceval's ribs were only fit to broil the Regent's heart on'.[19]

A proposition was put forward that the late Prime Minister should be accorded a public funeral, but this was taken no further by the House on the basis that the wishes of the family would have to be consulted on such an issue.[20] In any event, the proposal was rejected by the family.[21] No other parliamentary business was attended to that evening. That Tuesday night, at No. 10 Downing Street, Jane and the family said their final goodbyes to their beloved husband and father before his body was sealed in a lead coffin. Earlier the sculptor Joseph Nollekens had called at No. 10 and made a death mask of the Prime Minister's face.

When the House of Commons assembled the next day, Wednesday 13 May, even the radical MP Sir Francis Burdett, whom the mob had actually believed to be the assassin on the day of the murder, put his 'abhorrence' on record and described the killing as 'atrocious'.[22] The Commons then resolved itself into a committee of the whole House to consider the financial provision to be made for Perceval's wife and family. Many speakers once again referred to the late Prime Minister's selfless dedication to his country. It was stated how he had neglected a potentially lucrative career in the law to serve his country as a politician. The anti-slavery campaigner William Wilberforce said: 'A man of more real sweetness of temper; a man more highly blest by nature, was never known, or one in whom goodness of disposition was more deeply rooted.'[23] On Thursday 14 May the members of both Houses of Parliament travelled to Carlton House to present their address to the Prince Regent:

> The procession from the Lords, preceded by the Lord Chancellor, in his state carriage, and attended by upwards of sixty carriages, containing the members of the upper House, and the Commons, with the Speaker in his state carriage, accompanied by upwards of one hundred and sixty carriages, containing nearly 300 members, formed a most interesting spectacle, as did also that of the Lord Mayor and court of aldermen and all the officers of the corporation. Very few spectators were seen in the streets on this occasion.[24]

The petition from the House of Lords was presented at two o'clock and from the Commons at three.[25]

After several days of debate on the matter, the Commons agreed to vote an annuity of £2,000 per annum to Jane Perceval and, in addition, a grant of £50,000 to be vested in trustees for the support of the twelve children. It was also agreed that £1,000 would go to the eldest son, increasing to £2,000 on his mother's death.[26]

Also on Thursday, the Grand Jury met at the Sessions House, Clerkenwell.[27] A number of witnesses were heard, including Mr Francis Romilly, Mr William Smith, Mr Henry Burgess, Mr William Jerdan, General Gascoyne, Mr Vincent Dowling, Mr Joseph Hume and the Surgeon Mr Lynn.[28] Having heard the evidence, they went to the Court of Oyer and Terminer at Justice Hall in the Old Bailey and declared that they had found 'a true Bill against John Bellingham, for the wilful murder of the Right Honourable Spencer Perceval'.[29] His trial was scheduled for the following day.

On Friday 15 May, the day of Bellingham's trial, Lord Clive proposed, and Admiral Harvey seconded a motion in the House of Commons that:

> a monument be erected in the Collegiate Church of St Peter Westminster, to the memory of the late Right Hon. Spencer Perceval, First Commissioner of his Majesty's Treasury, and Chancellor of the Exchequer, who was assassinated within the walls of Parliament; as a mark of the deep sense which this House entertains of his public and private virtues, and of its abhorrence of the act by which he fell; and to assure his Royal Highness that this House will make good the expense attending the same.[30]

Some opposition members felt very uneasy about the idea, and this brought forth some dissension. It was argued that Mr Perceval's legacy was not sufficient to warrant such an honour. Lord Milton was of the opinion that the monument, instead of commemorating 'the virtues of Mr Perceval', would end up commemorating 'the vices of the person by whom he was destroyed'. He alluded to the case of the Duke of Buckingham, who had been assassinated in 1628 by a person 'who fancied he had been ill used' and in memory of whom no monument had been erected.[31] However, the matter was put to a vote and carried by 173 votes. The idea of a monument to the memory of Perceval at Westminster was not without its detractors from outside the House either. The *Freeman's Journal* wrote from the perspective of Ireland: 'It was fair enough, perhaps to pension off his numerous family, and to provide for the widow. . . But the Monument is another thing. It should never be given but for unequivocal services. Those of Mr Perceval, to say the most of them, were at all events questionable.'[32]

All attention now turned to the impending trial of John Bellingham.

Chapter 16

'THIS MELANCHOLY, BUT NECESSARY CATASTROPHE'

Throughout the week Bellingham's confidence regarding the justice of the act he had committed remained unshaken. He was not pleased to have killed Mr Perceval, but he regarded the action to have been necessary and justified in the circumstances. He remained calm and, to all those around him, seemed rational. On Tuesday morning, the day after the assassination, he awoke at seven o'clock in his prison cell and ate a breakfast of sweetened tea and two buttered rolls prepared by Keeper Newman himself to prevent the chance of poisoning by a third party. Later, Alderman Combe and a number of other magistrates came to his cell and found him willing to discuss freely and politely the events that had taken place. He even asked them about the direction that the fatal ball from his pistol had taken. When they told him that the downward direction of its journey through Mr Perceval's chest had led to speculation that he had fired over someone's shoulder, he told them clearly, with a somewhat indignant air, that he would never have endangered an innocent bystander in such a way. Had he not got an unhindered view of his victim, he informed them, he would not have fired.

It was recorded that a man called Hokkirk arrived at the prison that day asking to see the prisoner. Although he was refused access, he did give the authorities the information that Bellingham's father had died insane and that, in his opinion, Bellingham himself was suffering from the same condition. Yet those who spoke to the prisoner or watched his actions could see no sign of such insanity:

It was at first taken for granted, for it was impossible to believe such an act could be perpetrated by any other than an insane

man, that the man laboured under insanity, but it would be difficult to come to this conclusion from the manner and demeanour
of the prisoner . . . nothing appeared in his conduct to induce a
suspicion of his labouring under insanity. . .[1]

It is difficult to account for the composure and serenity in which
this unhappy criminal passes his time. If the worm of conscience
were gnawing him within, he could not sleep with such regular-
ity and soundness, nor demean himself with such ease, if not
cheerfulness, as he appears to do . . .[2]

In a letter written to his landlady on that day, Bellingham himself
alludes to this sense of calm. The letter addressed to Mrs Robarts,
No. 9 New Millman Street, reads:

Dear Madam,
Yesterday night, I was escorted to this neighbourhood by
a noble troop of Light Horse, and delivered into the care of
Mr Newman (by Mr Taylor the Magistrate and MP) as a State
Prisoner of the first class. For eight years I have never found my
mind so tranquil as since this melancholy, but necessary catastrophe, as the merits or demerits of my peculiar case must be
regularly unfolded in a Criminal Court of Justice, to ascertain
the guilty party, by a Jury of my country. I have to request the
favour of you to send me three or four shirts, some cravats,
handkerchiefs, night-caps, stockings, &c. out of my drawers,
together with comb, soap, tooth-brush, with any other trifle
that presents itself which you think I may have occasion for, and
enclose them in my leather trunk, and the key please to send
sealed, per bearer:– also my great coat, flannel gown, and black
waistcoat, which will much oblige,
　　　　Dear Madam, your very obedient Servant,
　　　　John Bellingham.
To the above please to add the prayer-book.[3]

After two o'clock he ate what was described as 'a hearty dinner'
and requested that he dine at that time every day.[4] He went to bed
at twelve o'clock that night.

On Wednesday morning he awoke from a sound sleep at seven o'clock and ate breakfast at nine. He was visited by a group comprising the sheriffs and a number of others. After their meeting it was clear to that group, as it was to all others who met him, including the prison staff, that he felt totally justified in his actions. He told them that, 'had he a million . . . lives to lose, they would not prevent him from pursuing his object in the same way'.[5] His solicitor, James Harmer, had a two-hour meeting with him in which the prisoner asked to have Henry Brougham and Peter Alley appointed to act as his counsel in court. He ate a dinner of 'roast beef and potatoes, with beer . . .'.[6] He was also visited that day by a Mr Fidler, who was a friend of his from their schooldays. The gentleman paid what was described as a brief cordial visit.[7]

Bellingham rose at seven o'clock on Thursday morning and had breakfast at eight thirty. The Solicitor for the Treasury, Charles Litchfield, paid a visit to the prisoner to inform him that his trial was to take place the following day. Bellingham was still quite calm and confident about his innocence. He declined to send a letter to his wife through Mary Stevens, who paid him a visit from Liverpool. He said that 'he would rather wait till the next day, that he might acquaint her with his liberation, which he confidently anticipated before the going out of the post'. When his solicitor arrived between four and five o'clock Bellingham refused to discuss the case with him any further. He spent the evening making notes, even running out of paper at one point and receiving a fresh supply from the Keeper of Newgate. His request for a few glasses of wine was, however, turned down, although he was later given a glass of porter. It was observed that he woke up at three o'clock in the morning and made a few further notes for about fifteen minutes before returning to bed and sleeping soundly until seven o'clock on Friday morning.

This was Friday 15 May, the day of his trial, which was scheduled for ten o'clock at the Old Bailey. Bellingham was shaved and had his hair cut short by a hairdresser. For the first time those at Newgate Prison noticed a brief change in his usually calm demeanour. He quickly vomited up what little of his breakfast he had eaten. He then broke down in tears, telling those around him that this was not from fear for his own destiny, but out of sympathy for his wife and children. However, he quickly recovered his composure. He was examined by the Newgate surgeon, William Box, who certified him fit to stand trial. When the time came for him to go, Keeper Newman came personally to lead the prisoner from his cell.

Chapter 17

THE TRIAL

It is ironic, in the light of the number of years that Bellingham had spent trying to get someone in authority to listen to his pleas for justice, that his trial was taking place only four days after he had carried out the assassination of the Prime Minister. The case had captured the public imagination and, to cope with the crowds expected around the Old Bailey that morning, large numbers of troops had been deployed. People began to arrive at seven o'clock, in the hope of gaining admission to the courtroom. One indication of the demand was the fact that the doorkeepers, who had begun by charging one guinea for admittance, were, by ten o'clock, charging three.[1] Those who did not manage to get in began to take up good vantage points along the street, while others used the windows of houses along Ludgate Street and Fleet Street in order to get a view of what was going on. So big was the crowd inside the courtroom, in fact, that the upper classes in society, including those from both Houses of Parliament, found themselves forced to mix with those from the lower classes. As reported in *The Times*, there was also a great number of ladies present, 'all led by the intense curiosity to behold the assassin, and to hear what he might urge in defence or in palliation of his atrocious act'.[2]

After ten o'clock the presiding judge, Sir James Mansfield, entered the court and took his place upon the bench. Mansfield had held the position of Lord Chief Justice of the Common Pleas since 1804, ironically after the position had been turned down by Perceval. Prior to that Mansfield had been Chief Justice of Chester. Although recognised to have a good knowledge of the law, he was not renowned for his eloquence from the bench and could demonstrate a volatile temper. He was joined by Baron (Sir Robert)

Graham, Mr Justice (Sir Nash) Grose and the Recorder. Among the other notable dignitaries present in court were the Lord Mayor, the Marquis of Wellesley, the Duke of Clarence and Lord Granville Leveson Gower.

When the prisoner was brought in, it was the first time that most of those present had seen the tall, thin figure of John Bellingham, with his tightly cut brown hair and sharp angular features. He was wearing a brown greatcoat, dark nankeen trousers and a yellow waistcoat with small stripes of black. He entered with 'a firm step and quite undismayed'.[3] He bowed respectfully before the court and, as ever, looked calm and collected. After all, as he saw it, this was the day he had waited so long for, the day when the justice of his case would finally be heard before a legitimate court of law.

Prosecuting was the Attorney General, Sir Vicary Gibbs, known as 'Vinegar Gibbs', a sobriquet earned as a result of his sour personality. Gibbs had been retained by Perceval in the position of Attorney General, having been first appointed to it by Portland. He shared Perceval's reactionary political views on issues such as parliamentary reform and Catholic emancipation and had been, like Perceval, a supporter of Princess Caroline during the Delicate Investigation. He was renowned in courtrooms for his propensity towards sarcasm and an attitude of loftiness. While he had a confidence bordering on arrogance, his grasp of the law and ability in legal argument were second to none. Assisting Gibbs were William Garrow, John Gurney, Mr Knapp and Mr Abbott. Bellingham was represented in court by Mr Peter Alley and Mr Henry Revell Reynolds.

Mr Alley began proceedings by immediately arguing for a postponement of the trial. He attempted to present the argument that his client was unfit to plead through insanity and that, if given enough time to bring forward witnesses, he could prove the fact. This was objected to by the prosecution, and Chief Justice Mansfield ruled that Bellingham would have to plead in any event, on the grounds that he could not hear anyone as counsel for the prisoner until the prisoner had pleaded. The indictment was then read by Mr Shelton, the Clerk of the Arraigns, and John Bellingham was charged with the wilful murder of the Right Honourable Spencer Perceval. The first count was under the oath of various witnesses and the second was under the verdict of the coroner's inquest.

The accused was then called upon to plead. At this point, Bellingham got to his feet and began to address the court:

> My Lords – before I can plead to this indictment, I must state, in justice to myself, that by the hurrying on of my trial, I am placed in a most remarkable situation. It so happens, that my prosecutors are actually the witnesses against me. All the documents on which alone I could rest my defence, have been taken from me, and are now in possession of the Crown. It is only two days since I was told by Mr Litchfield, the Solicitor of the Treasury, to prepare for my trial; and when I asked him for my papers, he told me that they would not be given up to me. It is, therefore, my Lords, rendered utterly impossible for me to go into my justification; and under the circumstance in which I find myself, a trial is absolutely useless. The papers are to be given to me after the trial, but how can that avail me for my defence? I am, therefore, not ready for my trial.[4]

The Attorney General began to give an explanation for the withholding of Bellingham's personal papers, when the Chief Justice interrupted and once again called upon the accused to plead. Bellingham finally did so by saying: 'Not guilty. I put myself upon God and my country.'

The Attorney General then proceeded to inform the court that they were indeed in possession of Mr Bellingham's papers. He stated that the prisoner had been informed that he was entitled to them prior to the commencement of his trial if his counsel requested them. Bellingham's counsel, Mr Alley, retorted by explaining to the court that he had been applied to only the day before and that he had never even seen Mr Bellingham prior to this. He once again petitioned the court for a postponement of the trial, although, at the same time, he wanted to make it clear to the public at large that he did not condone the crime:

> My Lords, it is now my duty, according to the instructions I have received, to make a regular application to you for the

postponement of this trial. However unpleasantly I might feel myself situated, – however disagreeable to one's honourable emotions it may be, – I yet will never shrink from my duty . . .[5]

He wanted to present to the court two affidavits in which it was asserted that the prisoner was insane:

I now, therefore, have to contend, that the jury ought not to be sworn in this case, if I can produce affidavits that the prisoner at the bar is not competent to rational actions, – that he is not in a state to meet this charge *sui juris*. The affidavits which I have, state, that whatever the appearance of the prisoner may be, – however plausible that appearance, he has been known by the deponent to be insane for years.[6]

One affidavit was from Ann Billett, who was, of course, Bellingham's cousin, although this point does not seemed to have been mentioned in court. Her affidavit stated: 'Many proofs . . . could be adduced of the prisoner's insanity, if sufficient time were allowed. In particular, Capt. Barker, an officer in a militia regiment, would be a witness of great importance.'[7] The other affidavit was from Mary Clarke, of Bagnio Court, Newgate Street, in which she stated that 'ever since the prisoner came, two years ago, from Russia, he was not of sound mind'.[8]

On the basis of these affidavits Mr Alley argued that 'the trial should be postponed to such a reasonable period, as would enable the prisoner to adduce such evidence as might tend to his advantage'. He complained that the time scale meant that he had not been able to get more evidence and witnesses regarding the sanity, or otherwise, of the accused from people resident in Liverpool. The Attorney General was having none of this, however, and he addressed their Lordships accordingly:

if you find that this is only an effort to postpone justice, if you think that witnesses have been purposely selected to impress a false belief on the court, then you must perceive that, by putting off the trial, not only the ends of justice will not be answered, but, on the contrary, they will be grossly violated.

Under such circumstances, I am sure, the application would not be attended to. Where, I would ask, has the prisoner been for four months preceding the act for which he is this day called upon to answer? Where has he been, and where are those persons who, during that time, have been in the habit of seeing him? Has Mrs Billett, or has Mrs Clark, witnessed his conduct? No, my Lords, they have not. He has been resident in this town, in the midst of a family, known to multitudes, and transacting business with as much sagacity, and with as perfect and masculine an understanding, as any person who now hears me possesses. None of those persons are called before you Lordships to prove the state of his mind – none of those who know, and could have given evidence of the fact, are brought before the Court: but a contrivance is resorted to – one woman, coming from Southampton, but generally residing in Dorsetshire, and another, living in this city, make affidavits of the prisoner's insanity; but neither of them have attempted to swear that he was in an infirm state of mind about the time that the crime was committed. I will call to your Lordships' recollection, what the prisoner has just now addressed to the Court, as a proof of his sanity – and I will also call to your recollection the anxiety which his Counsel manifested, to prevent his making those observations, which they conceived would influence the Court in coming to the decision, that he was not insane, which was contrary to what they wished. If, indeed, there was any ground for the plea of insanity, or of infirmity of mind, who is the best judge of it – and by whom could it be most satisfactorily proved? Would not his Counsel have sent a person conversant is such disorders, to examine the prisoner; some person, whose statement your Lordships would have regarded as of deep importance? No such course has been pursued: but affidavits, such as I have described, have been put in – evidently not to advance, but to retard and weaken justice . . .[9]

Mr Alley in his answer informed the court that they had, in fact, approached two of the most eminent doctors in the field, Dr Samuel Foart Simmons and Dr Thomas Munro. One of them had let them know that he was not available to attend court, while the other had not yet replied. He furthermore complained that even Bellingham's wife and family, who 'were most likely to be acquainted with his infirmity . . . could not arrive in London in time'.[10]

When, at this point, Mr Reynolds, the other member of Mr Alley's defence team, attempted to make a comment, he was informed by the Recorder that he was not entitled to do so at this time. Following a brief conference with his colleagues, Justice Mansfield ruled on the question of postponement. He stated that 'if there were proper grounds advanced for postponing the trial, he would coincide with the application – but no such grounds could be discovered in the affidavits'. He went on:

> They were both perfectly silent as to the conduct of the Prisoner since his residence in London – they were both silent as to his demeanour for months and months past, nay, for years. The first spoke of Liverpool as the Prisoner's established residence; the second related his return from Russia two years ago. Now, could it be supposed, that he went, or would be permitted to go, to Russia, if he were in a disordered state of mind? It was, there-fore, to be inferred that, when he set out for that country, his sanity was not affected. Two years ago, it seems, he returned. But where he had lived – who had been his companions – or with whom he had formed connections, since that period, both affidavits are silent. The question was not, then, whether he had, at any time, been guilty of extravagancies, but whether, at the time he committed the fact charged against him, he was in a situation to know what he was doing? Any affidavit of this kind should be clear as to the conduct of the individual for a con-siderable time before he had committed the crime, and up to a recent period. But here the affidavits were silent – every word in them might be true; and yet it might be as clear as the daylight, that, at the time he perpetrated the act, he might be in a sound state of mind. They had not spoken of that period during which the prisoner might have been meditating this act.[11]

Accordingly, he refused the application and ruled that the trial could proceed.

After a number of challenges, a jury was empanelled. It consisted of twelve men: Ephraim Lee, Thomas Whittington, Thomas Juggins, William English, James Osborne, John Bellas, Daniel Hayward, John Kennington, Lee Waters, Charles Russell, James King and George Gaton.[12]

Attorney General Gibbs was then invited to give his opening statement. He began by reminding the jury of the great man, the country's 'brightest ornament', whom it had lost through the assassination, and also by making them aware of their public duty:

> May it please your Lordships, Gentlemen of the Jury – A lamentable and painful task devolves upon me, to state to you the circumstances of this horrid murder – a crime perpetrated on a man, whose whole life, I should have thought, would have guarded and protected him against such an attack – who, I am sure, if enough of life had been left him to see by whose hand he had fallen, would have spent his last moment in uttering a prayer for the forgiveness of his murderer. But this is not a time for me to dwell on the private loss – the country has torn from it its brightest ornament – but the country has done justice to his memory. These, however, are not considerations by which you must permit yourselves to be swayed. It is not revenge, nor is it resentment, that ought to have any influence on your consideration of the question. You are to satisfy public justice – to take care by your verdict, this day, that the public shall not be exposed to the perpetration of such horrid crimes.[13]

He then informed them of the demands for compensation that Bellingham had made on the government as a result of the affair in Russia, and the reasonableness of the authorities' refusal of those demands:

> With respect to the Prisoner, who has committed this murder and assassination, I know nothing of his life, or how it has been spent, except so far as related to the circumstance of the case. He was in business, and acted as a merchant – in the course of his transactions he showed himself a man of sound understanding, in every act which he performed – he not only conducted his own

affairs with understanding, but he was selected by other persons
to manage theirs. Some three or four years ago, not finding his
affairs prosper in this country, he was entrusted by a house, I
believe, in the North, to execute business of great importance.
He went to Russia – and there, whether through his own misconduct, or by the justice or injustice of that country, I know not,
he was thrown into prison, and applied to His Majesty's Minister,
Lord Granville Leveson Gower, and to the Secretary of Legation,
Sir Stephen Shairp, for assistance and remuneration for certain
losses. They, for reasons which it is unnecessary, and would be
improper for me to state, refused to grant it. He then came to this
country, and went on in the pursuit of his affairs in the regular
mode. He found persons ready to avail themselves of his activity,
experience, and knowledge, and by them he was employed. But
he seems to have cherished in his mind a feeling of the propri-
ety of making an application to Government, to indemnify him
for losses which he said he had sustained through the means
of the Russian Government; and he applied to many persons in
this country, to assist him in procuring that recompense which
he conceived he was entitled to. The grounds of his application
were examined, as they always are, by his Majesty's Ministers,
who found them unworthy of attention, and therefore the claim
was rejected. He then had recourse to another contrivance,
which he hoped to have effected. As his Majesty's ministers did
not wish to interfere, he became desirous of having his case
laid before Parliament; to see if he had friends enough there,
to obtain that which he had in vain sought from Government.
He made applications to various Members of Parliament, who
declined complying with his request. He then applied to Mr
Perceval himself, the late Minister, to countenance his claims;
which, according to the forms of Parliament, was necessary to
be signified to the House, when pecuniary assistance was prayed
for. Governed by those principles of justice, which always regu-
lated and directed his conduct, he did not think himself justified
in acceding to the request, and he refused it.

Mr Gibbs then outlined to the jury the meticulous nature of
Bellingham's preparation for the crime:

From the moment the Prisoner found Mr Perceval would not countenance what he called a remuneration; from that moment the desire of revenge took root in his mind. He had been resident in this city for four months; and, from the time he found his application would not be received, he made preparation for effecting the horrible purpose, which he at last fatally accomplished. He provided himself with a brace of pistols, he purchased ammunition, and was ready to take advantage of the first opportunity which offered to prosecute his revenge: and for the purpose of greater certainty, he informed himself of the time when Mr Perceval usually attended the House. That everything might be complete, he procured to be added, to the common dress he wore, a pocket at the side, to receive one of the pistols. On the day when this atrocious act was committed, he placed himself in the lobby of the House of Commons, at the entrance, close to the door, and waited till the victim of his malignity was likely to appear. He prepared himself for the deed: and, just as he was passing the threshold, he discharged his pistol. It unfortunately took effect. Mr Perceval died almost instantaneously!

He then made their task clear:

Under these circumstances, you have to say, whether the person who stands at the bar be or be not the murderer? Whether he shall or shall not answer the justice of his country for the act he has performed? – Consider it not as the murder of so eminent a person. Consider it as the murder of a common individual. Suppose the meanest subject to have suffered as Mr Perceval did suffer, and pronounce your judgement as you would in that case! Is he or is he not guilty? To that point you must direct your attention – and I know of no reason to cause even a doubt.

Mr Gibbs turned next to the question of whether the trial should be postponed, as the defence wanted, to allow for the presentation of more evidence regarding the prisoner's insanity:

But, what remains? – This only remains – the attempt which was made this day to put off the trial on the ground of the Prisoner being fit for this or for any other crime, as he was afflicted with insanity. Let us consider this a little. The Prisoner is a man conducting himself, like others, in all the ordinary circumstances of life – who carries on business himself, none of his family or friends interfering – no pretence suggested that he was not able to superintend his own affairs. Not only managing his business himself, but employed by others, in consequence of the high opinion they entertained of his understanding. To them there appeared no defect, no blemish on his mind. What clearer proof can be given to show, contrary to the defence set up that this man was not what the law calls *non compos mentis* – that he was an unaccountable being? He manages his own affairs and the affairs of those by whom he is employed, in a manner that no persons complain of. What foundation is there then for raising, not a presumption, but a pretence or a suspicion of his insanity? I cannot answer that, for I have not occupied my mind with it – I know the cases where the plea of insanity will be received – when, for instance, a murder is committed by a person, whose mental infirmity may be considered as very nearly the absence of all mind. Against that defence, there is no argument. But I am this day to learn, whether the wickedness of the act, which the Prisoner is called on to answer, is to be considered an excuse for its perpetration.

Gibbs presented the jury with a hypothetical scenario to illustrate his point regarding accountability:

I can place my position in a stronger point of view by supposing a case. Let me suppose while the hand of this assassin was raised against the man whom he murdered that it was suddenly arrested by the stroke of death, and it pleased God, for the sake of the family, the friends, and the country, of Mr Perceval, to snatch the murderer from life. Let me suppose, on the morning of that day, the Prisoner had either made a will or entered into any obligation. Let me suppose that will or obligation to be called into question in a Court of Justice, and that his relations had interfered to do it away, because he was not in a state of mind to act for himself. Travelling through the whole life of this man, what ground could they adduce for such a proceeding? His every act appears rational, except one – and that is only irrational because it is so horrid that the imagination of man cannot fancy to itself the existence of so atrocious an act. Could a will or a bond so executed be disputed in law? Let me suppose that evidence was given of his having *intended* to accomplish that which, unfortunately, he did accomplish. Let the preparation and the attempt be stated – let it be said that the deed was all but carried into execution. Could these circumstances have been adduced in proof of a weak or insane mind, when he is shown to have exerted, in everything else, the most active, perfect, and sound understanding?

He argued that just because a crime is atrocious or barbaric does not mean that the perpetrator is necessarily insane:

And what does the argument of insanity in such a case amount to? It comes to this – you must conclude he was mad, because the deed is so atrocious, the act is so enormous, that none of those with whom we are in the habit of communicating in common life have ever even imagined such guilt. But how far would this argument go? It must arrive at this conclusion, that every act of gross and unusual atrocity would carry its defence along with it. That every act of peculiar horror would have, within itself, a certain defence. For the barbarity of the deed would be considered as proof that the mind which directed it was not in a state of sufficient sanity to judge whether the action was right or wrong! This is the only point for consideration, in forming a just conclusion, whether the prisoner possessed such a mind, at the time of the assassination, as to distinguish right from wrong. For, if his mind possessed that power, he is criminally accountable for the act . . .

At this point the Attorney General cited two precedents dealing with pleas of insanity. First, the case of Arnold:

In the year 1723, a person of the name of Arnold was indicted for having shot at and wounded Lord Onslow. He was supposed to have been murdered, but the noble Lord recovered. The act was proved beyond all controversy. The defence set up was insanity. It was proved that, from his childhood, he could not conduct himself like a common man. Every act of his life showed an insufficiency of understanding; to such an extent, that he was not competent to conduct his own affairs; nor would his friends, or, indeed, any person, permit him to transact his own business. But it was proved that he entertained a causeless hatred against Lord Onslow; that he had prepared himself for the attack; that he had purchased shot of a larger size than he generally made use of; that he had the act in view for some time before; and it was stated, by the learned Judge who tried the case, that if, from the circumstances adduced, a knowledge of right and wrong could be presumed, he was criminally accountable – and the jury being of the same opinion, he was found guilty.

Then, Lord Ferrers's murder of his steward, Mr Johnson:

The next was the case of Lord Ferrers, who was tried for the murder of Mr Johnson, his steward. Mr Johnson had resided in his Lordship's family from his childhood; and, when the noble Lord was separated from his wife, he was appointed receiver of the estates. Lord Ferrers then began to distrust, and dislike the man, of whom he conceived great jealousy. Johnson, it seemed, would not assist him in the furtherance of designs, which he considered unlawful. Against him his Lordship cherished an implacable resentment, and determined on revenge. He concealed it in his own breast, and made the necessary preparations for the foul deed. He sent for Mr Johnson, treated him with great civility, got the family out of the way, and, having enticed him to a room, he there shot him. It was argued on his trial, that he was a man without understanding. Many irrational acts of his Lordship were proved, and it was also deposed, that several of the family had died insane. It was clearly shown that he had acted with great insanity, not only in the business out of which the trial arose, but through his whole life. His solicitor had frequent conversations with him, and thought him so insane, that he refused to be employed by him, on that account, and on that alone. His physicians stated they believed him to be in an insane state of mind – and his relations considered him in such a situation that he was a fit object for a commission of lunacy – which they certainly would have taken out against him, but they were fearful that their actions might be perverted, and turned to their disadvantage if they could not satisfactorily make out the case. How were these facts answered? By the question put to the whole House of Peers, who tried the culprit, 'Whether, not withstanding all these acts, they believed, that, at the time he discharged his pistol, he had a mind capable of distinguishing right from wrong.' And the whole of his peers, with one *consentient* voice, pronounced him to be guilty. – He had judgement of death passed on him, and, on that judgement, so founded on the verdict of his peers, he was executed.

Gibbs concluded his opening statement by returning to the case at hand and affirming Bellingham's sanity and accountability for the crime committed:

Now, having pointed out these facts to you, and supposing that those persons were, to a certain degree, insane, with respect to civil affairs, suffer me to contrast their cases with that of the prisoner. Here there is no deficiency of understanding whatever – no opinion of others to that effect is adduced – on the contrary, he is entrusted with the management of their affairs. The question is whether, at the time the murder was perpetrated, he possessed sufficient sense to distinguish between right and wrong? What can you collect from the statement I have made (and I have made it as correct as the information I have received enabled me), from the systematic precision which his conduct evinced, that can support the plea of insanity? What conclusion can you draw, in favour of the idea which has been suggested, that the prisoner was not in a sane state of mind? Take from your recollection the horrid nature of the act, with the commission of which he is charged – a crime so great that one can scarcely suppose any human creature could be guilty of such an atrocity. Take from it its accumulated horrors, and the prisoner stands before you in a state of sanity. This is the point to which your attention must be directed.

Having prepared the jury adequately, Attorney General Gibbs was now ready to call the first witness on behalf of the prosecution.

Chapter 18

'OBSERVED A TUMULT'

The first witness called to the stand on behalf of the Crown was William Smith, the Member of Parliament for Norwich, and the future grandfather of Florence Nightingale.[1] He began giving his testimony in response to Mr Garrow's questions.[2]

On the 11th of this month (last Monday) I was going through the lobby towards the door of the House of Commons. As I was passing through the lobby, I stopped to speak to a gentleman whom I met with there; while in conversation with that gentleman I heard the report of a pistol, which appeared to have been fired close by the entrance of the door of the lobby.

By that door, do you mean the door by which members coming from their residences get into the house?

Yes, the first door of the lobby. This appeared to have been fired from that door; immediately upon hearing the report I turned my head towards the place from whence the noise appeared to have proceeded, and observed a tumult, and probably a dozen or more persons gathering about the spot, almost at the same instant a person rushed hastily from among the crowd, and several voices cried out shut the door, and let no one escape. The person who came from among the crowd came towards me, looking first one way and then another, and as I thought at the moment rather like one seeking for shelter, than as the person who had received the wound, but taking two or three steps towards me, as he approached he rather reeled by me, and almost instantly fell upon the floor, with his face downwards. Before he fell I heard a cry not very distinctly, what appeared to come from him, in which were the words, murder, or something very much like that. When he first fell I thought he might be slightly wounded, and expected to see him make an effort to rise, but gazing at him a few moments, I observed that he did not stir at all; I therefore immediately stooped down to raise him from the ground, requesting the assistance of a gentleman who stood close by me for that purpose. As soon as we had turned his face towards us, and not till then, I perceived it was Mr Perceval. We then took him in our arms, the other gentleman on his left side, and I on his right. We carried him into the office of the speaker's secretary, and seated ourselves on a table there with Mr Perceval between us also sitting on the table, resting on our arms. His face was at that time completely pale, the blood issuing in small quantity from each corner of his mouth, and as I then thought probably not more than two minutes had elapsed since the pistol had been fired there were not scarcely any signs of life remaining; his eyes were still open, but he did not appear to know me, nor take any notice of any person that came about him, nor had he uttered the least articulate sound from the moment that he fell. A few convulsive sobs, which lasted three or four minutes, together with scarcely a perceptible pulse, were the only signs of life remaining, and this continued but for a short time longer, and when I felt his wrist for the last time assisted by Mr Lynn a surgeon, who had arrived, it appeared to me that he was totally dead; I remained in the same situation with the body till we carried it into the speaker's house. I am incapable of giving any account of whatever passed afterwards in the lobby respecting the detention or conduct of the prisoner at the bar.

Had you afterwards any opportunity of seeing where Mr Perceval was wounded?

Mr Perceval still remained on my arm when Mr Lynn examined the wound; he came into the room, and examined the wound while we remained in the same posture. The body not having been moved at all; I saw the wound from which but little blood appeared to have issued.

Where was the wound?

The wound was very near the nipple of the left breast, a little above it and within it; the orifice appeared to me to be large for a pistol ball, and when Mr Lynn probed it; it seemed clearly that the ball had slanted downwards, but it appeared clearly that the ball had penetrated the cavity of the breast, for the probe did not touch it.

Mr Perceval, I believe, was a person of low stature.

Unquestionably.

State the hour of the day that this happened.

I recollect from various circumstances that it must have been between five o'clock, and a quarter after.

I know you have been long a member of that place, is that about the time that Mr Perceval, in his public situation, would come to the house?

It is about the time that Mr Perceval, in his public situation would come, and about that time he was constantly expected, and nearer to that time than any other.

Was the gentleman that assisted of the name of Phillips?

I believe it was.

Next to take the stand was Mr William Lynn:

I believe you are a surgeon residing in Great George-street, Westminster?

I am.

Were you sent for, and did you go to the House of Commons on Monday the 11th instant?

I did.

What time in the afternoon?

About a quarter past five in the afternoon.

What part of the House of Commons, or about it did you go to?

I went through the lobby into the passage to the speaker's secretary's room.

When you got there what did you see?

I saw Mr Perceval lay partly upon the table with his feet in two chairs one foot on each chair; I then saw some blood upon the white waistcoat and shirt; I turned it aside and saw an opening in the skin; I examined his pulse, he had no pulsation, and appeared quite dead.

Did you probe the wound?

I probed it, the probe passed three inches obliquely downwards and inwards, it being immediately over the heart, about the further

. Spencer Perceval, Tory Prime Minister from 1809 until his assassination in 1812. *(Mary Evans Picture Library)*

2. Bellingham fired his pistol directly at Perceval's chest fatally wounding him. (*Mary Evans Picture Library*)

. The Prime Minister had not uttered a single word since falling on the floor of the lobby, and the only noises to emanate from him after that were 'a few convulsive sobs.' *(Mary Evans Picture Library)*

4. John Bellingham assassinated the Prime Minister on Monday, 11 May 1812 and believed that he was quite justified in doing so. *(Mary Evans Picture Library)*

6. *Opposite:* The interior of the House of Commons where Perceval built up his political reputation. *(House of Commons Interior before the fire of 1834, from Ackermann's 'Microcosm of London' by T. Rowlandson (1756–1827) and A.C. Pugin (1762–1832) British Library, London, UK/© British Library Board. All Rights Reserved/The Bridgeman Art Library)*

5. A view of the Houses of Lords and Commons from Old Palace Yard. Perceval walked there that day from Downing Street. *(Pub. 1821 by Colnaghi & Co. (aquatint) by Havell, Robert the Elder (1769–1832) and Younger (1793–1878) Guildhall Library, City of London/The Bridgeman Art Library)*

7. William Pitt the Younger, Britain's youngest ever Prime Minister, who was an early admirer of Perceval's talents. *(National Portrait Gallery, London)*

8. Lord Granville Leveson-Gower, the British Ambassador at St Petersburg, whom Bellingham believed had not tried to help him in his time of need. 'If I had met Lord Gower,' he said in court, 'he would have received the ball, and not Mr Perceval.' *(National Portrait Gallery, London)*

9. Sir James Mansfield, Lord Chief Justice of the Common Pleas, said that Perceval was 'so dear, and so revered' he found it hard to suppress his feelings while presiding at Bellingham's trial. *(National Portrait Gallery, London)*

10. The Revd Daniel Wilson, Minister of St John's Chapel, Bedford Row, and later to become Bishop of Calcutta, called on Bellingham in Newgate prison to get him to repent his sin, but to no avail. *(Mary Evans Picture Library)*

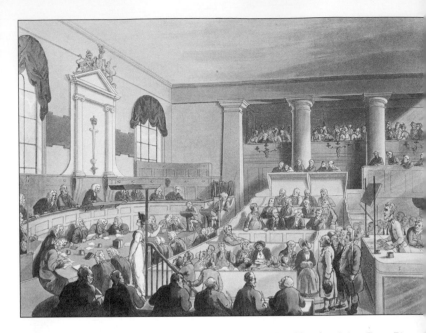

11. Bellingham's trial was held in a packed courtroom at the Old Bailey. *(Mary Evans Picture Library)*

12. Bellingham put forward a robust defence of himself in court. Opinion was divided on whether he had received justice. *(National Portrait Gallery, London)*

13. Opinion was also divided on how effective Prime Minister Spencer Perceval had been. *(National Portrait Gallery, London)*

rib: I had no doubt that the ball had passed into the heart, if not through it. It was a large pistol ball apparently.

Could you from the appearance judge, sir, that that was the cause of his death?

I have no doubt of that.

Henry Burgess, the solicitor, was called to the stand next and gave evidence regarding the prisoner's possession of pistols. He was examined by Mr Gurney:

You are a solicitor?

I am.

In the afternoon of Monday were you in the lobby of the House of Commons?

I was.

A little after five o'clock did you hear the report of a pistol?

I did.

From what part of the lobby did that report proceed . . .?

From the entrance.

What did you observe next after the report of the pistol?

I saw a person coming forwards along the lobby from the entrance towards the House, staggering, and just before he came to the pillars next the door I saw him put his hand to his breast, or nigh his breast, he said, oh, faintly, and fell forwards on his face; I heard some people say, that is the man, and I saw a man pointing towards a bench by the side of the fire place, at the side of the lobby. I immediately at the same instant went to the bench, I saw the prisoner sitting on the bench in great agitation, I looked at both hands, and saw his left hand on the bench, and in his hand, or under his hand I saw the pistol, I immediately took the pistol in my hand and asked him what could have induced him to do such a thing, or act; he replied, want of redress of grievance, and refusal by government; it was to that effect, I do not say these were the exact words; I said, you have another pistol in your pocket; he replied, yes; I asked him if it was loaded; he said, yes; I saw some person take it from the left side of the prisoner's person about the coat or breeches.

When you took hold of the first pistol which you found in his hand, or under his hand, in what condition was it?

It was warm, it had the appearance of having been recently discharged . . .

The pistol was then produced.

Is it a large or a small bore to the pistol?

I thought it was a very large bore. When he told me that the other pistol was loaded, I immediately put my hand into his right waistcoat pocket, and took out a pen-knife and a pencil, and a bunch of keys, and some money; at the same time I saw the pistol taken from him, and a bundle of papers.

Was the prisoner detained in custody?

He was.

Was he examined shortly afterwards?

Yes.

Was he taken upstairs in order, with other witnesses, to be examined before the magistrate?

He was.

Did you before the magistrate in the presence of the prisoner relate the facts which you have today related?

I did.

When you had concluded your narrative did he make any observation upon it?

He did, he said as nigh as I can recollect, I wish to correct Mr Burgess's statement in one part, but I believe he is perfectly correct in any other; instead of my hand, as Mr Burgess has stated, being on or near the pistol, I think he took it from my hand, or out of my hand; I do not know whether he said from my hand or out of my hand.

Did he make any other observation upon your evidence?

He did not.

Mr Alley then cross-examined the witness:

I take it for granted you have stated everything that occurred?

No, I cannot recollect everything that he stated; I have recollected everything of importance.

He said he had been ill used, and when you asked him why he did it, that is the reason he gave you, mere want of redress of grievance on the part of government?

Redress of grievance, and a refusal by government.

That is all he said to you?

No, he said, I will relate to you why I did it.

And when you asked him why he did it that is the reason he gave you?

That is nearly the reason.

He did not state any personal resentment to Mr Perceval?

He did not.

There were a great many persons in the lobby?

Not a great many, not more than twenty.

Do you mean at the time the pistol was fired?

I do. I do not think there were twenty at the time the pistol was fired.

There was an order given to shut the door of the lobby. Had that order been given before or after your conversation?

I will not pretend to say I heard the order given.

You say the man was very much agitated.

Very much.

Might not he have absconded after he had fired the pistol, before the door had been ordered to be shut?

I will not say.

Then Mr Gurney, re-examining on behalf of the Crown, asked a number of questions regarding how long the agitation of the prisoner had continued, to which the witness answered:

He was extremely agitated the whole time I was with him, afterwards, upstairs, he appeared perfectly calm and collected.

With respect to the possibility of escape from the firing of the pistol, must the prisoner have been within the lobby or without?

I don't know, I should suppose there is no doubt he was in the lobby, I have no doubt he was in the lobby in my own mind.

I believe down three steps from the door of the lobby there is an officer stationed?

Two steps from the lobby.

And then four or five steps down there is an officer?

There are persons belonging to the house stationed.
At the bottom of these four steps there are two persons stationed, are there not?
I generally see one, sometimes there are two, I generally see one.
Could any person go out of the lobby without going close by that person?
He must have gone within a yard of him or less.

General Isaac Gascoyne MP was then called upon to give his version of events. Mr Abbott began his examination by asking him if he was a member of the House of Commons:

I am.
Were you in one of the committee rooms on the afternoon of Monday last . . . ?
About five o'clock on Monday last I went to the House with a petition, to let Mr Perceval see it by his own desire, previous to that petition being presented to the House. Before five o'clock the House resolved itself into a committee of the whole House, to proceed further respecting the Order of Council. Mr Perceval then not being come down to the House, I postponed, till his arrival, presenting that petition, and went upstairs into the committee room, close by the balustrades which look down into the lobby, the door open towards that balustrade, it was merely the same thing as to hearing, as to being in the lobby of the House. I heard the loud report of a pistol shot, and almost instantaneously the cry of close the door. I rushed downstairs, through the House into the lobby; the door facing of the balustrade was open. The moment I came into the lobby, I saw a crowd collected about some individual whom I could not see, and to whom the attention of almost every person was directed, I mean the generality; a person near me, whom I should not know if I were to see him, immediately said, that is the man that fired the pistol, pointing to John Bellingham, who stands there, whose person I well knew, and whose name I was acquainted with; I flew towards him, he was then sitting with one or two others upon the bench, at the right hand side of the fire-place of the lobby, supposing your back turned towards that fire.

Between the fire-place and the entrance door of the lobby?

Just so. I seized him by the breast, I think, and as he lifted up his hand, it appeared to me that a pistol was in that hand, either cocked, or upon the half cock, it appeared to me cocked. The first impression in my mind was that it was to be used against himself. I saw the pistol in his hand grasped, I therefore kept down his arm with all my strength, and a person, whom I believe to be the last witness, Mr Burgess, whom I then did not know, took that pistol from under his hand, his hand being so held that there was little or no resistance from him. I heard that person ask him whether he had another pistol, I heard his reply – that he had; I proceeded to search for it, there were then others searching him. I put my hand into his coat pocket, I think one of the inside pockets, I had my hand in several of his pockets, I pulled out a bundle of papers, tied together with red tape; the pressure was great at that moment, I found myself closely pressed at that time, I was fearful of losing these papers and of losing the prisoner. I held up the papers, and Mr Hume, a member of the House of Commons, took the papers out of my hand, with my consent; it appeared to me at that time, as it were the prisoner was dragged from my hold, I have no doubt now but it was the effect of persons to secure him; at that time I thought it was to drag him out of the lobby. I fastened both my hands upon him, told him he could not escape, that I knew him well, and that I would not lose sight of him, he said he had submitted, as if it were not to use him ill, I believe he rather complained of my using his arm rather roughly, he said that he had submitted, that he was the person that fired the shot; some other questions were asked, but I cannot now distinctly speak to them, nor to the answers, but with the assistance of others he was dragged into the body of the house and placed at the bar, in the custody of the two messengers. I mentioned to him his name, which he admitted.

From the body of the house he was taken to another place where he and you were examined?

Yes.

You were examined, and that examination took place in his presence?

It did.

After you had made your deposition did the prisoner make any remark upon it?

Something to this effect: General Gascoyne is too correct for me to question what he has said. He must have been less agitated than I was; he complained of the violence to his arm.

When you first laid hold of him did he appear to be in a state of agitation?

He certainly appeared to be in a state of agitation, as any man would be, guilty of a crime, in a perspiration.

Did he appear to have recovered from that agitation after your deposition was over?

Completely composed, as I had known him before this occurrence happened.

You stated that you knew him, how lately before had you seen him?

The precise day I cannot mention, I can recollect some time in April, I saw him and conversed with him at my own house . . .

Mr James Taylor, the tailor who had supplied Bellingham with the specially modified coat, took the stand next. Mr Garrow began by asking him his address, which he gave as:

No. 11, North Place, Gray's Inn Lane.

Is that in the neighbourhood of Millman-street?

Very near it.

Do you know the prisoner at the bar?

I do know him.

How long have you known him?

Ever since the 5th of last March.

What business do you follow?

The profession of a tailor.

Have you ever been employed in the way of your business by the prisoner?

Only twice.

When first?

The first time that ever I saw Mr Bellingham was on the 5th of March; he came into my shop as a chance customer.

He came as a stranger?

Yes, he gave me an order for a pair of pantaloons and a striped waistcoat. I made them and took them home myself, and he paid me for them.

Where did you take them home to?

No. 11, New Millman-street, in Guildford-street.

Did you take them according to the directions that you received from the customer at the time of the order?

Entirely so, he gave me the directions in my hand; he wrote his own address in my presence.

You carried them home, and he paid you?

Yes, he approved of them, and he paid me.

Did you learn from him whether he kept the house, or was a lodger?

I do not know.

How soon after you carried home this first article did you see the prisoner again?

The next time was about the 25th of April, the other was on the 5th of March. On the 25th of April I met him in Guildford-street, he informed me that he had a small job to do, and if I would step back with him he would give it me immediately.

Did you go back with him to the same house that you took the former articles?

I did. When I got to the house he asked me into the parlour, he then went upstairs and brought me a dark coloured coat, he gave me directions to make him an inside pocket on the left side, so as he could get at it conveniently, he wished to have it a particular depth, he accordingly gave me a bit of paper about the length of nine inches.

He gave you a bit of paper about nine inches in length, did he bring that from upstairs, or from what other place did he produce it?

He brought it all downstairs together; I saw him go upstairs and come down; he brought the coat and the pattern paper.

How long had you waited from the time that he asked you to sit down and wait for his coming downstairs?

I suppose about ten minutes.

Did you execute that order?

I did, he was very particular to have it home that evening.

Did you carry it home yourself?

Yes, I delivered it to the maid-servant, I met him about six days ago in Gray's Inn Lane.

Lord Chief Justice Mansfield then asked Mr Taylor if anything passed between himself and the accused when they met in Gray's Inn Lane:

> Yes, I bowed to him, and he informed me that in the course of a few days hence he should have something for me to do; I never saw him from that till this morning.
>
> *Can you recollect what day this was?*
>
> It was about six days before I heard of the death of Mr Perceval.

The next witness was Mr John Norris, who was examined by Mr Garrow:

> *I believe, sir, you have frequent occasions to attend in the gallery provided for strangers in the House of Commons?*
>
> I have.
>
> *Did you go down to the house for that purpose on Monday last?*
>
> I did.
>
> *In passing to the staircase of that gallery do you necessarily go through the outer door of the house?*
>
> Certainly.
>
> *About what time did you arrive at that spot?*
>
> About five o'clock, or from five to ten minutes past five at the outside. I arrived at the door of the lobby.
>
> *Did you observe any person who is now here standing near that door?*
>
> I did, I observed the prisoner at the bar.
>
> *Describe particularly where he stood.*
>
> I observed him standing in the lobby, by the side of that part of the door that is generally closed.
>
> *It is a double door, and the other part open for the members to go through into the lobby?*
>
> Yes.
>
> *There is one half closed and the other half opened?*
>
> Yes, he stood at the lobby door, at that part which is generally closed.
>
> *How near might that be to where a person must pass the avenue, who are members?*
>
> Within an arm's length. I observed him, as if watching for some-

body that was coming; perhaps the impression is stronger on my mind now than it was then. I thought he appeared to be anxiously watching, and as my recollection serves me his right hand was within the breast of his coat in this way; I passed on to the staircase of the gallery.

How soon after you had passed that door where the prisoner was that you described did you hear any noise?

Almost as soon as I got on the top of the stairs that leads to the gallery for strangers, there is a sort of an anti-lobby as you pass part of that gallery there, I had just got into the upper lobby.

About twenty steps?

Yes, about that. When I got up there I heard the report of a pistol, I immediately heard the general confusion, and somebody said Mr Perceval was dead. Then I came downstairs.

Are you certain that the prisoner was the person that you thus saw at that place?

I am perfectly certain; I had frequently seen him before.

Had you any private acquaintance with him?

None; I had seen him in the gallery of the House of Commons, and about the passages of the House.

That is the gallery if any person wishes to be present at the debates?

It is.

Mr John Vickery was then examined by Mr Knapp.

You are an officer of Bow-street.

I am.

Did you go to the lodgings of the prisoner?

I received a paper, desiring me to go to No. 9, New Millman Street, it was last Monday.

Did you search his lodging?

I did, I found in a drawer upstairs in a bed-room, a pair of pistol bags, in the same drawer I found a small powder-flask, this pistol key . . . and a quantity of letters and papers; and I found a mould and some balls.

The witness was handed the pistol and the pistol key, which he demonstrated to be a corresponding pair. The ball that had been removed from Bellingham's loaded pistol was also produced and placed in the mould found in his room. Mr Vickery said that, in his opinion, the ball was made in that mould.[3]

The next to give evidence was the journalist Vincent George Dowling. He was first asked whether he was in the lobby of the House of Commons on Monday last:

> I was in the gallery when I heard the pistol discharged, I imme-diately rushed into the lobby.
> *Did you there see the prisoner at the bar?*
> I did; I took from his small clothes pocket, on the left hand side, this pistol.

The pistol that he had taken from Bellingham's pocket was produced in court.[4]

> *Did you keep it in your possession until it was examined to see whether it was loaded?*
> I examined it myself almost immediately after I took the pris-oner, it was loaded with powder and ball that is now in it. It was primed as well as loaded.

He was asked to check if the ball, which he was handed, would fit this pistol.[5] He did so and said:

> This ball fits one pistol as well as the other.
> *Are the pistols a pair?*
> They are; they bear the same maker's name.
> *Had you seen the prisoner ever before?*
> Several times. I had seen him several times in galleries in the House of Commons, and the avenues leading to it.
> *According to your best recollection about how long is it ago since you have seen him?*
> About a week or six days back, from my seeing him last Monday.
> *I apprehend you are frequently in the galleries during the debates?*
> Frequently; on one occasion I sat immediately next to him, while the House was in debate; I sat next to him about half an hour; I cannot say the precise time; there was a sort of general

conversation between him and myself, and some other person
that was sitting near me.

Mr John Addison Newman, the Keeper of Newgate gaol, was the
next witness called to the stand.

You are the keeper of Newgate?
Yes.
*The prisoner was brought into your custody after he was apprehended
on Monday last?*
He was. I have a coat I was desired to produce.
Is that the coat that he wore at the time he came into your custody?
I believe so; the prisoner has been wearing this coat till yester-
day, I believe. It was delivered to me by Bowman, the man that
came in with him.

Mr George Bowman, Newman's assistant, was also called upon to
give evidence:

You are an assistant to Mr Newman, are not you?
I am employed occasionally.
Then you are an assistant. Did you deliver any coat to Mr Newman?
I did . . .
Did you ever see that coat before?
I saw it in a room adjoining the chapel; the present prisoner
occupied that room.
The prisoner has been confined in that room since Monday last?
Yes.
Have you been frequently in that room while the prisoner was there?
I was there on Tuesday evening last between eight and nine
o'clock, and I remained there until eight or nine o'clock the fol-
lowing evening.

It was at this point that Bellingham asked for a chair, which was
brought to him.[6] During the proceedings he had managed to
maintain his usual calm demeanour. Occasionally he would
look around at the assembled crowd. At one point he removed
an orange from his pocket, which he pealed carefully and ate. At

another time he was seen to pick some leaves off a shrub on the bar in front of him, roll them between his hands and smell them.[7] Meanwhile the examination of Mr Bowman continued:

> *Do you know anything of this coat which is now produced?*
> I was in the room when the prisoner acknowledged this coat to be his coat; he said that in the scuffle at the lobby in the House of Commons the coat was torn, and that he wished to have it mended, it had been torn by some person endeavouring to take the papers from his pocket; he wished to have a tailor to mend the coat; there was a man in the chapel-yard in the room under the prisoner's room, that was a tailor, and the coat was lowered down to him by a string to the window to be mended.
> *Is that the coat?*
> It is the coat.

James Taylor, the tailor who had altered the coat for Bellingham, was then asked to confirm whether this was the same coat. To which he answered:

> Yes, sir, that is the same coat that I put the pocket in it, and this is the pocket I made in consequence of his pattern.

With that, the prosecution had concluded its case.

It was hoped that the evidence given by the witnesses had proven to the jury not only that the prisoner had murdered the Prime Minister, but also that he was responsible for what he had done. John Bellingham would now have an opportunity of countering those assertions.

Chapter 19

DEFENCE

The judge informed Bellingham that it was now time for him to make his defence and to bring forward any witnesses that he had to offer. At first the accused told the court that he was content to leave his defence to his counsel, but was informed that, apart from the examination of witnesses, his counsel could only offer him advice and that his defence was his own responsibility. Under common law at the time, those accused of capital crimes had to conduct their own defence unless a point of law was at issue.[1] They could merely receive assistance from their counsel in the examination and cross-examination of witnesses. In response to this, Bellingham's first action was to call once again for the return of his papers. He told the court: 'The documents and papers are necessary to my defence which were taken out of my pocket in the House of Commons, I beg to be indulged with them.'[2]

The Attorney General urged the court to prove first that the papers in court were, in fact, those taken from the prisoner. Therefore Mr Joseph Hume, MP for Weymouth, was called upon to give evidence. He confirmed that the papers in court were those of the prisoner: 'They are the whole, there is none kept back; I took them out of the hand of General Gascoyne. I saw him take them from the prisoner.'[3]

General Gascoyne similarly gave evidence that he had delivered all the papers in question into the hands of Mr Hume. At this point the papers were given to Bellingham and he went through them for some minutes before speaking. When he was ready, he got to his feet and began his defence by rejecting his counsel's argument regarding his insanity, even thanking the Attorney General for rebutting the argument.[4]

I feel great personal obligations to the learned Attorney General for the objections that he made to the defence set up by my counsel on account of insanity. It is far more fortunate for me that such a plea as that should be unfounded, and at the same time I am under the same obligation to my learned counsels for their zeal in my defence in setting up the plea that I am insane by the desire of my friends, or that I have been insane. I am not apprised of a single instance in Russia where my insanity was made public except in one single instance, when the pressure of my sufferings had exposed me to that imputation.

He then apologised for his style of oratory:

Gentlemen, I beg pardon. This is the first time I ever was in public in this kind of way, and you I am sure will look at the substance of what I say more than the manner of my offering it.

Then he turned his attention to the issue at hand:

Gentlemen, as to the lamentable catastrophe for which I am now on my trial before this court, if I am the man that I am supposed to be, to go and deliberately shoot Mr Perceval without malice, I should consider myself a monster, and not fit to live in this world or the next. The learned Attorney General has candidly stated to you that, till this fatal time of this catastrophe, which I heartily regret, no man more so, not even one of the family of Mr Perceval, I had no personal or premeditated malice towards that gentleman; the unfortunate lot had fallen upon him as the leading member of that administration which had repeatedly refused me any reparation for the unparalleled injuries I had sustained in Russia for eight years with the cognisance and sanction of the minister of the country at the court of St Petersburg.

He decided that, in order to explain his actions, he would give the jury a full account of the events as they had occurred from the beginning in Russia:

Gentlemen, I must begin to explain the origin of this unhappy affair, which took place in 1804. I was a merchant at Liverpool, in that year I went to Russia on some mercantile business of importance to myself, and having finished that business I was about to take my departure from Archangel for England; at that time a ship . . . was lost in the White Sea: she was chartered for England, and by the direction of her owners insured at Lloyd's coffee-house, but the underwriters at Lloyds refused to pay the owners for their loss. In consequence of some circumstances connected with this refusal, and the loss of the ship, they cast their suspicions at me, at the same time I had no concern in it whatever, I was about leaving the place; they writ up to Lloyd's coffee-house who had given the communication; I was seized as I was passing the Russian frontier by order of the military governor of Archangel, and thrown into prison;

He wasted no time in getting to the issue of what he perceived to be the inaction of the British authorities on his behalf:

I immediately applied to the British consul at Archangel, and through him to the British Ambassador, Lord Granville Leveson Gower, then at the Russian court, stating my case. Lord Gower wrote to the military governor of Archangel, desiring that if I was not detained for any legal cause I might be liberated as a British subject, but the governor answered that I was detained in prison for a legal cause, and that I had conducted myself in a very indecorous manner. From this time Lord Gower and the British Consul positively declined any further interference in the business, and I was detained in durance for near two years, in spite of all my endeavours to induce the British Minister to interfere with the Emperor of Russia for an investigation of my case. At length, however, after being banded from prison to prison, and from dungeon to dungeon, fed on bread and water, treated with the utmost cruelty, and frequently marched through the streets under a military guard with felons and criminals of the most atrocious description, even before the residence of the British Minister, who might view from his window, this degrading severity towards a British subject who had committed no crime to the disgrace and insult of the British nation. I was afterwards enabled to make my case known through the Procureur – it was investigated, and he obtained a judgement against the military governor, and the senate. Notwithstanding this decision I was immediately sent to another prison, and a demand was made on me for two thousand roubles, alleged to be due by me to a Russian merchant who was a bankrupt. I refused to pay this demand for a debt which I did not owe, and the Senate finding me determined to resist the demand, I was declared a bankrupt, and continued in prison under the pretence I had made answer that I could not pay it, because all my property was in England. No such answer was ever given by me; under this pretence I was detained in prison.

Gentlemen – It is a custom in Russia, that if a foreigner is declared a bankrupt, three months are allowed for all his creditors in Russia to make their claims, and eighteen months more for creditors resident in other parts of the world; but notwithstanding that, the three months had elapsed and not a single claimant appeared, although the Senate sent forth their clerks to enquire of all strangers who arrived, whether they had any demands against me.

Once again he underlined the fact that Lord Gower and his colleagues had not helped him:

Still I was detained in prison, and sent from gaol to gaol, and I was finally handed over to the College of Commerce; the two thousand roubles were still demanded of me, and Lord Gower refused to interfere in the business, and the Consul told me I must pay the money. I was not destitute of the means of payment, but I resisted the claim, on account of its gross injustice. When the Marquis of Douglas arrived in Russia I made my case known to him, and said I only wished it to be shown that the money was justly due, and I would pay it. The Marquis of Douglas made a representation, and stated that it was only desired that the justice of the claim should be shown and the money should be paid; this application was ineffectual, and I was still required to pay the two thousand roubles, or even twenty roubles, to acknowledge, in some degree, the justice of the demand; but I was aware if I had done this, I should justify the conduct of the Senate, and the military Governor of Archangel, against whom I had obtained a legal decision, with an acknowledgement that I had been unjustly treated. The necessary consequence would be that, for my supposed contumacy in bringing a false charge against the Senate and Governor, I should be sent to Siberia. I persisted in refusing to comply with the claims.

He informed the jury that not only himself, but also his wife and family, had suffered from this terrible injustice:

Gentlemen, all this while my wife, a young woman of only twenty years of age, with an infant at her breast, remained at St Petersburg, in expectation of my arrival, and at length, in the eighth month of her pregnancy, disappointed of her hopes, was obliged to set out, unprotected, on her voyage to England.

He told them how, while they consistently refused to help him, the British authorities had helped others:

At last, after a series of six years' persecution in the manner I have described, and after the repeated refusal of Lord Gower and the British Consul to represent my case to the Emperor, a circumstance occurred which proved, in a more particular degree, the peculiar negligence which I had experienced. A captain Gardiner, of a Hull ship, arrived at Archangel, he had a little squabble with the commander of a guard ship about a demand of a few roubles for pilotage, and yet this man's complaint was represented to the Emperor four times within a month by the British ambassador, while, for a series of six years' unparalleled persecution, I was not able to obtain any interference on my behalf.

He informed the court that finally, in 1809, he was released and, in his opinion, vindicated: 'I received at midnight, a discharge from my confinement, with a pass, and an order to quit the Russian dominions, which was in fact an acknowledgement of the justice of my cause.'

Having informed them of the background to his case, he then began to outline for them the considerable efforts he had made to get a hearing since his return from Russia:

On my return in England I laid a statement of my grievances before the Marquis Wellesley, accompanied by authentic documents, and claiming some redress for the injuries I had sustained through the British minister in Russia, which injuries it was impossible I should have suffered if they had not been sanctioned by that minister. The noble Marquis is now in Court, and could contradict my statement if false, but I represent the circumstances as they really were, and not as personally concerning myself but as involving the honour of the British Government. I was referred by the Marquis to the Privy Council, and from the Privy Council to the Treasury; and thus baffled from one party to another, I applied to Mr Perceval . . . but received for answer, from his secretary . . . that Mr Perceval could not encourage my hopes, that he would [not] recommend my claims to the House of Commons. I next memorialized his Royal Highness the Prince Regent, with a statement of my sufferings.

Bellingham then read to the court his petition to the Prince Regent and all the correspondence he had had with the various government departments, going through the sequence of events in detail. He explained to the court that he had received correspondence from Colonel McMahon, the Regent's private secretary, telling him that by some accident his first petition to the Prince Regent had been mislaid, and that he had had to rewrite the document. He went on to impress upon the court how the failure of all this correspondence to bear fruit affected him deeply:

Gentlemen – under these circumstances I was plunged into ruin, and involved in debt; and the learned Attorney General has admitted there was not a spot on my character until this fatal catastrophe, which when I reflect on it I could burst into a flood of tears. I was totally refused any redress. Gentlemen, what would be your feelings – what would be your alternative; as the affair was national, and as his Majesty's Ministers recommended me backwards and forwards from one to another. I wrote another petition to his Royal Highness, but was informed by a letter from Mr Ryder that his Royal Highness had not been pleased to give any commands on the subject.

Gentlemen. – As my petition was of a pecuniary nature I was informed by General Gascoyne that it was impossible to come into the house without the consent of one of his Majesty's Ministers, for which I thank General Gascoyne for his politeness in giving me that information, and as I was very well known in Liverpool, I could have got the signatures of the whole town. I began to flatter myself I should get redress, but instead of redress, his Majesty's Ministers, and the Chancellor of the Exchequer, told me I was not to expect anything. I was obliged to give notice about six week since to the magistrates at the public office Bow-street, in a letter stating my grievances, entreating their interference, by application to Government, and adding that, if all redress was refused me, I must be obliged to do myself justice . . .

He then read out the letter he had written to Mr Read, of Bow-street, before continuing:

I received an answer from Mr Justice Read, saying that the office could not interfere. But I found that Mr Read, as was his duty, had represented the circumstance to government, and on a subsequent application to the Treasury I was informed that I had nothing to expect, and that I was at liberty to take such steps as I thought fit.

He had then arrived, he explained to the jury, at the point at which he felt he had no other option but the one he had taken:

Finding myself thus bereft of all hopes of redress, my affairs ruined by my long imprisonment in Russia through the fault of the British minister, my property all dispersed for want of my own attention, my family driven into tribulation and want, my wife and child claiming support, which I was unable to give them, myself involved in difficulties, and pressed on all sides by

claims I could not answer; and that justice refused to me which
is the duty of government to give, not as a matter of favour, but
of right; and Mr Perceval obstinately refusing to sanction my
claims in Parliament; and I trust this fatal catastrophe will be
warning to other ministers.

The terrible event that had occurred was, after all, as he saw it, the
fault of the politicians alone:

If they had listened to my case this court would not have been
engaged in this case, but Mr Perceval obstinately refusing to
sanction my claim in Parliament I was driven to despair, and
under these agonizing feelings I was impelled to that desperate alternative which I unfortunately adopted. My arm was
the instrument that shot Mr Perceval, but, gentlemen, ought I
not to be redressed; instead of that Mr Ryder referred me to the
Treasury, and after several weeks the Treasury sent me to the
Secretary of State's office; Mr Hill informed me that it would be
useless to apply to government any more; Mr Beckett added,
Mr Perceval has been consulted, he would not let my petition
come forward.

Gentlemen, A refusal of justice was the sole cause of this
fatal catastrophe; his Majesty's ministers have now to reflect
upon their conduct for what has happened. Lord Gower is now
in court. I call on him to contradict, if he can, the statement I
have made, and, gentlemen, if he does not, I hope you will then
take my statement to be correct. Mr Perceval has unfortunately
fallen the victim of my desperate resolution. No man, I am sure,
laments the calamitous event more than I do. If I had met Lord
Gower he would have received the ball, and not Mr Perceval. As
to death, if it were to be suffered five hundred times, I should
prefer it to the injuries and indignities which I have experienced
in Russia, I should consider it as the wearied traveller does the
inn which affords him an asylum for repose, but government,
in the injustice they have done me, were infinitely more criminal than the wretch, who, for depriving the traveller of a few
shillings on the highway, forfeits his life to the law. What is the
comparison of this man's offence to government? or, gentlemen,

what is my crime to the crime of government itself? It is no more than a mite to a mountain, unless it was proved that I had malice propense towards the unfortunate gentleman for whose death I am now upon my trial. I disclaim all personal or intentional malice against Mr Perceval.

Bellingham spoke for well over an hour.[5] When he had concluded his statement he sat down. Onlookers noticed that he was in an agitated state, and he then began to weep uncontrollably. He asked for a glass of water, which was brought to him. He continued in this distressed state for some time, as his legal team prepared to call their first witness to the stand.

Chapter 20

'A STATE OF PERFECT DERANGEMENT'

The first witness called on behalf of the defence was Mrs Ann Billett, Bellingham's cousin.[1] When asked where her residence was located, she replied:

At Ringwood, near Southampton.
When did you arrive in London?
Last night.
What induced you to come to London?
I thought I knew more of Mr Bellingham than any other friend that would come forward. I have known him from his childhood.
Where did he live latterly?
In Liverpool.
Do you know how long ago it is that he left Liverpool to come to London?
I think that he came at Christmas.
Do his wife and children now reside there?
Yes, they do.
What situation of life has he been in?
Something in the mercantile . . . business.
Did you know his father?
Yes, he died insane in Titchfield-street, Oxford-street; he died there in a state of insanity.

The witness was cross-examined by the Attorney General:

Do you know that of your own knowledge?
Yes, and my knowing of it was a great inducement of bringing

me to London, and within this last three or four years it is
known to myself and Mr Bellingham's friends that he has been
in a state of perfect derangement with respect to this business
he has been pursuing.

Have you had an opportunity of seeing him in London lately?
No, not lately; it is more than a twelvemonth ago that I saw him.
At that time how was he?
Deranged, when he spoke of this business.
Do you know for what purpose he was in London at that time?
Pursuing the same plan.
Before that had you seen him at Liverpool?
I saw him at Liverpool about a year and a half ago.
In what state of mind was he at that time?
He was in a deranged state when anything of this was men-
tioned to him. I did not mention it to him because of the state of
mind he was in.

Mr Garrow then continued the cross-examination of the witness
on behalf of the prosecution:

*This purpose of being in London a year ago was for the purpose of
pursuing the same object, what do you mean by pursuing the same
object?*
That of going to government for redress of grievances.
*And to use your own words in your own opinion you considered he
was in a state of perfect derangement?*
Yes, I do. He has been more than three years in a state of
derangement, and since he has been in London he has been pur-
suing the same plan, and for a long time before that. When he
was in Russia . . . he was pursuing the same object. As soon as
he returned home all his friends were well convinced that was
the case.
I think you spoke of him as a married man?
Yes, he has a wife; she carries on the millinery business at
Liverpool.
I suppose that he had some male friends?
Yes.
Do you know that he was engaged as a merchant?

Yes.

Do you know any of the persons that he was engaged in business with?

No.

Do you not know the name of any one person that he was in business with at Liverpool?

No, not one. I was in the house with his family at Liverpool, I did not know anybody that he was concerned in trade with. I was in the house more than a week. I would wish to mention one circumstance which strongly confirmed me in my opinion, and a strong mark of insanity. Two years ago last Christmas he had been telling me of his great schemes that he had pursued, he said that he had realised more than an hundred thousand pounds, with which he intended to buy an estate in the west of England, and to take a house in London; I asked him where the money was, he said he had not got the money, but it was the same as if he had; for that he had gained his cause in Russia, and our government must make it good to him; this he repeatedly said to me and his wife, but neither she nor I gave any credit to it; he then told Mrs Bellingham and myself, to convince us of the truth of it, he would take us to the secretary of state's office; he did so, and we saw Mr Smith the secretary. When Mr Smith came to us, he told Mr Bellingham that if he had not known that he had ladies with him, he would not have come at all. Mr Bellingham then told him the reason he had brought us, that it was to convince us that his claim was just, and that he should very soon have the money. Mr Bellingham said – 'Sir, my friends say that I am out of my senses, is it your opinion, Mr Smith, that I am so.' Mr Smith said, 'it is a very delicate question for me to answer, I only know you upon this business, and I can assure you that you will never have what you are pursuing after', or something to that effect. We then took our leave of Mr Smith, and when we got into the coach, he took hold of his wife's hand, and said, 'now I hope my dear, you are well convinced all will happen well, and as I wished', and as he had informed us, to which we felt indignant, that he should have taken us to an office, and made us appear in the light he did.

How long is this ago, pray ma'am?

This was last Christmas two years.

I think you stated that he has been in town from last Christmas?

Yes.

Has he been staying in London all that time?

Yes.

Has he been pursuing the same plan?

I understood all along that he was here pursuing the same object at the public offices.

And upon that object you always considered him in a perfect state of derangement?

I did.

Mr Smith received you with politeness and attention?

Yes he did.

How long did you remain in town after that?

Till the next midsummer.

In the same family with the prisoner?

No, I saw him frequent.

Was he under any restraint at that time?

Not at that time.

Were you in habits of intimacy with his family?

Yes.

If he was coerced you must have known it?

I think I must.

If there had been any restraint do you think it would have happened without your knowing it?

I do not know that it could.

Where did he live when you were in London, at the time you went to the secretary's office?

I think Theobald's road; his wife was in town then, she was on a visit with me.

And he was living by himself at the time that all his friends thought him in a state of perfect derangement?

Yes . . .

Has he been left to act upon his own will as much as me, or . . . any body else?

Yes. I believe he was.

Did you ever communicate to the government that he was in a deranged state?

No.

After your visit to Mr Smith, at the secretary of state's office, he remained in town, and after that, neither you nor his wife gave any intimation to Mr Smith that he was a deranged man, or to any of the officers of government?

No.

How long is it ago since you saw him?

More than a twelve month ago.

Did it consist with your knowledge that he carried fire arms about him?

No.

Did you ever know him confined for a single day?

No.

The prosecution having no more questions for Ann Billett, the defence called Mary Clark to give evidence:

Where do you live?

No. 7, Bagnio court, Newgate-street. I have known the prisoner since his return from Russia, I have known him several years, but I have known most of him since he returned from Russia, about two years and a half, I have been in company with him several times.

Can you form any judgement respecting the state of his mind ever since he came from Russia?

It is my opinion that he has been disordered in his mind. I have seen him six or seven times; the last time I saw him was last January; I saw him at No. 20, North Street, Red Lion Square, I did not see any particular derangement then, I had but very little conversation with him then, he said he came upon business, he might not stay above ten days or a week, I did not see him above ten minutes at that time.

The Attorney General then cross-examined the witness:

He came up from Liverpool to London. He came up alone?

Yes, he left his wife, and he came up alone, to the best of my knowledge, he told me that he was come on business.

He transacted business for himself then, did not he?
I did not know anything about his business.
You do not know anybody that transacted business for him do you?
No, I heard that he was confined in Russia.
For all that, he was suffered to go about here in this country?
I do not know of any control over him.
Or do you know of any medical person being consulted about him?
No, I do not know.
You do not know of any precautions that were taken to prevent him from squandering his property, in this state of derangement, do you?
I do not.
You do not know of any course pursued to him by his friends that would not be pursued to any rational man?
I do not.

Mrs Robarts, Bellingham's landlady at No. 9 New Millman Street, did not attend court but sent her servant, Catherine Figgins, to give evidence in her place.[2] She was asked why Mrs Robarts was not in court although a subpoena had been served upon her, to which she replied:

My mistress is unwell . . .
Was it in her house that the prisoner lodged?
Yes, he lodged there four months . . .
Do you recollect the day he was taken in custody?
Last Monday.
On the day before, on Sunday, did you make any observations on the conduct of the prisoner?
I did rather, I thought he seemed confused, and was so for some time.
Had you made that observation for some time before?
I had.
On the day before he was taken, tell me whether anything particular occurred in the house?
No.
Were you at home on that day?
I was out in the evening about two hours and a half.
On the Monday, before you went out, had you noticed anything particular?

I noticed a word and his actions; I thought he was not so well as he had been for some time past.

Mr Garrow then cross-examined:

How long had you lived with Mrs Robarts?
Only two months.
Why he had been there four months, had not he?
Yes. My sister lived there before me.
Mr Bellingham was respected by the family, I believe?
Yes, I believe they respected him very much.
Did he dine at home?
Very seldom, he dined once with the family.
What hours did he use to keep?
Very regular hours, a remarkable regular man.
What place of worship did he go to?
He went with Mrs Robarts and her little boy in the morning.
They went to the Foundling did not they?
Yes.
That was the last Sunday of all?
Yes.
Did he dine at home that day?
Yes, he dined alone, and I think it was too late for them to go to the Magdalene; my mistress and Mr Bellingham went to the Foundling in the evening; the service of the Foundling is over in the evening between eight and nine.
He went to bed as usual?
Yes.
What time did he go out the next day?
The first time about twelve o'clock; he came home to accompany my mistress and her little boy to the European museum about one, and they went off altogether.
Had they a coach?
No, they walked, my mistress and her little boy came home about a quarter after five.
Then they came home without Mr Bellingham?
Yes.
Were his pistols usually in the bags or loose?

I never knew that he had pistols.

Though you had attended him in his room for two months, you did not know that he had pistols, did you use to brush his clothes?

No.

What was the tailor's name that brought home a coat that had a little job done to it?

I never knew his name; I remember a man bringing home a coat.

How long before the last Sunday was it that the tailor brought home a coat that there had been a little job done to it?

That is three weeks or a month ago.

Did he pay the washer woman's bill on the Monday?

Yes, there was a dispute about what was to be paid for washing a dressing gown; he settled the bill before he went out that morning; he breakfasted at home.

Are you sure that you never saw either of these pistols?

Yes.

Nor noticed the bag for pistols?

No, I never noticed anything of the kind.

Did you ever know of any surgeon or apothecary attending him?

No.

Miss Figgins was then allowed to step down and Bellingham's counsel, Mr Alley, had the door-keeper call at the door to see if any witnesses had arrived from Liverpool to give evidence on his client's behalf. It emerged that two people had arrived to give evidence regarding the degree to which the prisoner was deranged, but, on being allowed to see Bellingham, they realised that he was not the person they knew.

At this point, since under the law at that time lawyers for the defence were not permitted to make an address summarising the case to the jury, Bellingham's defence was concluded.[3] Bellingham himself had wanted to call a number of other witnesses such as Lord Leveson Gower, Sir Stephen Shairp, Marquis Wellesley, Mr Litchfield and Mr Ryder.[4] He was persuaded not to do so by his legal team, in the belief that they could only do his case more harm than good. The evidence of witnesses such as Lord Gower, Stephen Shairp and the Marquis Wellesley would add nothing to his legal team's desire to have him declared insane, and might only reinforce in the minds of the jury how sane and carefully planned his actions had appeared. The defence felt that they could do no more to convince the jury of either the innocence or the insanity of its client.

Chapter 21

VERDICT AND SENTENCE

Gentlemen of the jury, you are now to try an indictment which
charges the prisoner at the bar with the wilful murder . . . of Mr
Spencer Perceval . . . who was murdered with a pistol loaded
with a bullet . . . a man so dear, and so revered as that of Mr
Spencer Perceval, I find it difficult to suppress my feelings.[1]

These were the opening words of Lord Chief Justice Mansfield's
summing-up statement to the jury, and, indeed, he did find it hard
to suppress his feelings. As he spoke, he was so overcome with
emotion that on a number of occasions he had to pause, was perceived to speak in a weak voice and even began to weep bitterly.
It is recorded that 'his lordship was sincerely affected, and burst
into tears, in which he was joined by the greatest portion of the
persons in court'.[2] His statement continued:

to say anything of the distinguished talents and virtues of
that excellent man might tend to excite improper emotions in
the minds of the jury . . . gentlemen . . . form your judgement
upon the evidence which has been adduced in support of the
case, undressed by any unfair indignation which you might feel
against his murderer, by any description, however faint, of the
excellent qualities of the deceased. Gentlemen, you are to try
the unfortunate man at the bar, in the same manner, as if he
was arraigned for the murder of any other man. The law pro-
tects all his Majesty's subjects alike, and the crime is the same
whether committed upon the person of the highest and most
distinguished character in the country, as upon that of the
lowest. The only question you have to try is whether the prisoner

did wilfully and maliciously murder Mr Spencer Perceval or not. It is not necessary to go very minutely into the evidence which has been produced to the fact . . .

Sir Mansfield then referred to the evidence given by a number of the witnesses:

Mr Smith, Surgeon Lynn and Mr Burgess clearly substantiated the fact that the deceased had died in consequence of a pistol shot which had been discharged into his breast, and that the hand of the prisoner was the hand which had discharged that weapon.

He rebutted the justification given by Bellingham for his actions:

from what I could collect from the prisoner's defence, it seems to amount to a conclusion that he conceived himself justified in what he had done, by his Majesty's government having refused to redress some supposed grievances. Such dreadful reasoning could not be too strongly reprobated. If a man fancied he was right, and in consequence conceived that that fancy was not gratified, he had a right to obtain justice by any means which his physical strength gave him. There is no knowing where so pernicious a doctrine might end. If a man fancies he has a right, and endeavours to assert that right, is he to put to death the persons who refuse to give him any reparation to that which he supposes himself entitled. By the same reason every person who presided in a court of judicature refusing to give to a suitor in an action, what he requires, would be liable to revenge equally atrocious.

He similarly denied the defence of insanity:

In another part of the prisoner's defence, which was not, however, urged by himself, it was attempted to be proved, that at the time of the commission of the crime he was insane. With respect to this the law is extremely clear, if a man is deprived of all power of reasoning, so as not to be able to distinguish whether it

is right or wrong to commit the most wicked, or the most innocent transaction, he could not certainly commit an act against
the law; such a man, so destitute of all power of judgement,
could have no intention at all. In order to support this defence,
it ought to be proved by the most distinct and unquestionable
evidence, that the criminal was incapable of judging between
right or wrong. There is no other proof of insanity which would
excuse murder, or any other crime.

He goes on to identify a number of varieties or 'species' of insanity:

There are various species of insanity. Some human creatures
are void of all power of reasoning from their birth; such could
not be guilty of any crime. There is another species of madness
in which persons are subject to temporary paroxysms, in which
they are guilty of acts of extravagance. This is called lunacy.
If these persons commit a crime when they are not affected
with the malady, they are to all intents and purposes amena-
ble to justice: so long as they can distinguish good from evil,
so long are they answerable for their conduct. There is a third
species of insanity, in which the patient fancies the existence
of injury, and seeks an opportunity of gratifying revenge, by
some hostile act; if such a person is capable, in other respects,
of distinguishing right from wrong, there is no excuse for any
act of atrocity which he might commit under this description
of derangement.

He then returned once again to the specifics of Bellingham's
defence:

The witnesses who have been called to support this extraordinary defence have given a very singular account to show that
at the commission of the crime the prisoner was insane. What
might have been the state of his mind some time ago was perfectly immaterial. The single question is, whether, at the time
this act was committed, he possessed a sufficient degree of
understanding to distinguish good from evil, right from wrong,
and whether murder is a crime not only against the law of God,

but against the law of his country. Here it appears that the prisoner had gone out like another man; that he came up to London by himself, at Christmas last, that he was under no restraint, that no medical man had attended him to cure his malady, that he was perfectly regular in all his habits, in short there was no proof adduced to show that his understanding was so deranged as not to enable him to know that murder was a crime. On the contrary, the testimony adduced in his defence has most distinctly proved, from a description of his general demeanour, that he was in every respect a full and competent judge of all his actions.

The judge then made some comments on the evidence of Ann Billett, Mary Clarke and Catherine Figgins before advising the jury 'to take all the facts into their most serious consideration'. He concluded with the words: 'If you have any doubt, you will give the prisoner the benefit of that doubt; but if you conceive him guilty of the crime alleged against him, in that case you will find him guilty.'

The jury remained in their box for two and a half minutes, discussing the case among themselves, before they made it known that they wanted to retire to the jury room. Bellingham was seen to examine carefully the faces of each jury member as they walked out of the courtroom. Fourteen minutes later they returned with their verdict. Once again Bellingham scrutinised their expressions carefully as they took their positions. Their names were called out and the foreman was asked to announce their verdict. He replied in a voice described as 'faltering': 'Guilty upon the indictment for murder, and upon the Coroner's Inquisition.'[3] Many people noticed that Bellingham looked surprised. He was addressed by Mr Shelton: 'John Bellingham, you stand convicted of the wilful murder of the Right Honourable Spencer Perceval; what have you to say why the court should not give you judgement to die according to law?' To this Bellingham made no reply. Then the Recorder, speaking in a manner described as 'solemn and affecting',[4] proceeded to pass sentence:

Prisoner at the bar! you have been convicted by a most attentive and a most merciful jury, of one of the most malicious and

atrocious crimes it is in the power of human nature to perpe-
trate – that of wilful and premeditated murder! A crime which
in all ages and in all nations has been held in the deepest detes-
tation – a crime as odious and abominable in the eyes of God
as it is hateful and abhorrent to the feelings of man. A crime
which, although thus heinous in itself, in your case has been
heightened by every possible feature of aggravation. You have
shed the blood of a man admired for every virtue which can
adorn public or private life – a man whose suavity and meekness
of manner was calculated to disarm all political rancour, and to
deprive violence of its asperity. By his death, charity has lost one
of its greatest promoters; religion, one of its firmest supporters;
domestic society, one of its happiest and sweetest examples; and
the country, one of its brightest ornaments – a man whose ability and worth was likely to produce lasting advantages to this
empire, and ultimate benefit to the world. Your crime has this
additional feature of atrocious guilt, that in the midst of civil
society, unarmed, defenceless, in the fulfilment of his public
duty, and within the very verge of the sanctuary of the law,
your impure hand has deprived of existence a man as univer-
sally beloved, as pre-eminent for his talents and excellence of
heart. To indulge in any conjecture as to the motive which could
have led you to the commission of this atrocious deed would
be to enquire into all that is base and perfidious in the human
heart. – Assassination is most horrid and revolting to the soul
of man, inasmuch as it is calculated to render bravery useless
and cowardice successful. It is therefore that the voice of God
himself has declared, 'that he that sheddeth man's blood, by
man shall his blood be shed'. In conformity to these laws, which
God hath ordained, and men have obeyed, your disgraced and
indignant country, by the example of your ignominious fate,
will appreciate the horror of your offence, and set up a warning
to all others who might hereafter be tempted to the perpetration of a crime of so deep a dye. A short time, a very short time,
remains for you to supplicate for that mercy in another world,
which public justice forbids you to expect in this. Sincerely do
I hope that the short interval that has elapsed since the commission of this atrocious offence has not been unemployed by

you in soliciting that pardon from the Almighty which I trust
your prayers may obtain, through the merits of your Redeemer,
whose first attribute is mercy. It only now remains for me to pass
the dreadful sentence of the law, which is –

That you be taken from hence to the place from whence you
came, and from thence to a place of execution, where you shall
be hanged by the neck until you be dead; your body to be dissected and anatomised.[5]

After all Bellingham's efforts, over a number of years, to bring his
case to public attention, his trial had lasted only a matter of eight
hours.[6] Throughout it all, he had remained convinced that he
would be acquitted, even whispering to his solicitor, James Harmer,
during the judge's summing-up, that he ought not to forget to
send his wife a note by evening post telling her of his acquittal. As
the verdict was read out, he was heard at one stage to utter, very
quietly, the words 'My Lord'. Thinking that he wished to address
the judge, Mr Newman informed him that he was not permitted, at
that time, to speak. After his sentencing he was led from the dock,
stumbling slightly as he went. Those who observed him as he left
could see very few signs of panic or horror in his demeanour. All
that was evident was a red flush upon his cheeks, hair that was wet
with perspiration and an 'imperceptible convulsive motion of the
lip'.[7] As news of the verdict and sentence spread to the people outside the court, there was an eerie quietness among them as they
began to move slowly away.

Meanwhile, inside the courtroom there was an unseemly
squabble over the exhibits. William Jerdan managed to get possession of Bellingham's opera glasses and a copy of his petition dated
21 January 1812, written in his own handwriting, and initialled
by Joseph Hume. Charles Litchfield, Solicitor to the Treasury, put
the pistols in his bag, but was then accosted by Sheriff Birch, who
claimed that it was his duty to take 'custody of all property belonging to prisoners convicted . . . in that court . . .'. Litchfield refused to
give them up, and the Attorney General had to intervene and calm
Birch down by telling him that 'they would be disposed of in the
proper manner'.[8] In the end they were lodged in the Office of the
Secretary of State.

In a final twist, witnesses from Liverpool did, in fact, arrive, but only when it was too late for them to be of any use to Bellingham's defence. A Mr Statham, the Town Clerk of Liverpool, arrived with three witnesses from there, just as the jury was retiring from the courtroom for their deliberations.[9] The group from Liverpool had in their possession a number of papers, which they claimed the mayor of that town had thought would be relevant to the business of the trial. But as they arrived when the hearing of witnesses was concluded, Mr Statham did not even notify the officials of their presence. He made their presence known the following morning and duly applied for expenses on behalf of his witnesses.[10] It is impossible now to evaluate whether the evidence of these witnesses and the papers in their possession would have been beneficial or detrimental to the case of John Bellingham. They may well have been beneficial, since Statham did try later to get financial assistance for Mary Bellingham. The following day *The Times* newspaper related the outcome of the trial to its readers:

> The fate of the murderer Bellingham is now decided, and we think it superfluous to make any comment on the nature and enormity of his offence. If ever there was one who for shedding man's blood deserved that his blood should by man be shed, this is that person.[11]

Chapter 22

'THWARTED, MISREPRESENTED AND ILL-USED'

Following his trial, John Bellingham was returned to Newgate Prison, where he was placed in one of the fifteen cells that were reserved for condemned prisoners. A small window allowed light into this small room, which was just 9 feet by 6 feet. Its heavy door, 4 inches thick, had a small hole in it to allow a modest flow of air. As was the practice, the condemned man was kept in the presence of two keepers at all times to prevent him from committing suicide. The prison officials once again found him calm, polite and cooperative. On entering the cell he looked around for a moment, taking in his new surroundings, before asking for a cup of tea. He was informed that, by law, as a condemned prisoner, he was now entitled only to bread and water, news that he seemed to accept stoically. There was a bucket of water already in the cell and he was brought some bread, which he ate. He said that he found his new cell unpleasant. He was heard to make the comment that he would be happy when he was 'out of existence'.[1] That night he was noticed to jump a number of times during his sleep, as if suffering from nightmares.

On Saturday morning Bellingham woke a little later than usual, at nine o'clock. He again asked for tea and later for a jelly, but was given only a loaf of bread and two quarts of spring water.[2] Permission for the door of his small cell to be left open was given by Mr Newman, so that the prisoner could have extra space for exercising. Bellingham expressed his gratefulness for this mercy, and he walked up and down the passageway outside his cell twice that day in the company of two attendants.[3] He asked one of his keepers to read to him from the New Testament and showed particular interest in the fourth and fifth chapters of St John's First Epistle. He remained in a serene mood as the chapters were read, commenting only that he would 'soon be with his heavenly father, and released from all trouble'. He said that he 'wished for the time of his final exit to come'.[4]

Around the same time on Saturday morning the funeral of the Prime Minister was taking place. Perceval's remains were removed in a large procession of carriages from No.10 Downing Street to the Church of St Luke at Charlton, near Woolwich, in Kent.[5] At the front of the procession were the mutes and attendants on horseback. Next came the plain hearse drawn by six horses. This was followed by six coaches carrying the mourners, the first of which was occupied by Lord Arden and his chaplain, the second by the Lord Chancellor, the Earl of Liverpool, the Earl of Harrowby and the Home Secretary, Richard Ryder.[6] Twenty-five carriages carrying the Cabinet ministers, Mr Perceval's relatives, and others followed on.

As this solemn procession passed through the streets of London, shops were closed as a mark of respect, and the crowds watched silently and respectfully. The bells of the Abbey and St Margaret's Church could be heard pealing as the cortège neared Westminster Bridge. It came to a temporary stop at George Street and Parliament Street as a mark of respect towards the deceased and to allow a moment's reflection on the terrible event that had occurred. From Newington Butts to the church a party of the City Light-Horse, of which Perceval had been a member, accompanied the procession.[7] The body of the Right Honourable Spencer Perceval was laid to rest in the family vault at St Luke's Church. The inscription on the coffin read:

Right Honourable Spencer Perceval,
Chancellor of the Exchequer, First Lord of the Treasury,
Prime Minister of England,
Fell by the Hand of an Assassin in the Commons House of
Parliament, May 11,
A.D. 1812, in the 50th Year of his age; born Nov. 1st, A.D. 1762.

Meanwhile, back at Newgate, Dr Brownlow Forde, the prison chaplain or ordinary as they were known, visited Bellingham from a little after eleven until twelve o'clock.[8] Brownlow Forde, who was a vehement opponent of the death penalty, spent a considerable amount of time praying with the prisoner.[9] Bellingham's main concern during their meeting seemed to be that his wife and family would not be left destitute.[10] Dr Forde would visit him frequently over the next few days to offer him comfort and spiritual guidance.

At a quarter to nine on Saturday night, Mr Newman and one of his men came to see how the prisoner was. Bellingham told them that he was well and would soon be out of his troubles.[11] As they left, they locked the door to his cell behind them and at nine o'clock Bellingham went to bed. Again it was noticed that he awoke a number of times during the night. At three o'clock on Sunday morning he asked for some bread and water, which was given to him. He got up at nine o'clock after his cell door was opened, and was given some soap and water to wash.

As sentence had been passed upon him, it was decided by the sheriffs that from that point on he would have no visitors except with written permission.[12] It seems that a Scottish clergyman named Nicholas was, consequently, refused admission.[13] On Sunday morning, when he was visited by Alderman Matthew Wood, he told his visitor: 'Government think to intimidate me, but they are mistaken, I have been guilty of no offence, having only done an act of public justice.'[14]

Although it was Sunday, Bellingham, as someone convicted of murder, was not entitled to attend religious services. However, the Revd Daniel Wilson, Minister of St John's Chapel, Bedford Row, and later to become the Bishop of Calcutta, called on the prisoner to tend to his spiritual needs. Revd Wilson later published a rather troubled account of this visit.[15] The Revd Wilson was accompanied by a gentleman believed to have been James Stephen MP, the political colleague and friend of Perceval.[16] In fact, Stephen probably organised the meeting. It seems that he visited the prisoner earlier in the day and asked him if he would be willing to meet the Revd Wilson. Stephen was a religious man, a devoted campaigner on many moral issues, and he, like Wilson, would have had a religious motivation for the visit, a desire to get Bellingham to admit to the sinfulness of his act and thereby to save his soul. As the men entered his cell, the prisoner rose to welcome them warmly. Wilson explained to him that he had come to discuss matters of God with him, and Bellingham replied: 'Undoubtedly, no topic can be more interesting to me.'[17] The clergyman began to talk of a range of topics such as 'the condition of men as sinners before God; The evil nature of sin; the purity and excellency of God's holy law . . .'.

> I told him, that as God saw the thoughts and intents of the heart, and noted every sinful imagination, desire, and motive, as well as all the sins of the temper and conduct, our transgressions were by far more numerous, as well as more aggravated, than we could possibly conceive . . .[18]

Having continued in this way for some time, the Revd Wilson then asked Bellingham if he understood what had been said. 'Perfectly,' he replied, 'I know myself to be a sinner. We come into the world sinners.'[19] Although the Revd Wilson was not convinced that he really understood, he decided to continue in a similar vein. After some time he asked Bellingham if he would be willing to confess, forsake his sins and 'seek humbly to God for salvation'. At first Bellingham said that he wished to do this, and asked how these blessings of pardon and grace were to be obtained. But then after some more discussion he said, in a manner that the Revd Wilson later described as 'indifference mingled with confidence, without the least shadow of real contrition', that he had confessed his sins before God and, he hoped, in his mercy.[20] Revd Wilson told him that a 'merely cursory acknowledgement of sin is totally distinct from true repentance'.[21]

> The heart must be affected, the judgement convinced, the conscience alarmed, and the whole soul filled with sorrow and compunction. There must be a hungering and thirsting after salvation from a deep and abiding sense of our guilt and condemnation . . . There must be an entire change of heart, a new and spiritual life, a genuine and humble sorrow for every sin, before we can have the least hope that we are in the way of salvation.[22]

'I confess my sins,' Bellingham replied, 'but I cannot say I feel that sorrow you describe, nor that earnest hungering of mind after salvation.' Wilson described the tone in which he spoke as 'calm and unfeeling'.[23] Having tried for a little longer, the clergyman stopped and spoke in a more direct manner to the prisoner: 'I can go on no further. Till there be some impression on your heart, some relenting, some desire after a Saviour, some conviction of the need of religious contrition, all I can say will be in vain.'[24]

The Revd Wilson describes Bellingham's manner as mild, 'not at all resembling the ferocity or coarseness of the ruffian'.[25] They then prayed together.

James Stephen decided that he should now attempt to get Bellingham to face the 'atrocity of his last dreadful crime'. First, he made the point that perhaps Mr Perceval had never known of his case, that he had never actually seen the documents relating to it. That they had been passed from civil servant to civil servant, from office to office, without the Prime Minister's direct knowledge. Bellingham paused for a moment on hearing this. Then he said: 'O, he must have known of it.'[26] Stephen next brought to his attention the argument that, even if he had known of his case, perhaps he might have found it 'impossible or improper to accede to his request'.[27] In order to bring to his attention the kindness and thoughtfulness of Perceval's temperament, he introduced to him the story of a Mr Dickenson from No. 3 Princes Court, Drury Lane. When Dickenson wrote to him requesting a change to the system of pressing men into the navy, the Prime Minister had paid for the schooling of one of the man's children and 'twenty pounds towards the boy's board and clothes'.[28] Stephen handed Bellingham the letter written by Perceval, dated 27 April 1812, which included the words:

> I received your letter to which you refer, and if I had found any means of complying with the request contained in it, I would have answered it; but that was not the case. I should hope, that if I do not comply with any such request, you have sufficient proof that my non-compliance is not owing to a disinclination to serve you.[29]

Bellingham read the letter carefully for some time, before saying: 'This was very kind to be sure!' But, although the words were reasonable, the Revd Wilson found his tone 'most chilling'.[30]

The Revd Wilson told Bellingham how Mrs Perceval and her children had knelt around the body of the Prime Minister, their loving husband and father, and offered up prayers for his murderer:

> Thus . . . while you, on a mere presumption of injury in your own mind, have assassinated a man who had never personally injured you, and whose amiable and benevolent character you cannot but acknowledge, his widowed partner, whose injuries from you are incalculably greater than any you can even pretend to have received from Mr Perceval, has, in all the poignancy of her anguish, been offering up prayers to God on your behalf.[31]

For a moment Bellingham hung his head down, deep in thought. Then he said: 'This was a Christian spirit! She must be a good woman. Her conduct was more like a Christian's than my own, certainly.'[32] Encouraged by this, the Revd Wilson continued to probe in the hope of bringing about a true repentance:

> if I were to allow you all you wish, that you were injured in the most aggravated manner, still, can that warrant, in any degree, an act of blood? Can that justify you in taking what you are pleased to call justice into your own hands; and, on your own private opinion, without inquiry, without trial, without judge or jury, without one form of law, to hurry a fellow-creature, one who never offered you any offence, without a moment's time for reflection or prayer, into eternity, by the treacherous blow of an assassin? For Mr Perceval . . . died I believe, almost immediately.[33]

'Yes,' Bellingham replied in a detached manner, 'he lived but a few minutes'. The calm matter of the answer was once again chilling to the Revd Wilson. In response to the clergyman's pressure, Bellingham referred to his being denied justice. Wilson persevered with his argument:

Can your opinion of justice being refused you, warrant your becoming the judge and executioner in your own cause? Was your view of your own case to be considered as infallible? Or, supposing your opinion correct, still can any provocation whatever palliate the foulest and most dreadful of all social enormities, the taking away the life of another? Would you have justified anyone who, on the pretence of an affront, should have dared to have planted a dagger in the bosom of your wife or child? Or, supposing you had yourself been in Mr Perceval's situation, the prime minister of the realm, with all the private and public virtues of that excellent statesman; supposing further, what must be the case with every minister, that you were surrounded with petitioners whose cases it was absolutely impossible for you fully to investigate, and who were all equally positive in their claims; and that, in addition to this, you had of course all the weighty concerns of the empire pressing upon you; I ask, what should you have thought of a petitioner, merely because he had been disappointed in his application, imagining himself, a private individual, justified in assassinating you, the chief minister of the crown, incapable of intending him the smallest evil, and, at the very worst, only mistaken in your judgement, whilst in every other act of your life you were exemplary and benevolent?[34]

At this point the Revd Wilson thought that he was getting through to Bellingham. He noticed tears in his eyes and Bellingham seemed unable to answer. But his answers soon proved to be as consistent as ever. When Wilson described the crime as 'one of the foulest crimes which has ever disgraced our national character', and accused Bellingham of being 'the man who alone is insensible of its enormity!', Bellingham replied: 'I have confessed my sins before God, and trust to a general amnesty of them.'[35] Wilson, annoyed at this idea, replied: 'This is the very deceit which is hardening your heart, and sealing your ruin to eternity . . . does the guilt of blood demand no more compunction than this?'[36]

Their debate continued in this religious vein. The Revd Wilson put the question to him: 'Can you now . . . possibly imagine that you are justified, in the sight of God, in this act?'

'To stand before God', Bellingham replied, 'is a very different thing from standing before men; and the Scripture says "Thou shalt do no murder."' Noticing that he looked tired and realising that the irons on his legs must be hurting him, the Revd Wilson asked him if their long conversation was making him weary. 'By no means,' Bellingham answered, 'what can be more agreeable to me? I should be glad if you could stay with me the whole night.'[37]

Bellingham told them that he had spent a long time thinking about the assassination and that he was 'as sorry as any man could be, for Mrs Perceval and the family'.[38] Their theological discussion lasted for two hours until they were interrupted by the Keeper of the Prison. At this point the Revd Wilson had to leave, but James Stephen remained with Bellingham. As Bellingham lay on his bed, Stephen read to him the 51st Psalm. Bellingham told the politician how his father had died when he was young. He said his mother was a very good and pious woman whose dying words were that 'she wished to meet him in heaven'.[39] He wept as he told Mr Stephen of this.

Stephen then left him but returned to see him some hours later. That visit again finished without Stephen, with his Christian sensibility, being convinced about Bellingham's degree of repentance for what he had done. For his part, the visit with Bellingham had left the Revd Wilson exasperated. He had genuinely hoped to show Bellingham the error of his ways and to elicit from him a sincere repentance and confession for his sins. But, in reality, no one could convince Bellingham that his actions had not been merited and justified. The Revd Wilson knew that he had failed:

A more dreadful instance of depravity and hardness of heart has surely never occurred. We see here a man of some education, of good natural parts, cool and argumentative in his turn of mind, mild and pleasing in his manners, and, as it should appear, of considerable expertness in commercial affairs; a man who enjoyed the advantages of early religious instruction, who was not unacquainted with the Holy Scriptures, and who preserved, till the day preceding his atrocious crime, an attention to some external duties of religion. We behold this man commit an act of blood, horrid almost beyond example: and this, not under the sudden irritation of passion, but with the most cool, determinate and cautious malice. We see him confide his dark purpose to no one associate, but, after a long and desperate preparation, wreak his vengeance on the very walls of Parliament, with fearless obstinacy. We then perceive that he makes no attempt to escape the provoked justice of his country, but avows and defends his deed, devising to himself a new and terrific code of right and wrong, and by the weakest evasion attempting to distinguish his motives from the designs of an assassin . . .[40]

Late on Sunday night, Joseph Butterworth, an acquaintance of Bellingham's, who was a bookseller on Fleet Street, visited him. Having brought Butterworth to the cell, Newman was about to leave when Bellingham asked if he could bring him a pen, ink and paper. Mr Newman said he would bring them when he returned later for Mr Butterworth. Butterworth was a religious man, very involved both in charitable work and in the British and Foreign Bible Society. He and Bellingham spent their time together talking and praying. Butterworth asked him about a query that was still bothering some people: 'had you or had you not some other person or persons concerned with you in the murder of Mr Perceval?' To which Bellingham answered clearly: 'No: I do most solemnly declare I had not.'[41] About an hour later, Newman returned to escort Mr Butterworth away and he brought with him the writing materials for the prisoner. That night Bellingham wrote his last poignant letter to his wife:

My Blessed Mary,

It rejoiced me beyond measure to hear you are likely to be well provided for. I am sure the public at large will participate in, and mitigate your sorrows. I assure you, my love, my sincerest endeavours have ever been directed to your welfare. As we shall not meet any more in this world, I sincerely hope we shall do so in the world to come.

My blessing to the boys, with kind remembrance to Miss Stevens, for whom I have the greatest regard in consequence of her uniform affection for them. With the purest intentions, it has always been my misfortune to be thwarted, misrepresented and ill-used in life; but, however, we feel a happy prospect of compensation, in a speedy translation to life eternal. It's not possible to be more calm or placid than I feel, and nine hours more will waft me to those happy shores where bliss is without alloy.

Yours ever affectionate,

John Bellingham.

Sunday Night, 11 o'clock .

Dr Forde will forward you my watch, prayer book, with a guinea and note. Once more, God be with you, my sweet Mary. The public sympathise much for me, but I have been called upon to play an anxious card in life.[42]

He included a note in which he blamed his conviction on the failure of his counsel, Mr Alley, to call his list of witnesses:

I lost my suit solely through the improper conduct of my Attorney and Counsel, Mr Alley, in not bringing my witnesses forward (of which there were more than 20), in consequence, the Judge took advantage of the circumstance, and I went on the defence without having brought forward a single friend – otherwise I must inevitably have been acquitted.

He was still convinced that he had been justified in both his cause and his actions.

Chapter 23

EXECUTION

rumour had circulated that Bellingham was to be taken
from Newgate Prison and brought to Palace Yard,
Westminster, where he would be hanged on a tempo-
rary gallows. The story went that it would be fitting for him to be
executed near the place where the heinous crime had been committed. Earl Grey heard the rumour and was very much against
the idea, regarding it as imprudent. He related his concerns to both
the Chancellor and Lord Ellenborough.[1] Grenville was similarly
against it, writing to his brother that 'Bellingham is . . . to be hanged
in Palace Yard. If so, our judges are as mad as Bellingham.'[2] In the
event, the hanging was not carried out at Westminster. Most politicians seemed to realise that holding the execution in such a place
would represent a 'call to arms' to every anti-government, disgruntled and rebellious group in the country. They would see it as an
ideal opportunity to congregate and express their ire against the
authorities. Such an occasion would undoubtedly lead to violence.

Early on the rainy morning of 18 May 1812, the crowds began
to gather around the site of the execution at Newgate Prison even
as the gallows was being prepared. Newgate Street soon filled up,
with many paying up to two guineas each to get a vantage point
at a window or on a rooftop. Before long the crowd spilled over
onto Holborn and into Giltspur Street. A witness described the Old
Bailey as 'paved with umbrellas'.[3] Interest in the case seemed to
be common across all social classes, and even Lord Byron stayed
awake all night to see Bellingham 'launched into eternity'.[4]

In case of crowd trouble, 5,000 troops were quartered near
Lambeth. After all, the ominous words 'Rescue Bellingham or
die' had been written on a number of walls around London.

Barricades were erected and signs were put up to warn the public of what had happened at the hanging of Haggerty and Holloway. On that occasion an estimated crowd of 40,000 had gathered to see the executions of these two men, convicted and condemned to death for a murder committed in Hounslow. The numbers present that day were unmanageable and when a pieman bent down to pick up his fallen basket, his accidental tripping-up of a woman spectator was enough to cause a crush in the crowd and the subsequent panic.[5] Thirty-two people died as a result and perhaps up to a hundred were injured. *The Times* had warned people on 16 May:

> If any should in the present instance become the victims of their own curiosity, either through the pressure of crowd, or any other accident, they will hardly deserve compassion. We repeat this warning in the most impressive terms we are able.[6]

And again on the day of the execution:

> Every precaution to secure public tranquillity has been adopted. A strong body of military has already arrived, and will be posted in Smithfield, and to the south of Blackfriars-bridge. We do not object to this, though we fear no tumult from public disapprobation of the sentence which rids the country of one of the most hardened and unpitiable villains that has ever disgraced it . . . Our fear is from the curiosity of the people; and . . . the danger of a catastrophe like that which occurred at a former execution.[7]

Notices from the police were displayed on all the approaches to the Old Bailey: 'Beware of entering the crowd! Remember, thirty persons were crushed to death by the crowd when Haggerty and Holloway were executed.'[8] However, it seems that this time the crowd on the streets was not so large as to be unmanageable.[9]

As is usual in such cases, the press had begun the process of vilifying John Bellingham. *The Times* described him as 'a turbulent, untractable, profligate adventurer' and said that his behaviour towards his wife 'had been for many years neglectful and unaffectionate'. It also stated that he 'seldom visited her but for the purpose of obtaining money'.[10] Another paper said that 'he was extravagant in his younger days, and by no means a pattern of domestic happiness since his marriage, not withstanding the feeling allusions to his wife in his defence would seem to indicate the contrary'.[11] Most of these comments were sensational and unfair. It is true to say that he had been away from his family for a considerable amount of time, but he had been confined in Russia, and since his return to England had been in the grip of an obsession too strong for him to resist. From reading some of the articles one would have thought that he cared nothing for his wife and children. In fact, he does seem to have loved them dearly and even believed, in accordance with his flawed logic, that he was pursuing his claims for their benefit. He had made this clear when talking to Mary Stevens: 'he was determined to have justice done him and he should be undeserving the name of a parent if he did not endeavour to make some provision for his children.'[12]

He could perhaps be described as 'untractable' but never accurately as 'turbulent' or 'profligate'. The assertion that he visited Mary only 'for the purpose of obtaining money' was equally false. In any event, in the last months of his life he had inherited that sum of money from his mother and he had his new business interests and was not in need of money. True, it had not been easy for Mary, and their married life had been shattered as a result of the controversy in Russia and subsequent events, but their letters do show love and affection between them to the end, even to the extent that Mary shows a flash of jealousy when he addresses Mary Stevens in too friendly a manner. As he approached his execution, Bellingham's major concern was for the future welfare of Mary and the children. The fact that many of the accusations made against his character were overplayed in the press was admitted by the *Liverpool Mercury*, a publication that had access to local knowledge about the Bellinghams: 'it appears he has . . . been considerably misrepresented, as we hear from very good authority, that the alleged separation from his wife was wholly unfounded; and that he was always remarkably solicitous about the welfare of his family.'[13]

One of the stories being circulated about him was that he had been, at one time, a bankrupt. The story ran that he operated a

Block Tin Manufactory at No. 97 Oxford Street in 1794 and became a bankrupt in March 1794, after which he set fire to his own house.[14] It was reported that he was discharged of his bankruptcy in March 1799. One correspondent to the *Gentleman's Magazine* was convinced, following research, that the story was false:

> In the private Memoir of the late unhappy John Bellingham, published in your last Supplement . . . it is asserted that he was a Tinman in Oxford-street, and a Bankrupt in the year 1794. I beg to refer you to Smith's List of Bankrupts, and think you will find this assertion to be wrong, no such name appearing for that, or any other year, between 1786 and 1806. As a friend to truth and justice, you will correct this mistake in your next magazine.[15]

There is no direct evidence to back up this story of bankruptcy and it seems unlikely to be true. Furthermore, it has been argued that Bellingham would have found it difficult to find employment, and would probably not have been sent oversees on behalf of a business, had he been a bankrupt.[16]

There are also doubts regarding the authenticity of another story covered in the press accusing him of failing to fulfil the terms of a commercial contract in Hull around 1802 and being put in prison as a result. This story, like the others, although probably not true, contributed to a generally negative portrayal of Bellingham's character: 'the monster *Bellingham*, – this self-redresser of imaginary wrongs . . .'.[17]

In his prison cell, between six and seven o'clock that Monday morning, Bellingham was awakened. He complained that it was too early an hour.[18] Perhaps this was because his first sleep the night before had been a short one out of which he had awoken to hand Walker, one of his observers in his cell, a shilling. He thanked the man for his kindness and told him that he wished it were a guinea. He then slept soundly for the rest of the night. He read from his prayer book for half an hour before Dr Forde arrived. Bellingham greeted him graciously with a shake of the hand. He was then led to the room for the condemned prisoner repeating 'the declaration which he had frequently before made, that his mind was perfectly calm and composed, and that he was perfectly prepared to meet his fate with resignation'.[19] He received the sacrament of Holy Communion from Dr Forde. Once he and Dr Forde had concluded their prayers, he was told that the sheriffs were ready, to which he answered: 'I am perfectly ready also.'[20] He was then led to the Press Yard at around half past seven.

Bellingham was wearing a brown greatcoat and the striped waistcoat and trousers that he had worn at his trial. He was not as neat in his appearance as he would have liked and had, in fact, complained that morning at not being permitted to shave, regretting the fact that he would 'not be able to appear as a Gentleman'.[21] In attendance in the yard was a group of invited gentlemen, including the two sheriffs William Heygate and Samuel Birch, and the Lord Mayor. On entering the open air Bellingham was heard to remark: 'Ah! It rains heavily.' A man came forward with a hammer. Bellingham placed his foot upon an anvil and the man began the process of removing his chains. He gave instructions to the man carrying out the task: 'Mind, mind – take care, take care. Strike it in the centre, and more firmly, then you will accomplish it.' As the man continued with his work, Bellingham glanced around the yard a number of times at the assembled group of men. His look was noticed to be one of calmness and dignity: 'His face possessed the same character and colour as on Friday during his trial. – no emotions of fear or compunction were visible.'[22]

Once the chains were off, he was led back to the room for condemned prisoners, where he was joined by the Lord Mayor, the two sheriffs and a number of other 'worthy' gentlemen. A conversation then took place between Bellingham and the Sheriffs. Mr Sheriff Birch took the opportunity of asking him the question that he had been asked so many times by now: whether anyone else had been involved with him in the deed, and if 'it was perpetrated on any public ground'. He once again gave the negative assurance that was desired. Sheriff William Heygate joined in the conversation. He was satisfied that Bellingham had acted alone. He noticed that Bellingham 'manifested no signs of displeasure or impatience'.[23] Bellingham requested that Heygate make Mr Perceval's family aware of the fact that he sympathised with them. Heygate later wrote of his impression following this conversation:

the motive for the horrible act he brought himself to commit was
an absurd and vague idea of bringing to a public hearing and
decision at the bar of a Court of Justice, his complaints against
the Russian Government . . . for this end he would have sacrificed
any other public characters if they had fallen in his way . . . his
conduct was entirely unconnected with any public question . . .[24]

He noted that Bellingham 'met death with composure and fortitude, but not with eagerness or triumph'.[25] By now Bellingham
had had enough of all this talk and turned away saying:
'Gentlemen I am ready.' He was told that he had ten minutes more
to wait.[26]

He was then instructed to change into a pair of Hessian boots.
The executioner, William Brunskill, set about binding his hands
and arms in the appropriate manner. Bellingham was at all times
calm and cooperative, turning back his own sleeves and joining his
hands together. He did express some concern about the strength
of the rope but was informed that it would bear his weight easily.
He implored the executioner and his assistants to do everything
properly so that he would not suffer any more than was necessary
and was assured that they would do so. When the executioner ges-
tured to loosen his cravat, telling him that he was doing it so that
it could be more easily removed when they reached the scaffold,
Bellingham said: 'Certainly do so, it is perfectly all right.'[27]

He was then led from the room. Some observers noted that as
he left he bent his head to his shoulder as if to wipe away a tear.
He was brought through a number of dark narrow passageways
and outside to the front of the debtors' door, the place of execution that had replaced Tyburn since 1783. Prisoners at their cell
windows could be seen straining their necks to get a glimpse of
this infamous prisoner as he passed by. Once outside, he was con-
fronted, for the first time, by the sight of the scaffold on which he
was to die. He walked calmly up the steps of the scaffold 'with a
light step, a cheerful countenance, and a confident, a calm, but not
an exulting air'.[28] He was led to stand in the correct position: 'On
his appearance, a confused noise arose among the mob, from the
desire and attempts of some to huzza him, counteracted by a far
greater number who called silence!'[29]

Bellingham did not respond to the noise from the crowd. The noose was placed around his neck without any hint of a struggle. When asked if he had any final message to send, he began to speak again of his treatment in Russia, until told by Dr Forde that this was inappropriate and he ceased. When Dr Forde asked him how he felt, he replied: 'I thank God for enabling me to meet my fate with so much fortitude and resignation.'[30] When the executioner approached to place the blindfold cap over his head, Bellingham asked if 'the business could be done without it'. He was told that this was impossible and his final request was denied. As the cap was being tied a number of people called out: 'God bless you! God save you!' When asked by the prison chaplain, Dr Forde, if he heard, he said that he could hear them but could not make out the words of what they were saying.

The executioner had now concluded his preparations and the prisoner was ready. Bellingham and the clergyman prayed together loudly for about a minute, before the clock began to strike eight o'clock. On the seventh stoke the executioner knocked out the supporting bolt and allowed the only assassin ever of a British Prime Minister to fall to his death. As was the usual practice, out of sight, the executioner's assistants were pulling on the prisoner's legs in an effort to cut short his sufferings. Witnesses noticed that Bellingham made hardly a move after the drop. Among the crowd there was a 'most perfect and awful silence'.[31]

William Cobbett, who had watched from the window of his cell, described the scene: 'The crowd was assembled in the open space, just under the window at which I stood. I saw the anxious looks; I saw the half-horrified countenances; I saw the mournful tears run down; and I heard the unanimous blessings.'

The crowd remained silent and after about ten minutes began to move slowly away. The body of John Bellingham was left to hang there for an hour in accordance with the law of the day. Then it was cut down and loaded on a cart, onto which climbed the executioner's assistant and a boy. With the City Marshal leading the way on horseback, the body was brought along Newgate Street, down St Martin's-le-grand Street, up Little Britain Street, to Duke Street and the house of the beadle of the Company of Surgeons at St Bartholomew's Hospital. It was followed all the way by a solemn crowd, while many more looked on from open windows. As this macabre procession made its way, the executioner's boy raised the sack covering the body a number of times to satisfy the curiosity of onlookers.

The body of John Bellingham was dissected in the packed Anatomical Theatre of St Bartholomew's Hospital, by the surgeon Sir William Blizard. In an obvious example of press hyperbole, a number of papers reported that Bellingham's heart continued to beat for four hours after the execution: 'The expanding and contracting powers continued perceptible till one o'clock in the day – a proof of the steady, undismayed character which he preserved to the last gasp. It is said of some men, that the heart dies within them; but, here, the energies remained when life was extinct.'[32]

It had taken only a week for Bellingham to be tried, convicted and executed. In the days that followed, a number of macabre items began to appear on sale. Buttons, reputed to have come from the assassin's coat, were selling for 'a dollar'. The executioner sold the coat in which Bellingham had been hanged for £10. At the end of May Greenwich Fair was the venue for a very unusual spectacle. The admittance fee was six pence to the booth in which the audience could witness the firing of the 'actual' pistol used by Bellingham to assassinate the Prime Minister.[33] While the claims of the showman that the pistol was genuine, and that he had paid 'an immense sum' for it, were indubitably false, it is fairly certain that he made a good profit from the event.

Chapter 24

Aftermath

In the aftermath of the assassination of Spencer Perceval and the execution of John Bellingham, those who had been affected by the terrible turn of events were left to deal with the conse-quences. One such person was Lord Granville Leveson Gower. Lord Gower's inability, failure or unwillingness, as ambassador, to assist Bellingham in Russia had been central to the whole affair. His con-tribution to the demise of both Bellingham and Perceval was, as one would expect, much debated in both the public and private arenas. Such was the controversy that on 17 May Lord Gower had felt the need to write a letter to Lord Castlereagh, in which he defended his actions pertaining to the Bellingham affair. He tabled that letter in the House of Commons on 20 May 1812, and the papers printed it for the general public to read.[1]

It appears upon the trial of John Bellingham, for the murder of Mr Perceval, that the prisoner in his defence endeavoured to justify that atrocious act on the ground of his Majesty's gov-ernment having refused to compensate him for the injuries and oppression he states himself to have suffered in Russia, during the time that I had the honour of representing his Majesty in that Country. He complained particularly of my conduct, and that of Sir Stephen Shairp, his Majesty's consul general, as having sanctioned, by our silence and neglect to interfere in his behalf, the unjust treatment, as he considered it, of the Russian Government.

I was subpoenaed by the prisoner to attend the trial; I did attend, and expected anxiously to be called upon, to state, upon oath, all I could recollect of the circumstances of his case in Russia. In this expectation, however, I was disappointed; my testimony was not called for; and after having heard the most serious accusations of gross neglect of duty and want of common humanity, brought forward by the prisoner, against myself and Sir Stephen Shairp, I had not the opportunity afforded me of publicly refuting those charges. Although I am perfectly aware that the assertions of a man, standing in the situation of Bellingham, can, unsupported by any other testimony, have no weight whatever with the sober and reflecting part of the public, yet I should be wanting, I think, to the interests and honour of the government of this country, as well as to my own character and reputation, if I did not endeavour to do away any possible misapprehension upon this subject, by as ample a statement of circumstances, as my memory, of transactions which passed some years ago, will allow me to furnish . . .

He recounted the events as they had unfolded in Russia according to his point of view:

In the year 1805, I remember receiving a letter from John Bellingham, complaining of his being detained in prison at Archangel, and claiming my protection, against what he conceived to be the injustice of the constituted authorities of that port; I remember that immediately upon the receipt of this letter, I consulted with Sir Stephen Shairp, who agreed not only to write a letter to the governor general, requiring an explanation of the circumstances of which Bellingham complained, but also his own mercantile correspondents, British residents at Archangel, for their opinion of the conduct of the Russian government towards the complainant.

It appeared from these inquiries that, Bellingham having been engaged in commercial business with the house of Dorbecker and Co., pecuniary claims were made by each party against the other, and that these claims had been by the governor general referred for decision to four merchants, two British merchants being appointed on the part of Bellingham, and two other persons on the part of Dorbecker. By the award of those arbitrators, Bellingham was declared to be indebted to the assignees of Dorbecker, the sum of 2,000 roubles. This sum Bellingham, notwithstanding this decision, refused to pay.

He acknowledged that there was no evidence supporting the claim that Bellingham had written the letter regarding the sinking of the Russian ship:

It also appeared from the communication received from Archangel that a criminal suit had been instituted against Bellingham, by owners of a Russian ship which had been lost in the White Sea. They accused him of having written an anonymous letter that had been received by the underwriters in London, in which letter it was stated that the insurance of the ship was a fraudulent transaction; and payment for the loss of her had been in consequence resisted. No satisfactory proof was adduced against Bellingham, and he was acquitted of this charge. But before the termination of this suit, he attempted to quit Archangel, and being stopped by the police, whom he resisted, he was taken to prison; but was soon after liberated, in consequence, I believe, of a second application to the governor from Sir Stephen Shairp.

He related the story of how Bellingham came running into his residence for help:

About this period I quitted Russia; and I have no recollection of hearing anything more of John Bellingham, till after my arrival at St Petersburg upon my second embassy. He came running into my house one evening, and solicited me to allow him to remain all night, in order to avoid being retaken into custody by the police, from whom he had escaped. I complied with the request, though I could not, upon any ground, assume to myself the power of protecting him from legal arrest. It appeared that the award of the arbitrators of Archangel had been confirmed by the senate, to which body Bellingham had appealed; and he was in consequence delivered over to the custody of the College of Commerce . . . there to remain till he discharged the debt of the 2,000 roubles. This custody was not very strict, for he was allowed to walk wherever he pleased, attended by a police officer belonging to the college. He came frequently to my house, and at various times received from my private secretary small sums of money, to support him during his confinement. Confined as he was by the legal authorities of the country, I could on no pretence make any application for his release; but I remember well, in conversation with the minister for foreign affairs, expressing my personal wish that the Russian government, seeing no prospect of recovering the sum of money required from him, would liberate him from prison, on condition of his immediately returning to England.

Very soon after this conversation, all diplomatic intercourse ceased between the two courts; and the course of public events necessitated my quitting Russia in the abrupt manner with which your lordship is well acquainted.

Lord Gower was not the only politician to defend the system by which Bellingham had felt so let down. On the day following Perceval's assassination Castlereagh made the comment in the House of Commons that 'the particular occurrence which brought on the calamity in question was produced by the conscientious discharge of public duty on the part of his Right Hon. friend, who would not permit a claim to be successfully preferred to government, for which he was satisfied there was no just foundation'.[2]

Even though most people acknowledged that Bellingham had committed a terrible act, there was still a great deal of sympathy for him among the general public and elsewhere. Lord Gower's letter, in particular, inspired much correspondence in reply,[3] much of which was negative and some of which was threatening:

before many days are pass'd you'll meet the fate poor Bellingham design'd you. He was my friend from earliest youth and has left a glorious example to the world that a glorious death, after revenge, has nothing frightful in it when compar'd with a life of poverty, distress and oppression. Beware the fate which waited Caesar on the ides of March – your fate is decreed therefore prepare for death.

Other replies were just downright insulting:

> From as much as I have read of your Letter . . . I judge you to be a
> mean spirited & cowardly ministerial fool. Are you not, my Lord,
> ashamed of publishing such a letter, when you are well assured
> that the only person, who could have any chance of refuting
> any part of it (poor Bellingham) is long since murdered . . .

One member of the public was even inspired to write a poem in
support of Bellingham's cause in which he was highly critical
of Lord Gower's involvement in the affair. He explained that Mr
Perceval had promised him recognition for his poetic talents. But
now, he claimed, as the Prime Minister was dead, financial necessity would force him to publish his work, unless, of course, Lord
Gower could make it financially possible for him to burn it. He sent
Lord Gower some lines of verse to help him make up his mind:

> There liv'd in princely pow'r
> A sycophant, a courtier, call'd Lord ——
> It shames the place that gave this reptile birth,
> And shames his embassy, & *Sharp* may shame
> Makes us forget his base, unmanly name . . .

The poet virtually canonised the memory of Bellingham:

> An honest tradesman, of superiour sense,
> Bless'd by experience, and by eloquence,
> His credit good, unsullied was his name,
> He paid with pleasure every honest claim.[4]

William Cobbett was particularly dismissive of Lord Gower's
letter. In a rather bitter open letter written to the Prince Regent
from prison on 4 June, Cobbett gave his forthright views on the
matter. He believed that Bellingham had been right to expect the
protection of his country while he was in Russia:

> Mr Bellingham, by entering the territory of Russia, did not get
> rid of his obligations of allegiance to the King, and, of course,

he did not thereby forfeit his right to all the protection which the treaties between England and Russia warranted our government in giving him. It is an old and incontrovertible maxim, that protection and allegiance go hand in hand; that one cannot be without the other; and, as no one will pretend, that it would not have been treason for Mr Bellingham, while in Russia, to have plotted the death of the King; so, no one can pretend to deny, that he was entitled to the protection of the representative of that King.[5]

He stated that he found it 'next to impossible not to believe' Bellingham's version of events that the accusations made against him in Russia were false:

Lord G.L. Gower (*since the death* of Mr Bellingham) has written and caused to be published a letter in vindication of his own conduct and that of the Consul; but, to say nothing of the circumstance of the other party not being alive to answer them, Lord Gower, in stating that Mr Bellingham was imprisoned for the debt of 2,000 roubles, does not say a word about the charge ever having been acknowledged to be a false one . . . Indeed, this letter of Lord Gower does nothing, in my opinion, either in the way of self-exculpation, or in that of inculpation against Mr Bellingham. The declaration of the two parties are opposed to each other. Mr Bellingham says he was neglected, and abandoned to the scourge of tyranny; Lord Gower says he was not; and, it must be left to the world to judge between them.[6]

Cobbett complained that vast sums of money were spent every year on maintaining ambassadors and consuls in foreign countries and that, if not to help in such cases, why else should they be maintained: 'If anyone had, in the year 1808, or at any other time, complained of the immense expense of the diplomatic body, the answer would have been, that it was necessary, amongst other things, for the protection of the interests of English merchants trading to foreign countries.'[7]

Not only was Cobbett critical of Lord Gower's lack of action in Russia; he was equally scathing about the role played by Perceval's

Government at Westminster: 'what is the business of a government, if it be not its business to attend to the complaints of those, who have no means of redress in courts of law? The end of all government, is, the good of those who agree to live under it; what good is there without protection; without the means of obtaining redress of wrong?'[8] After all, he argued, what Bellingham sought was not compensation but a hearing:

> he could obtain no hearing; no investigation; no trial of his claim . . . he was bandied about from office to office, from Secretary to secretary; and . . . could obtain nothing like investigation anywhere.[9]

> The merits of Mr Bellingham's case, therefore should have been fully investigated . . . Mr Perceval had not paid due attention to the claim of Mr Bellingham . . .[10]

Cobbett was not the only one to place blame on those in authority. Among the people who had failed to help Bellingham were the members of the House of Commons who had been petitioned by him, the Prince Regent, the Home Secretary, a host of civil servants who had passed his letters and petitions from department to department and the magistrates of Bow Street.

Of course, those affected most by the assassination and subsequent execution were the two widows left behind with young families to support. Perhaps surprisingly, there was a great deal of sympathy for Bellingham's widow. Most people did not hold Mary Bellingham responsible in any way for the extreme action taken by her husband. On 20 May an anonymous letter appealing for help on her behalf was sent from an anonymous citizen of Liverpool to Lord Gower:

> [John Bellingham's] punishment could not be too ignominious. But, my Lord, that punishment has not been confined to the villain who was the cause of it, but is extended to his innocent wife and family. His wife, independent of the shock which she must inevitably have received at such an event, is left totally unprovided for, with three helpless children dependent upon

her exertions for a livelihood. She has been at once deprived of
the support of her husband, and of all the little property she was
possessed of, which his expensive residence during five months
in London has squander'd, and at the same time, her delicate
frame has received a blow which totally incapacitates her to
attend to her affairs for the present in order to procure immediate subsistence for herself and Family . . .

According to the prisoner's confession it was only the chance
of fortune which saved you from the fate of Mr Perceval. This
consideration, however, I trust will not stimulate you to turn a
deaf ear to the miseries of his unoffending family . . . In the prisoner's explanation of his motives for committing the barbarous
deed, he seems most certainly to have been unjustly persecuted,
and he imputes some degree of neglect to your Lordship, which,
whether false or true, he states to be the remote cause of his
unjustifiable conduct. Your Lordship was perhaps the only
person living that was aware whether you could have assisted
him under his (perhaps supposed) grievances, or whether your
services would have been totally unavailable to him. His sense
however of the injury he imagined he had unjustly sustained
has, it appears, been the origin of his ruin – and possibly now
that he has suffered the awful sentence which has hurried him
away to a final account, you may now perhaps feel a degree of
regret that his application did not meet your more attentive consideration. This, however, is mere conjecture and your Lordship is
most probably convinced that every means consistent with your
situation was exerted on his behalf, and that ingratitude was the
only return for your kindness. Even, however, if this is the case,
it is honourable to return good for evil and independent of every
other motive to commiserate and assist the unfortunate objects
of my solicitation – probably the idea that the prisoner did in his
own mind conceive you had neglected his claim to your support
may, now that he is no more, induce you to befriend his wretched
family. To relieve the miserable is always worthy of a good man
but when the father's children and widow are the objects of distress an act of benevolence is then doubly useful and is certain
to meet with its reward . . . And I hope that no presentiment that
such conduct would be construed by the prisoner's wife into a

tacit confession of this imputation of neglect will prevent your
lordship's extending the hand of benevolence to alleviate the
complicated calamity of the innocent sufferers. No, it would be
a confirmation of the general opinion that your duty has been
completely fulfilled and that your humane heart was open to the
access of calamity even in the offspring of your enemy . . .[11]

The letter may have had some effect on Lord Gower. In any event
through George Canning he asked Peter Bourne, son of the Mayor
of Liverpool and John Drinkwater, the son of a former mayor, to
find out who the anonymous author of the letter was and also
to give Mary Bellingham £50. Drinkwater, however, objected to
the whole idea, believing that giving compensation in this way
to Bellingham's family was sending a bad message to the 'lower
classes of society'. Notwithstanding these objections, Drinkwater
was persuaded to cooperate, and on 28 May he and Bourne arrived
at Mary's house at No. 46 Duke Street. Drinkwater described the
scene: 'Mrs Bellingham was sitting at the upper end in deep mourn-
ing. Her late Husband's Picture was suspended over the chimney
piece, & the House altogether appeared to be well furnished.'[12]

Drinkwater began by reading a letter from George Canning.
Miss Stevens then entered the room and she joined Mary as they
listened to him read both the anonymous letter and another from
Lord Gower himself. Mary told them that she had no idea who the
author of the anonymous letter was. She thanked them for Lord
Gower's gift of £50. According to Drinkwater, she remarked that
her husband had shown signs of insanity for some time and it now
gave her some comfort to believe that he was insane at the time
he committed 'the dreadful act'. She also said that she understood,
from her dealings with Sir Stephen Shairp, that Lord Gower had
had no authority to intervene in the Russian affair. She had tried
many times to convince her husband that his fight for compensation from the government was futile, but she had been unable to
convince him of this.[13]

In order to raise money for his daughter and her children, Mary
Bellingham's father decided to have a play, which he had writ-
ten some time earlier, printed and put on sale. The play, entitled
St Patrick's Night, was advertised in the press:

St Patrick's Night; a Comic Opera in Two Acts.

A subscription is set on foot in England, for the Widow of John Bellingham and her three fatherless Children, now left destitute of support; – her Father, willing to contribute his Mite, will Print by Subscription, for their use and benefit, the above-mentioned Play, written by him . . . revised, corrected, and adapted for the present day.

Price 5s. – on superfine wove Paper 10s 6d. . . . Subscriptions received by John Neville . . . and by all Booksellers in Town and Country.

NB The Names of such Subscribers as wish it, shall be printed with the Work.[14]

However, this kind of public appeal for funds led to an adverse reaction from some quarters. One publication stated: 'We are by no means disposed to visit the crimes of the guilty on their innocent posterity; but it is one thing not to punish them, and another to reward them for those crimes.'[15]

Mary Bellingham understood these sentiments and felt the need to distance herself from the play and the advertisement. She wrote to the newspapers on 6 June and made it very clear that she had nothing to do with it. She had not asked for it and, in fact, hoped that it would not go ahead. She also gave a solemn undertaking not to profit from it in any way.[16] There were other attempts to help Mary and the children, including a private subscription set up by the Deputy Mayor of Liverpool, John Bridge Aspinall, and the Town Clerk, Richard Statham, who had arrived at Bellingham's trial, with a group of people, too late to give evidence.[17]

On 10 June Mary wrote to Lord Gower informing him that she was 'left totally destitute'. She told him that she had 'three most interesting, lovely children . . . whose future welfare and good conduct through life must depend in a great measure upon the education I shall be enabled to give them'. She sought his Lordship's help:

I hope you Lordship will not deem me impertinent or presuming on your kindness in thus stating my unhappy situation, my character upon inquiry I trust would be found a deserving one, and if thro' your Lordship's interest the great and wealthy could be induced to contribute to alleviate suffering almost too great for human nature, I doubt not but the feelings of their own hearts would be superior to any thanks I could offer.[18]

In the months that followed, Mary attempted to carry on her millinery business with her partner, Miss Stevens, until its final closure toward the end of the year. The following advertisement was placed in the *Liverpool Mercury* on 13 November:

M. Bellingham presents her best respects and sincere thanks to the Ladies of Liverpool and its Environs, who have favoured her and her Partner, Miss Stevens, with their Orders; she is sorry to inform them that she has been reduced, by unprecedented misfortunes and distress, to the necessity of compounding with her Creditors for ten shillings in the pound, in order to pay which, she is obliged to offer her Millinery, Dresses, &c which she has selected in London for this Season, with her Whole Stock in Trade, at Cost Price, for Ready Money. On Tuesday next, the 17th, she opens her Rooms for this purpose, when she most earnestly solicits the attendance of her Friends and the Public. At the same time requesting the liquidation of all debts due to the firm of Bellingham and Stevens – with the most painful sensations she feels the necessity of adopting this measure, having no other means of supporting herself and three Fatherless Children than what may arise from her present line of Business, 46 Duke Street.[19]

Soon after this, it seems that Mary began to use her maiden name, Neville, in an effort to escape the infamy of her late husband's name. She may well have been the Mary Neville who lived at No. 14 Seymour Street in 1818 and at No. 71 Islington Street, Liverpool, in 1821.[20]

Mrs Jane Perceval, although in a much more advantageous position socially and financially than Mary Bellingham, was similarly left in a tragic situation with the loss of her husband and a large family to rear on her own. The firmly held religious faith of the family was demonstrated by the anecdote related by the

Revd Wilson to Bellingham during his visit to Newgate Prison that Jane had prayed together with her children for the salvation of the assassin's soul. It is only what the evangelical Perceval would have wanted. At first it was difficult for the Percevals to get any privacy to mourn the man who, although a prime minister to the country, was a much-loved husband and father to them. Jane went to stay with her friends, the Ryders, for a few days, but nowhere could she escape the talk of her husband's murder. The people of London spoke of little else, the papers were full of it and the balladeers had already begun to compose their songs about it. Even when she took her three eldest girls to St Martin's Church on the Sunday following the assassination, they were forced to listen to a sermon entitled 'Thou shalt do no murder'.[21] Lord Arden, the brother of the late Prime Minister, wrote of Jane's fortitude under these difficult conditions: 'Mrs Perceval though exquisitely and deeply sensible of the loss she has sustained, has with the most becoming fortitude composed her mind to meet the situation in which it has placed her . . .'.[22] In January 1815 Jane married a Lieutenant-Colonel Sir Henry Carr, who died in 1821. She lived on until 1844, dying at the age of 74.

Of course, the suffering of the Perceval children needs no description. The late Prime Minister had been very affectionate and close to his children. Perhaps the lasting effects of such a horrific event upon a child are best illustrated by the story that, when his youngest daughter Frederica died, eighty-eight years later in 1900, she was reported to be still in possession of a rug from the Houses of Parliament stained with the blood of her dying father.[23]

Notwithstanding the private suffering of the Perceval family, William Cobbett objected strongly and publicly to the grants of money awarded to them in the aftermath of the assassination, at least in the absence of any proper investigation into Bellingham's case. His words were uncompromising:

These grants cannot be grounded upon any merits of the parties to whom they are made. Of these parties the public know nothing at all. They consist of a widow and her twelve children, and doubtless, they are an afflicted widow and children. But, Sir, the circumstances of widowhood, and of numerous family, and of deep affliction, are no grounds, and do not all together form any ground for a claim upon the public purse. If they did, how many thousands would be in affluence, who are now in the poor-house . . .[24]

There were other people less immediately connected with the assassination who were, although in a much lesser way, affected by it. Events of this magnitude, even in modern times, capture the public imagination and inevitably lead to reports of related supernatural phenomena. Soon after the assassination there came the usual reports of those claiming to have experienced supernatural premonitions of the event. The most famous of these was allegedly experienced by Mr John Williams, a banker and mining engineer from Cornwall.[25] Williams claimed to have experienced a dream in early May in which he imagined himself standing in the lobby of the House of Commons. He saw a small man enter wearing a blue coat and white waistcoat. Then he saw another man dressed in a snuff-coloured coat with yellow buttons, take a pistol from under his coat and point it at the small man. He described what happened next:

The pistol was discharged, and the ball entered under the left breast of the person at whom it was directed. I saw the blood issue from the place where the ball had struck him; his countenance instantly altered, and he fell to the ground. Upon inquiry who the sufferer might be, I was informed that he was the Chancellor. I understood him to be Mr Perceval who was Chancellor of the Exchequer. I further saw the murderer laid hold of by several of the gentlemen in the room.[26]

Williams claimed that he woke up and told his wife about the dream immediately. She dismissed it as merely a dream and told him to go back to sleep. He did this, but experienced the same dream twice more. He wife still paid no attention to it. The following day he told his brother and a business partner about the dream and that he was thinking about going to London to warn Mr Perceval. They dissuaded him from this course of action, saying that he would be seen as a fanatic. But then, on 13 May, Williams's son ran into their house shouting 'Father, your dream has come true! Mr Perceval has been shot dead in the lobby of the House of Commons.' On a subsequent trip to London, Williams was able to purchase a print representing the murder of Spencer Perceval. He was amazed by what he saw: 'I found it to coincide in all particulars with the scene which had passed through my imagination in my dreams. The colours of the dresses, the buttons of the assassin's coat, the white waistcoat of Mr Perceval, the spot of blood upon it, and the countenance and the attitude of all those present, were exactly what I had dreamed.' Williams's story was treated with such veracity that he was asked to recount it before two representatives from the Admiralty, who, it seems, believed him.

By those convinced of such paranormal premonitions a lot was also made of the fact that on the reverse side of Perceval's will were written the words 'delivered a copy of this to Jane, – 1st April 1812'.[27] Many believed that the act of sending his will to Jane in April, only weeks before his death, was an indication of the fact that he too had had a premonition of his own death. Others pointed to a prediction in 'Old Moore's Almanac' for 1812, which stated that the position of the planets 'may tend to frustrate the ablest designs for the public service, if not hasten the death of some great man'.

As always in cases of this type, there was an abundance of conspiracy theorists who read much into Bellingham's act of violence. Even though Bellingham repeated the denial a number of times, they would not accept that Perceval's assassination was not part of some revolutionary, anti-government plot. Even the Sheriffs of London were suspicious enough about it to be asking Bellingham if he was involved in such a plot as he was preparing to mount the gallows. One particularly colourful conspiracy theory linked the assassination of Perceval to the claims of the watchmaker Karl Wilhelm Naundorff to be Prince Louis-Charles, the son of King Louis XVI and Marie Antoinette, and the rightful heir to the throne of France. Prince Louis-Charles had been imprisoned during the French Revolution and was believed to have died of poisoning in prison. But it was always claimed by some that he had, in fact, survived and escaped from prison. Karl Naundorff was one of many who clamed to be Prince Louis-Charles. One French pamphlet suggested that Perceval was assassinated because he was in possession of information regarding the mystery.[28] The spread of conspiracy theories such as these are a reflection of how disturbing and worrying people found the assassination to be.

Chapter 25

'Injudicious and improper'

The issue of John Bellingham's trial and execution led to a great deal of debate and diversity of opinion. While some had no misgivings at all about Bellingham's conviction and punishment, others were worried about the nature of the justice he had received. Two major issues in particular stood out: the haste with which the trial had been held, and the issue of whether Bellingham should have been found to be insane.

The length of time that elapsed from Perceval's assassination to Bellingham's execution had been only a week and the trial itself had lasted for only one day. Although such expediency was not unusual in the eighteenth and nineteenth centuries, it is clear that the defence lawyers, having met their client only the day before, felt that they had not been given a sufficient period to prepare their case. Many at the time, and since, have agreed that the haste with which Bellingham was tried and convicted denied him and his counsel the opportunity to prepare an adequate defence. The scarceness of time even meant that not all those who wanted to give evidence could do so. As William Townsend, writer and barrister, wrote in 1850: '[Bellingham] was executed without the least sympathy for his hurried fate, or the slightest public manifestation of feeling that justice in mercy had been withheld from him.'[1] Lord Holland wrote in a similar vein: 'Such hurry was by many thought harsh and illegal, and by more injudicious and improper . . . the accused should be allowed full opportunity of proving . . . his defence.'[2]

Only days after the trial, on 21 May, a contributor to the press voiced his concerns about the time allotted for the trial. Although he believed 'the verdict of *Guilty* against Bellingham to be in complete consistence with the oath they [i.e. the jury] had previously taken', he felt that 'the ends of impartial justice might equally have been attained, had there been less of *precipitance* in the bringing on of the trial of this man'.[3]

More time might, consistently with the ends of justice, have been allowed to his friends to have come forward and . . . [say] what they knew of his state of mind. All doubt on the subject would, in that case, have been dissipated; and his Judges would have been less liable to be biased by those natural feelings of indignation which his monstrous crime naturally engenders.[4]

In 1855 Samuel Warren, Queen's Counsel and Recorder of Hull, also felt uneasy about the trial: 'We can with difficulty record calmly that Bellingham's counsel, fortified by strong affidavits of the prisoner's insanity, and that witnesses knowing the fact could be brought from Liverpool and elsewhere, applied in vain for a postponement of the trial.'[5]

The aforementioned contributor to the newspaper on 21 May also referred to that other crucial issue at the heart of the trial of John Bellingham – the question of his sanity and competence to stand trial:

here, we have exposed to our view a man, on the eve and in the direct contemplation of an act, at which human nature, depraved as it is, shudders – cool and collected, employing himself in the innocent office of explaining the subjects of a gallery of pictures, in the most indifferent and unconcerned manner, whilst at the very moment he had the weapons of the destruction of a fellow-creature loaded in his pocket. After the commission of the horrid crime, we see him equally tranquil, equally indifferent to the dreadful fate which awaited him, as to the enormity of the deed he had just performed. When conducted to prison he sleeps soundly, eats heartily, and, whenever an allusion is made to what he has done, endeavours to defend it, as if an act of that atrocity could be defended. We have heard of many cases of uncommon firmness of mind, but this is beyond our conception of what human nature, in a state of sanity, is able to perform. Because on every common subject a man is rational and sensible, we are not absolutely to decide upon his soundness of mind. Many insane persons are so, and may be conversed with for a long time without exhibiting any particular symptoms of derangement, until one chord is touched, which at once discovers the unfortunate maniac. Such appears to us to be the fact with this wretched man. On every subject, save one, he seems sensible and rational – but rouse his feelings relative to his sufferings in Russia and elsewhere, and all the madman quickly appears.[6]

On this question of Bellingham's sanity, Sheriff Heygate, who spoke to the prisoner just before his execution, believed that 'he entertained no adequate notion of the enormity of his crime, having, by a singular perversion of judgement, formed to himself in a considerable degree, a justification of the murder of Mr Perceval, although he reprobated murder in the abstract'.[7]

There were many who, although conceding that Bellingham was insane at the time of the murder, felt that insanity was no defence. One contributor writing on the issue believed that he was no more mad than most other criminals and murderers and that was no excuse for murder: 'The fact is, that our passions may be carried to frenzy, but that is no excuse; for if it were there would be no such thing as justice. Bellingham was mad – allowed; but so was Felton, so was Lord Ferrers; yet neither could or ought to be saved. But Bellingham appears not only to have more sense, but more ability than either of those.'[8]

Romilly was of a similar opinion: 'No person can have heard what the conduct and demeanour of this man have been since he was committed or can have read his defence, without being satisfied that he is mad, but it is a species of madness which probably, for the security of mankind, ought not to exempt a man from being answerable for his actions.'[9]

Latham Browne, writing in 1882, disagreed: 'That Bellingham was, if one may use the term, morally, though not legally, mad, few would now doubt . . . Surely if a man is mad, he is not responsible for the act he commits during his madness. If he is not responsible, is it less than murder to make him answerable for his actions?'[10]

Knapp and Baldwin, when compiling their famous Newgate Calendar around twelve years after the event, said of Bellingham: 'his general character was that of strict integrity – a kind husband and father – loyal in his political opinions – and punctual in the observance of religious duties; and the whole tenor of his life, with the exception of the Russian affair, on which it was supposed he was insane, proves him to have been a well-intentioned man'.[11]

Lord Brougham's opinion of the trial, writing in 1871, was that it was 'the greatest disgrace to English justice'.[12] According to him, as regards the fact that Bellingham was deranged, 'there can be no manner of doubt'.

William Cobbett was another critic of the way in which Bellingham had been treated throughout the whole affair. In considering this it must be noted that he was not one who held a principled opposition against the death penalty for the crime of murder. He would later write that 'the murderer is always positively excluded from any and from all mitigation of punishment. He shall always be put to death.'[13] But he did not see Bellingham as a murderer in this sense. Imprisoned in Newgate in 1812 for libel, Cobbett was one of those who actually witnessed the scene of Bellingham's execution and said of him: 'He was one of those unhappy men who are driven to a state of insanity by not being able to bear misfortunes, and especially misfortunes proceeding from what they deem wrongs.'[14]

Writing in more recent times, Gillen argues that, as Bellingham was unable to recognise the wrong of the act he had perpetrated, this in itself defines him as insane.[15] Lovat-Fraser goes further in arguing that the acceptable criterion of criminal responsibility laid down by the Chief Justice would be seen as 'imperfect' in more modern times.[16] He writes: 'When indignation over the crime had subsided, it was realised that grave injustice had been done.'[17] Ray in his *Medical Jurisprudence* also states a belief in Bellingham's insanity:

His fixed belief that his own private grievances were national wrongs; that his country's diplomatic agents in a foreign land had neglected to hear his complaints and assist him in his troubles, though they had in reality done more than could have reasonably been expected of them; his conviction, in which he

was firm almost to the last, that his losses would be made good
by the Government, even after he had been repeatedly told,
in consequence of repeated applications in various quarters,
that the Government would not interfere in his affairs; and his
determination on the failure of all other means to bring his
affairs before the country, to effect this purpose by assassinating the head of the Government, by which he would have an
opportunity of making a public statement of his grievances
and obtaining a triumph, which he never doubted, over the
Attorney-General – these were all delusions as wild and strange
as those of seven-eighths of the inmates of any lunatic asylum
in the land.[18]

It is interesting to consider that the McNaghten Rules, under
which insanity later came to be judged in English courts, may well
have led to a different outcome in Bellingham's case. Thirty-one
years later, in 1843, Daniel McNaghten shot and killed the Prime
Minister's secretary, Mr Edward Drummond, believing him to be
the Prime Minister, Sir Robert Peel. The trial was postponed to
allow for evidence of his insanity to be adduced. During the course
of the trial McNaghten's counsel, Alexander Cockburn, QC, who
was later Lord Chief Justice, referred to the Bellingham case:

Gentlemen, it is a fact that Bellingham was hanged within one
week after the commission of the fatal act, while persons were
on their way to England who had known him for years, and who
were prepared to give decisive evidence of his insanity. He was
tried – he was executed, not withstanding the earnest appeal of
Mr Alley, his counsel, that time might be afforded him to obtain
evidence as to the nature and extent of the malady to which
Bellingham was subject . . .[19]

McNaghten was found not guilty 'on the ground of insanity'. In
response to the public outcry that followed the verdict, members
of the House of Lords were required to define the law respecting
crimes committed by the insane, which they did by presenting
five questions and answers. From these came the legal convention that a person could not be held responsible for a crime if it

was proven that 'at the time of committing . . . the act, the party accused was labouring under such a defect of reason, from disease of the mind, as not to know the nature and quality of the act he was doing; or, if he did know it, that he did not know he was doing . . . wrong'. Not only did Bellingham not have the advantage of the McNaghten Rules, but neither had he any right of appeal, as the Court of Criminal Appeal was established only in 1907.

But, notwithstanding later legal developments, the pertinent question is whether Bellingham should have been found to be legally insane according to the law as it stood at the time of his court case?[20] Goddard points to the fact that he did plan the crime well in advance, having had his coat specially modified to conceal the firearms, practising the use of those firearms, attending the House of Commons so as to learn about the topography of the place and to become acquainted with the faces of the members of government. But he was not, according to himself, specifically planning to assassinate Spencer Perceval. In fact, he stated that he would have shot Lord Granville Leveson Gower had he come upon him that day. It has been pointed out[21] that the judge, Sir James Mansfield, set out what he called the 'third species of insanity' as an instance 'in which the patient fancied the existence of injury, and sought an opportunity of gratifying revenge, by some hostile act'.[22] But did he apply the test for this?[23] Mansfield ruled that, even if a person was deranged, 'if such a person was capable, in other respects, of distinguishing right from wrong, there is no excuse for any act of atrocity which he might commit under this description of derangement'.[24] But to fall under his 'third species' definition seems to require that a person was seeking revenge, and it can be argued that Bellingham was not seeking revenge.[25] He was obsessed by the injustice that he perceived had been done to him and he shot Perceval, it can be argued, in order to achieve justice and not to exact revenge. In reality, the degree of Bellingham's sanity or otherwise was never properly investigated in court. Not enough time was allowed for further witnesses to come from Liverpool to testify to the fact, and he was not examined by medical professionals. This means that the question of his sanity, or otherwise, from a legal point of view will now never be fully determined.

Added to all this there is the issue of Justice Mansfield's some-what biased and emotional summing-up statement to the jury. He openly stated in court that he was so affected by the assassination of Perceval that he found it difficult to suppress his personal feel-ings. He had to pause a number of times, his voice grew weak and he even wept in front of the jury. It is difficult to say whether these were genuine displays of emotion or a blatant attempt to influence the jury. Although he stated that he wanted the jury members to form their judgement 'upon the evidence which has been adduced in support of the case', there could have been very little doubt in the mind of anyone in the courtroom that day regarding the ver-dict most desired by the judge, especially since he referred to the late Prime Minister using phrases such as 'the distinguished tal-ents and virtues of that excellent man' and 'the excellent qualities of the deceased'.[26]

To the end, of course, Bellingham was firm in his commitment that he had been denied justice. He was convinced throughout that, upon a hearing of his case, he would be found not guilty of murder and that he would receive the compensation to which he believed he was entitled. Indeed, many would accept that Bellingham was subjected to awful and, most probably, unjust treatment in Russia. It can be argued that the British authorities in Russia and at home were negligent in failing, at least, to give his case a credible hearing. But his response to his frustration and sense of injustice was disproportionate and wrong. So blinded had he become by his own quest for justice that he was unable to see the injustice that he had inflicted upon another innocent man and his family. He seems to have been unable in any real way, apart from a few lapses here and there when he was moved to tears, to recognise the wrong that he had done and to empathise with the sufferings of the Perceval family.

Chapter 26

LEGACY

The sense of shock and abhorrence experienced by most people regarding the assassination of the Prime Minister was felt, even more keenly, by those in Parliament. This meant that in the immediate aftermath of the tragedy not much critical comment was made about the achievements of the late Prime Minister. The poet Thomas Moore summed this up:

> In the dirge we sung o'er him no censure was heard,
> Unembittered and free did the tear-drop descend;
> We forgot, in that hour, how the statesman had erred,
> And wept for the husband, the father and friend.
>
> Oh! proud was the meed his integrity won,
> And generous indeed were the tears that we shed,
> When in grief we forgot all the ill he had done,
> And tho' wronged by him living, bewailed him, when dead.[1]

This mood was underlined by various acts carried out in the Prime Minister's honour, such as the erection in June of the memorial in Westminster Abbey. On the fifth of that month £105 was voted by Northampton Corporation towards the erection of a monument to him in All Saints' Church. A medal was struck in his memory by the government, with one side featuring an image of the late Prime Minister and the other a figure pointing to a broken pillar representing the loss that had been suffered by the country.[2] A tablet in his honour was purchased by his legal colleagues at Lincoln's Inn bearing a Latin epitaph composed by the Bishop of Oxford.[3] Also in June the Honourable Society of Lincoln's Inn paid its tribute to the late Prime Minister by asking his widow to nominate two of her sons for vacant chambers and by offering to pay the fees for their legal education. Jane Perceval chose her eldest, Spencer, and her eighth child, Dudley. A year later the tellership of the Exchequer was also awarded to Spencer. Even Perceval's one-time greatest rival in the competition to become Prime Minister, George Canning, wrote of him: 'In truth, he was a man with whom one could not be personally at variance; and our rivalry had been a rivalry of circumstances which neither of us could command – not of choice, still less of enmity.'[4]

Eventually, however, it was essential that the assassination be consigned to the past and the political business of the country attended to. The members of the incumbent administration expressed to the Prince Regent their willingness to remain in office, with any of their number that he decided to select as Prime Minister. Consequently, on 8 June 1812, after the usual political posturing and negotiation, Lord Liverpool was appointed to the position. On 23 June 1812 the controversial Orders in Council were at last repealed. However, relations between Britain and America had deteriorated to such an extent that five days earlier on the 18 June a formal declaration of war had been made upon Britain by the American Congress in Washington. History, as ever, marched onwards.

Those who were committed supporters of Perceval, of course, continued to speak of him with the highest of regard: 'an attentive husband, a fond and instructive father, an affectionate friend, and an active servant of the public . . .'.[5] William Wilberforce wrote in his memoirs: 'Perceval had the sweetest of all possible tempers, and was one of the most conscientious men I ever knew; The most instinctively obedient to the dictates of conscience; the least disposed to give pain to others; the most charitable and truly kind and generous creature I ever knew.'[6]

But, as time passed, and things began to return to normal, a more balanced assessment of the legacy of Spencer Perceval began to emerge. Those who had felt it was inappropriate in the period immediately following his death began, now, to express their true opinions on the achievements of the late Prime Minister. Naturally, one of the first and most topical criticisms to emerge referred to his failure to accommodate adequately the problems of John Bellingham. In answer to this criticism his supporters pointed to Perceval's reputation, contrary to what had happened in Bellingham's case, as a charitable man who was always willing to help people in need. They pointed out that it was not always easy to give assistance in these cases and that, as Prime Minister, he was inundated with such requests. In support of this argument some of the newspapers carried the story of a civil servant who had worked abroad for many years on behalf of the government. When the man experienced financial difficulties and asked for help, Perceval gave him £100. The man later became ill, but, before he died, arranged for the money to be returned. Subsequently, the man's daughter wrote to Perceval, through a third party, again requesting financial assistance. His reply to the third party was printed:

> I have this moment received your letter from Miss ——. It is extremely interesting, and certainly seems to be written by a person of a very amiable character. The distress it represents is very great, and the claim for some consideration on the part of his Majesty is well founded. But I have no doubt you will easily imagine how many cases of nearly similar distress are daily arising by the death of public servants, whose salaries could not enable them to make provision for their family, and whose widows and children are therefore left in great distress . . .[7]

In this letter Perceval promises to pass the case on to the Duke of Portland but warns that the Duke has many such 'claims upon him, which are extremely urgent'. He says that he is afraid 'it will be extremely difficult, if not impossible, for him to do it immediately, or very soon'. He ends the letter by saying:

> In the mean time, if you would trouble yourself to be the conveyer of a hundred pounds . . . It is a sum which I advanced him without any intention or wish that he should repay it, and which has been returned to me since his death, at his request in his last illness. I consented to receive it only upon the terms of . . . [returning] it to his family, if, upon enquiry into their circumstances, they should be found to want it . . .[8]

The intention of publicising this story was to show not only the charitable nature of the late Prime Minister, but also to emphasise how difficult it was for every request for assistance to be facilitated by Government. This contention, however, was not accepted by everyone. Those who argued that Perceval had not done enough to help Bellingham, pointed to the case, which had occurred some time earlier, of Isabella Erskine, Countess of Glencairn. She too, like Bellingham, had petitioned the Prime Minister for compensation and she too had failed to receive a satisfactory hearing. Interested by the similarities between her story and Bellingham's, the press re-examined the details of her complaint in the weeks following the assassination.[9] Her claim referred back to the time when Isabella was married to William Lesie Hamilton, who, in 1777, became the Solicitor General, and later Attorney General, of the Leeward Islands in the West Indies. The Countess claimed that 'almost the whole weight and expense of the Administration fell upon Mr Hamilton, including the public table kept for the Officers, the collection and communication of intelligence to the Governments of the neighbouring islands, and to the naval and military officers commanding the forces on the station'.[10]

Unfortunately, the ship carrying the documentary evidence of his expenditure during these years was lost at sea and the gentleman himself died soon afterwards. Subsequently, Isabella married the Earl of Glencairn and her late husband's expenses were neither sought nor received. But then Isabella's circumstances changed when the Earl died before he had inherited a vast fortune from his mother, leaving his widow in a difficult financial situation. She began to petition the government for compensation in the amount of £15,000 as a result of her first husband's expenditure in the West Indies. To back up her case she acquired the testimonies of a number of prominent people, including no less a person than Lord Nelson. Through Mr Wilberforce, Lady Glencairn managed to get an interview with Perceval at Downing Street in 1812. The fact that this produced no favourable result angered her greatly and she published an account of her futile attempts to get her case heard. The Countess placed the blame for her failure squarely upon Perceval's shoulders. In her publication she revealed a number of letters that she had sent to him, as well as a memorial to the King and the testimonies of those who were supporting her claim. Lady Glencairn also accused the Prime Minister of making some very damning comments about Lord Nelson. She reported his words as:

> I am sorry to find, Lady Glencairn, that you rest so much on the force of Lord Nelson's opinion; with me, you could offer no name of less weight; I never thought of Lord Nelson and his services as the world has; So far otherwise, that I considered his death as the salvation of the country: for had he lived, he, in one way or another, would have ruined the nation, and emptied the Treasury.[11]

Perceval denied these comments and wrote to Wilberforce saying that it was as if he had 'damned the King and blasphemed My Maker in the same conversation'.[12] Indeed, it could be argued that the nature of the comments attributed to him by the Countess do look to be out of character for the usually polite, mild-mannered Perceval.

Apart from the analysis of Perceval's record in personal cases like those of John Bellingham and Lady Glencairn, other commentators began to point to what they perceived as his more general political failures. The Marquis of Wellesley was one of the first to attack Perceval in this way. He had criticised Perceval's political leadership in a resignation letter written before the assassination. In it he objected to Perceval's handling of the war and his attitude to Ireland. He declared the late Prime Minister to be 'incompetent to fill that office, although sufficiently qualified for inferior stations'.[13] In allowing his letter to be published in *The Times* soon after the assassination, on 20 May, he was criticised for bad taste, and the adverse reaction negatively impacted upon his chances of becoming Prime Minister.

There were other more general criticisms of the late Prime Minister and his policies:

> As a minister . . . the burning of Copenhagen, the fatal and fruitless expedition to Walcheren, our increasing misunderstanding with America, and the ruinous consequences of our orders in council, all rest upon the shoulders of Mr Perceval and his colleagues in office.[14]

With every private virtue, however, which could adorn a human being, he was . . . the most mischievous of all the bad ministers who, for these thirty years past, have been placed at the head of affairs in this country . . . As minister of finance, he was profuse, and deficient of vigour . . . he seemed to suppose, that rectitude of intention was alone a sufficient reason for self-confidence; and therefore feared nothing because he meant well . . .[15] since the Revolution England has not had a more incapable and unpopular minister, than this unfortunate gentleman . . .[16]

He [Perceval] was more intent upon oppressing Ireland than liberating Spain, and seemed more desirous to overawe the citizens of London, by his barracks in Marylebone Park, than to regain the liberties of Europe . . . as a politician, he was weak and pitiful, and, as an orator, it is easy to form a correct idea of his talents by a reference to his speeches. In these there will be found no glow of eloquence – no ardour of expression – . . . there was nothing to be found but cautious argument, legal subtleties, and personal recrimination; he well knew how to irritate his adversary, but not how to oppress or convert him; he had neither the majestic energy of Pitt, nor the argumentative force of Lord Holland; in ideas and language he was cold and tame, his only warmth was to be found in his temper, not in his eloquence; his views of religion and internal policy were equally as narrow as his general politics; for arts and literature he had no esteem; he neither courted nor fostered them, and if they flourished under his Administration, it was in spite of his neglect and his frowns.[17]

William Cobbett was, of course, one of the fiercest critics of Perceval's politics. Cobbett objected to Perceval's views on the control of the press and he felt that the tragic assassination of the Prime Minister only lent further weight to his argument for a greater degree of freedom in this area. In fact, he indirectly attributed Perceval's assassination to his policies on the freedom of the press. It was his view that, because of the policies of Perceval's government, no paper would have dared publish Bellingham's story. To do so they would have had to accuse Lord Gower and

Sir Shairp of 'neglect of duty'. This, argues Cobbett, would equate to accusing those gentlemen of a crime 'and would amount, therefore, to a libel':

> if he had a free press open to him; if he had found the press ready to receive and promulgate his complaint: if he had had this method open to him of making his wrongs known to the world, it is likely that he would thereby have been satisfied, or, at least, appeased so far as to have prevented him from doing what he did. If he had found an opening through the press, he would have seen his affair discussed.[18]

He also complained about what he saw as Perceval's poor record in government, criticising such policies as high taxation, the Walcheren expedition and 'his conduct relative to the inquiry into the transactions of the Duke of York and Mrs Clark'.[19] Charles Verulam Williams in his book written shortly after Perceval's assassination was equally critical: 'Notwithstanding the general sympathy first expressed at Mr Perceval's untimely fate, it seems the fall of the Man rather than that of the Minister has been most deplored . . . since his demise, most of his measures have already been openly or tacitly condemned.'[20]

In the years since his death, the reputation of Spencer Perceval has not risen to equal that of the countries most renowned leaders. Although the only Prime Minister of Great Britain to have ever been assassinated, he has, for the most part, been overlooked by history. Dickens may have been able to rely on his readers' knowledge in order to understand his reference to Perceval in *The Pickwick Papers*: 'Could the man Weller, in a moment of remorse, have divulged some secret conspiracy for his assassination? It was a dreadful thought. He was a public man: and he turned paler, as he thought of Julius Caesar and Mr Perceval.'[21] But, in more modern times, perhaps no such knowledge could be relied upon.

Perceval's critics point to his reactionary views on a number of topics. He did much to retard the development of an attitude of freedom towards the workings of the press. He was involved in a number of high-profile legal cases in which that freedom was put on trial, such as the Peltier case and the prosecutions of William

Cobbett. He also fought hard throughout his career to stymie any moves towards a reform of the parliamentary system or the abolition of sinecures. It is interesting, however, to note that, although he resisted the idea of change in the granting of sinecures, he did not derive any great benefit from them himself. Apart from the meagre Surveyorship of the Meltings, he never accepted a sinecure. He also, of course, refused the salary to which he was entitled as Chancellor of the Exchequer. When a sinecure worth £2,700 a year, called the tellership of the Exchequer, became available through the death of the incumbent in 1810, it would have been reasonable to expect Perceval to reserve it for his eldest son.[22] This is especially so since he had such a large family to support and was not in possession of a large fortune. Instead, he chose to have it awarded to Charles Yorke, who was a supporter of his and whom he believed was in need of it. King George III mentioned the matter to him in a letter dated 28 January 1810: 'His Majesty cannot in sufficient terms express his sense of the liberality and public spirit which Mr Perceval shows upon this occasion, when an opportunity occurred of making a handsome provision for one of his numerous family, and where indeed it had occurred to His Majesty to have proposed such an arrangement to him.'[23] Lord Palmerston expressed similar sentiments when he wrote: 'It is a great instance of self-denial and disinterestedness on the part of Perceval that with his large family he did not give it . . . to his son.'[24]

Perceval is viewed, with some justification, as an enemy of the Catholic religion. His own religious views meant that he did all he could to retard the growth of Catholicism. He saw Catholics as a threat to his own religion and to the stability of the state, especially where Ireland was concerned. He fought against the idea of granting Catholic emancipation and consistently opposed any motion for additional funds towards the provision of Catholic education. His policies, particularly with regard to the Orders in Council, are also blamed for the war with America that began shortly after his death. It is, perhaps, an indictment of his policies that many of the changes to which he was opposed were later introduced, such as the freedom of the press, the reform of Parliament, Catholic emancipation and, indeed, the repeal of the Orders in Council.

Perhaps his most lasting political accolade is the determination shown by him in his continuance of the war against Napoleon: 'It is no doubt to be regretted that Perceval was unable to abolish the sinecure system, to recognise the Catholic claims, but from the point of view of history it is far more important that he determined, at all costs, to carry on the war in Spain, and was strong enough to rise above all the petty intrigues of the men who might have supported him.'[25]

The war was long and difficult. It had already been going on for many years when Perceval first came to the Cabinet table. When he was appointed Prime Minister, Napoleon looked unstoppable. But, at the time of Perceval's assassination, Wellington had turned the tide of the war in the Iberian Peninsula and Napoleon would soon make the serious mistake of focusing his aggression on Russia. Wellington could not have achieved what he did without the support and determination of the Prime Minister. 'If Perceval had been less determined, or less able, Wellington would have been withdrawn from the peninsula in the spring of 1810. But Perceval was not likely to yield. From his first entry into Parliament, he had been the most consistent of all the opponents to French ambition.'[26]

This was a fact that Wellington himself acknowledged in later years, though at the time of the war he was often quite critical of Perceval's policies.[27] Perceval was also, of course, Chancellor of the Exchequer during this very costly war and brought in five financially prudent budgets, which made it possible to continue funding the war when many thought it impossible to do so.

This stoic attitude portrayed by Perceval in his continuance of the war was a reflection of his general character. He was determined, resilient and full of energy. The primary driving force of his life was his evangelical faith. He was dogmatic, perhaps bigoted, in religion and conservative in politics. As one writer has put it: 'A champion of the old regime, he fought on until his death in defence of a George III tradition and the policy of Pitt.'[28] Not for him the decadence and shifting fashions of the regency period.

He was recognised by all sides of the political divide to be intelligent, principled and honest. His abilities were held in high esteem by those who worked closely with him, and even the Prince Regent, who had been an enemy of his, learned to respect and trust him and, in recognition of that ability, maintained him in power when he need not have done so. He had been in Parliament only a very short time when the great William Pitt the Younger was thinking of him as a likely successor. Although his style of oratory was not superlative, with a reported slight hesitation at the beginning of each sentence, the straightforward clarity and obvious sincerity of his speeches in the House of Commons, born out of his firm religious faith and political principles, gave them impact. When he first took office as Prime Minister very few gave his government a good chance of survival. However, survive it did and in the process managed to negotiate a number of very politically difficult situations. Apart from the war, there were crises such as the illness of King George III, the regency question and the scandal involving the Duke of York and Mrs Clark, all of which led to contentious debates in the House. Perceval handled them all with great political skill. By the end the members of his Cabinet were appreciative of his skills and had become a much more closely knit group than they had been at the beginning.

Perceval was still under 50 years of age at the time of his assassination and had been Prime Minister for only three years, so it is difficult to judge what impact he would have made upon his country had he been able to live out his natural life span. Admittedly, at the point of his death, he was very unpopular with a great number of the general public, and, as his life was cut short before he got the opportunity to endear himself to the nation in the fashion of a William Pitt the Younger or a Lord Nelson, we cannot know if he ever would have. He was not the greatest Prime Minister perhaps, not the most visionary, not the most tolerant with respect to religion, not a statesman to equal the greatest in the world, but an honest, direct and hard-working individual. Benjamin Disraeli would later in the House of Commons make the comment, referring to the killing of President Lincoln, that 'assassination has never changed the history of the world'.[29] Whether the assassination of Spencer Perceval by John Bellingham changed the history of Britain, and in what way and by how much, we can never be sure.

Notes

References abbreviated here are given in full in the Bibliography

Chapter 1

1. D. Gray, *Spencer Perceval: The Evangelical Prime Minister, 1762–1812* (Manchester: Manchester University Press, 1963), p. 426.
2. BL, Perceval MSS, Malmesbury to Perceval, 2 January 1811.
3. W. Jerdan, *The Autobiography of William Jerdan* (4 vols; London: Arthur Hall, Virtue & Co., 1852), vol. 1, p. 134.
4. Among those in the lobby at that moment were Lord Francis Osborne and Mr Nicholas Colborne, who were walking across the lobby about to leave, Colborne having stopped momentarily to chat to an acquaintance of his near one of the pillars; Mr Henry Burgess, a solicitor from Mayfair, was standing close to the door to the House hoping to meet Mr Samuel Whitbread; another solicitor, Mr Boys from Margate, was standing nearby; Mr Francis Romilly, a clerk, was standing by a pillar to the right of the door leading to the House of Commons; William Smith, MP for Norwich, had been on his way into the chamber but, just as the Prime Minister entered, was chatting to someone he had met on the way; standing close to the fireplace was Francis Phillips from Longsight Hall near Manchester.
5. Eyewitnesses vary on the words he actually used. Jerdan (*Autobiography*, vol. 1, p. 134) thought he said: 'Oh God!' or 'Oh my God!', while Henry Burgess heard the cry 'Murder, murder' and the Prime Minister say 'Oh!'. See T. Hodgson, *A Full and Authentic Report of the Trial of John Bellingham, Esq. . . . Also the Arguments of Counsel on Both Sides and Bellingham's Own Defence at Length . . .* (London: Sherwood, Neeley, and Jones, 1812), pp. 25–6.
6. Ibid., p. 30.

Chapter 2

1. Hodgson, *A Full and Authentic Report*, p. 24.
2. Jerdan, *Autobiography*, vol. 1, pp. 136, 137.
3. Parliamentary Debates, vol. 23 (5 May–30 July 1812), p. 166.
4. *Freeman's Journal*, 21 May 1812.
5. Parliamentary Debates, vol. 23, p. 167.
6. Ibid., p. 167.
7. Ibid. pp. 162, 163; *The Times*, 12 May 1812.
8. Parliamentary Debates, vol. 23, p. 164.
9. *Freeman's Journal*, Saturday 16 May 1812.
10. Hodgson, *A Full and Authentic Report*, p. 24.
11. Ibid., p. 23.
12. *Courier*, 12 May 1812; Hodgson, *A Full and Authentic Report*, p. 23;
    M. Gillen, *Assassination of the Prime Minister* (London: Sidgwick
    & Jackson, 1972), p. 13; Anon., *An Account of the Trial of John
    Bellingham for the Wilful Murder of the Right Hon. . . .* (Brighton:
    John Forbes: 1812), p. 8.
13. P. Treherne, *The Right Honourable Spencer Perceval* (London: T.
    Fisher Unwin, 1909), p. 196, quoting Lord Holland.
14. *The Times*, 13 May 1812.
15. Ibid.
16. Ibid.

Chapter 3

1. *Burke's Peerage and Baronetage* (London: Fitzroy Dearborn, *c.*
   1999), p. 956.
2. Treherne, *The Right Honourable Spencer Perceval*, p. 211.
3. *Burke's Peerage and Baronetage*, p. 956; Treherne, *The Right
   Honourable Spencer Perceval*, p. 17; *Gentleman's Magazine* (May
   1812), pp. 499–501.
4. *Gentleman's Magazine* (May 1812), p. 499; *Burke's Peerage and
   Baronetage*, p. 957; Sir B. Burke, *A Genealogical and Heraldic
   Dictionary of the Peerage and Baronetage of the British Empire*
   (London: Harrison, 1857), p. 359.
5. For the nickname 'Little P', see S. Walpole, *The Life of the Right
   Hon. Spencer Perceval* (2 vols; London, 1874, 1912), vol. 2, p. 320,
   and Gray, *Spencer Perceval*, p. 15. For his performance at school,
   see Gray, *Spencer Perceval*, pp. 4–5.
6. Gray, *Spencer Perceval*, p. 6, seems to doubt this story, which he gets
   from *Public Characters, 1809–10*, p. 505.
7. Gray, *Spencer Perceval*, p. 7; *Burke's Peerage and Baronetage*, p. 957.
8. Gray, *Spencer Perceval*, p. 8.

9. Sir Samuel Romilly, *Memoirs* (3 vols; London: John Murray, 1841), vol. 1, p. 9; *The Diary of the Right Honourable William Windham, 1784–1810*, ed. Mrs Henry Baring (London, 1866), p. 71.

10. Walpole, *Life*, vol. 1, p. 12, seems to suggest that Jane's father may have known about the wedding.

11. BL, Harrowby MSS, vol. 8, fo. 146, Perceval to Dudley Ryder; see also Walpole, *Life*, vol. 1, p. 12.

12. Treherne, *The Right Honourable Spencer Perceval*, p. 24.

13. Pitt to Perceval, 2 January 1796, as quoted in Walpole, *Life*, vol. 1, pp. 20–1.

14. Walpole, *Life*, vol. 1, pp. 23–5; Gray, *Spencer Perceval*, p. 13.

15. Walpole, *Life*, vol. 1, p. 26.

16. Gray, *Spencer Perceval*, p. 14.

Chapter 4

1. BL, Perceval MSS, Perceval to Redesdale, 4 December 1802; Gray, *Spencer Perceval*, p. 38.

2. The country was 'shaken to its roots' according to N. Davies, *Europe: A History* (London: Pimlico, 1997), p. 737.

3. Walpole, *Life*, vol. 2, p. 320; Treherne, *The Right Honourable Spencer Perceval*, p. 32.

4. Treherne, *The Right Honourable Spencer Perceval*, p. 32.

5. BL, Perceval MSS, draft of speech at the Crown and Rolls; Gray, *Spencer Perceval*, p. 16.

6. W. Roberts, *The Portraiture of a Christian Gentleman* (London, 1829), pp. 169–70, as quoted in Gray, *Spencer Perceval*, p. 16.

7. For Perceval's donations to charity, see Gray, *Spencer Perceval*, pp. 16, 17.

8. For child factory workers, see ibid., p. 56; for slavery, see ibid., p. 18.

9. See N. Davies, *The Isles: A History* (London: Macmillan, 1999), p. 632.

10. See Parliamentary Debates, vol. 9 (5 March–14 August 1807), pp. 8–12, for speech given on 5 March 1807 on Roman Catholics Army and Navy Bill.

11. *Edinburgh Review* (July 1812), p. 29; Gray, *Spencer Perceval*, p. 19.

12. *Gentleman's Magazine* (June 1812), p. 589; see also Walpole, *Life*, vol. 1, pp. 31, 32; *National Advertiser*, 20 May 1812.

13. *Gentleman's Magazine* (June 1812), p. 589.

14. Pitt to Lord Mornington, 26 January 1798, as quoted in Treherne, *The Right Honourable Spencer Perceval*, pp. 39, 40, and Gray, *Spencer Perceval*, p. 41.

15. *Gentleman's Magazine* (June 1812), p. 590; Gray, *Spencer Perceval*, p. 41.
16. Walpole, *Life*, vol. 1, p. 83. Gray, *Spencer Perceval*, p. 44.
17. *Parliamentary History*, vol. 35, p. 367, June 1800; Hodgson, *A Full and Authentic Report*, p. 4; Gray, *Spencer Perceval*, p. 44.
18. Walpole, *Life*, vol. 1, p. 88.

Chapter 5

1. *Cobbett's Complete Collection of State Trials and Proceedings for High Treason and Other Crimes and Misdemeanours from the Earliest Period to the Present Time* (Hansard, 1809–26), vol. 28, pp. 520–619.
2. Ibid., pp. 520–619.
3. Ibid., pp. 520–619; Gray, *Spencer Perceval*, p. 55; *Gentleman's Magazine* (June 1812), p. 591.
4. Walpole, *Life*, vol. 1, pp. 122–3.
5. Ibid., p. 136.
6. Ibid., p. 136.
7. Ibid., pp. 140, 153.
8. R. Wilberforce and S. Wilberforce, *The Life of William Wilberforce* (5 vols; London: John Murray, 1838), vol. 3, pp. 248, 249.
9. Perceval to Redesdale, 23 January 1806, as quoted in Walpole, *Life*, vol. 1, p. 173.
10. Walpole, *Life*, vol. 1, pp. 191, 192.

Chapter 6

1. C. Hibbert, *George III: A Personal History* (London: Penguin, 1999), p. 251.
2. Gray, *Spencer Perceval*, p. 83, quoting Colchester, *Diary and Correspondence*, vol. 2, p. 69; Brougham, Lord Henry, *The Life and Times of Henry, Lord Brougham, by himself* (3 vols; New York: Harper Brothers, 1871), vol. 2, p. 63; Treherne, *The Right Honourable Spencer Perceval*, p. 66; Walpole, *Life*, p. 201.
3. Hibbert, *George III*, p. 328.
4. David, *Prince of Pleasure*, p. 253.
5. Gray, *Spencer Perceval*, p. 83; the quotations come respectively from J.W. Ward (1st Earl of Dudley), Robert Huish and Sir Samuel Romilly. See also Treherne, *The Right Honourable Spencer Perceval*, p. 67.
6. Walpole, *Life*, vol. 1, p. 205–8, denies that Perceval used the case as a stepping stone to power.
7. Gray, *Spencer Perceval*, pp. 85, 86.
8. For the various amounts paid see Gray, *Spencer Perceval*, p. 87,

Treherne, *The Right Honourable Spencer Perceval*, p. 69, and C.V. Williams, *The Life and Administration of the Right Honourable Spencer Perceval* (London, 1812), p. 319. In any event 'The Book' was published some years later after Perceval's death.

9. Gray, *Spencer Perceval*, p. 89, quoting Lord Glenbervie, *The Diaries of Lord Glenbervie*, ed. F. Bickley (2 vols, London, 1928), vol. 2, pp. 128, 129.

Chapter 7

1. Gray, *Spencer Perceval*, p. 73.
2. *Gentleman's Magazine* (June 1812), p. 591.
3. Williams, *The Life and Administration*, p. 21.
4. Ibid., p. 22.
5. Wilberforce and Wilberforce, *Life*, vol. 3, p. 307.
6. Gray, *Spencer Perceval*, p. 95.
7. Ibid., p. 305.
8. *Gentleman's Magazine* (June 1812), p. 591.
9. Walpole, *Life*, vol. 1, p. 251.
10. Gray, *Spencer Perceval*, p. 141.
11. *Gentleman's Magazine* (June 1812), p. 592.
12. W. Hinde, *George Canning* (London: Collins, 1973), p. 200.
13. Williams, *The Life and Administration*, p. 133.
14. Parliamentary Debates, vol. 12 (19 January–7 March 1809), p. 892, statement made on 20 February 1809.
15. BL, Perceval MSS.
16. Williams, *The Life and Administration*, pp. 136, 137.
17. Lord Colchester, *The Diary and Correspondence of Charles Abbot, Lord Colchester* (3 vols; London: John Murray, 1861), vol. 2, p. 181; Gray, *Spencer Perceval*, p. 207; Walpole, *Life*, vol. 1, p. 329.
18. Walpole, *Life*, vol. 1, p. 347; Hinde, *George Canning*, p. 218.
19. Gray, *Spencer Perceval*, p. 223.
20. Walpole, *Life*, vol. 1, pp. 358–76.
21. Hinde, *George Canning*, p. 228; Gray, *Spencer Perceval*, p. 243.
22. C.J. Bartlett, *Castlereagh* (London: Macmillan, 1966), pp. 96, 97; Hinde, *George Canning*, p. 227.

Chapter 8

1. *Report on the MSS of Earl Bathurst* (Historical Manuscripts Commission, 1923), p. 118.
2. Gray, *Spencer Perceval*, p. 121.
3. Parliamentary Debates, vol. 15 (23 January–1 March 1810), pp. 500–2, 21 February 1810.

4. Williams, *The Life and Administration*, p. 165.

5. It has been argued that this may have been a symptom of the debilitating illness called porphyria, which is a blood disease that upsets the body's chemical balance.

6. S. David, *Prince of Pleasure: The Prince of Wales and the Making of the Regency* (London: Little, Brown & Co., 1998), p. 310.

7. Treherne, *The Right Honourable Spencer Perceval*, pp. 156, 157.

8. Walpole, *Life*, vol. 2, p. 185, 186.

9. Treherne, *The Right Honourable Spencer Perceval*, p. 157; Walpole, *Life*, vol. 2, p. 192.

10. A. Aspinall, *The Correspondence of George, Prince of Wales 1770–1812* (8 vols; London: Cassell, 1963–71), vol. 7, pp. 135–6; see also pp. 190, 191.

11. David, *Prince of Pleasure*, p. 316.

12. Treherne, *The Right Honourable Spencer Perceval*, pp. 159, 160; Walpole, *Life*, vol. 2, p. 194.

13. Treherne, *The Right Honourable Spencer Perceval*, p. 160; Walpole, *Life*, vol. 2, p. 196.

14. Treherne, *The Right Honourable Spencer Perceval*, p. 169.

Chapter 9

1. Aspinall, *Correspondence*, vol. 8, pp. 370–1.

2. Ibid.

3. David, *Prince of Pleasure*, p. 328.

4. Parliamentary Debates, vol. 21 (7 January–16 March 1912), p. 1094, 3 March 1912.

5. Ibid., p. 1151, 3 March 1812.

6. Ibid., p. 1153, 3 March 1812.

7. Parliamentary Debates, vol. 23, p. 71, 7 May 1812.

8. BL, Perceval MSS, Arden to Bishop of Bristol, 30 July 1812.

9. Gray, *Spencer Perceval*, pp. 430–1.

10. Ibid., p. 431.

11. *The Times*, 14 May 1812; *Freeman's Journal*, 18 May 1812.

12. *Salisbury and Winchester Journal*, 25 May 1812; see also Gillen, *Assassination*, p. 27.

13. BL, Perceval MSS, copy by Spencer Perceval junior of a paper written by his father dated 11 March 1800; see also Gray, *Spencer Perceval*, p. 12.

Chapter 10

1. There is some disagreement over Bellingham's actual birthplace: *The Times*, 13 May 1812, says that he was born at St Neots, as

does Treherne, *The Right Honourable Spencer Perceval*, p. 197; Gray, *Spencer Perceval*, p. 455, and Walpole, *Life*, vol. 2, p. 297, both say that he was 'a native of St Neot's'; *Freeman's Journal*, 27 May 1812, states that he was not a native of St Neots; D. Wilson, *The Substance of a Conversation with J. Bellingham, the Assassin of the Late Right Hon. S. Perceval, the Day Previous to his Execution . . .* (London: John Hatchard, 1812), p. 32, states that he was born in London.

2. Gillen, *Assassination*, p. 43.

3. Wilson, *Substance*, p. 32; *Gentleman's Magazine* (May 1812), p. 664.

4. Gillen, *Assassination*, p. 43.

5. *Gentleman's Magazine* (May 1812), p. 664.

6. Wilson, *Substance*, p. 33; *Gentleman's Magazine* (May 1812), p. 665.

7. There is some confusion over the name of this ship. Bellingham himself refers to it as the *Sojus* in his printed petition (see TNA: PRO 30/29/6/11). In *The Whole Proceedings . . . Held at Justice Hall, in the Old Bailey on Wednesday the 13 May, 1812 and Following Days; Being the Fifth Session in the Mayoralty of The Right Hon. Claudius Stephen Hunter, Lord-Mayor of the City of London* (London: R. Butters, 1812), it is referred to as the *Soleure*, as it is in *The Times*, 16 May 1812; For more on this see Kathleen S. Goddard, 'A Case of Injustice? The Trial of John Bellingham', *American Journal of Legal History*, 46/1 (2004), p. 4, note 34, and Gillen, *Assassination*, p. 53.

8. BL Add MS 48216; Gillen, *Assassination*, pp. 53, 55.

9. BL Add. MS 48216.

10. Ibid., a sworn statement made by Bellingham to the Revd Benjamin Beresford, certified by Alexander Shairp, brother to Stephen Shairp the British Consul-General in Russia, on 1 June 1807.

11. Bellingham's printed petition in TNA: PRO 30/29/6/11 and BL Add. MS 48216.

12. BL Add. MS 48216, dated 4 March 1805.

13. BL Add. MS 48216, dated 12 May 1805.

14. BL Add. MS 48216.

15. Bellingham's printed petition in TNA: PRO 30/29/6/11 and BL Add. MS 48216.

16. BL Add. MS 48216.

17. Ibid.

18. Ibid.

Chapter 11

1. Bellingham's printed petition in TNA: PRO 30/29/6/11 and BL Add. MS 48216.
2. Ibid.
3. BL Add. MS 48216.
4. Ibid., 30 July 1807.
5. See Chapter 23; Parliamentary Debates, vol. 23, pp. 240–3; *Freeman's Journal*, 27 May 1812; Williams, *The Life and Administration*, pp. 254–8.
6. BL Add. MS 48216.

Chapter 12

1. BL Add. MS 48216, statement of Mary Stevens.
2. *Freeman's Journal*, 20 May 1812; *Gentleman's Magazine* (May 1812), p. 665; Gillen, *Assassination*, p. 70.
3. From her evidence at the trial, as given in *The Whole Proceedings . . . in the Old Bailey*, pp. 263–74.
4. BL Add. MS 48216, Bellingham to Marquis of Wellesley.
5. BL Add. MS 48216; see also Hodgson, *A Full and Authentic Report*, p. 75; *The Whole Proceedings . . . in the Old Bailey*.
6. Hodgson, *A Full and Authentic Report*, p. 77.
7. Ibid., p. 75; *The Whole Proceedings . . . in the Old Bailey*.
8. Walpole, *Life*, vol. 2, p. 299.
9. BL Add. MS 48216; Hodgson, *A Full and Authentic Report*, p. 75.
10. Gillen, *Assassination*, p. 73.
11. Ibid., p. 73.

Chapter 13

1. BL Add. MS 48216, Mary Stevens's statement.
2. BL Add. MS 48216.
3. Hodgson, *A Full and Authentic Report*, p. 69.
4. TNA: PRO 30/29/6/11; BL Add. MS 48216; see also Hodgson, *A Full and Authentic Report*, pp. 71–4; *The Times*, 14 May 1812.
5. TNA: PRO 30/29/6/11; BL Add. MS 48216; see also Hodgson, *A Full and Authentic Report*, p. 77; *The Times*, 14 May 1812.
6. TNA: PRO 30/29/6/11; BL Add. MS 48216; see also Hodgson, *A Full and Authentic Report*, p. 78; *The Times*, 14 May 1812.
7. *The Times*, 14 May 1812.
8. BL Add. MS 48216.
9. Hodgson, *A Full and Authentic Report*, p. 79; *The Whole Proceedings . . . in the Old Bailey*.

10. Hodgson, *A Full and Authentic Report*, pp. 79, 80.
11. Ibid., p. 80.
12. *The Whole Proceedings . . . in the Old Bailey*; Hodgson, *A Full and Authentic Report*, p. 80.
13. Hodgson, *A Full and Authentic Report*, p. 80.
14. Gascoyne mentioned this meeting when he gave evidence at the inquest and Bellingham's trial.
15. BL Add. MS 48216.
16. Ibid.

Chapter 14

1. BL Add. MS 48216, Mary Stevens's statement.
2. Ibid.
3. Ibid.
4. Hodgson, *A Full and Authentic Report*, p. 86; *The Whole Proceedings . . . in the Old Bailey*.
5. *Freeman's Journal*, 8 June 1812, quoting from *Liverpool Mercury*.
6. All these quotes are from BL Add MS 48216, Mary Stevens's statement.

Chapter 15

1. Parliamentary Debates, vol. 23, p. 217.
2. *Freeman's Journal*, 16 May 1812; *The Globe* carried the story on 12 May, and *The Mercury* on 15 May.
3. See Gray, *Spencer Perceval*, p. 459, n. 1.
4. Gillen, *Assassination*, p. 18, quoting from BL, Perceval MSS.
5. Hodgson, *A Full and Authentic Report*, p. 44; *The Times*, 15 May 1812.
6. BL, Perceval MSS, Lady Redesdale to Margaret Walpole, 12 May 1812.
7. Some of the newspapers give the venue for the inquest as the Cat and Bagpipes, but the Rose and Crown is given in the Coroner's Report.
8. The evidence given by these witnesses comes from Hodgson, *A Full and Authentic Report*, p. 25; *The Times*, 12 May 1812; *Gentleman's Magazine* (May 1812).
9. Parliamentary Debates, vol. 23, p. 168.
10. Ibid., p. 169.
11. Ibid., p. 174.
12. Ibid., p. 176.
13. Ibid., p. 175; Hodgson, *A Full and Authentic Report*, p. 35.
14. Parliamentary Debates, vol. 23, p. 178.

15. *Morning Chronicle*, 13 May 1812.
16. *Freeman's Journal*, 18 May 1812.
17. *Nottingham Journal*, as quoted in Gillen, *Assassination*, pp. 33, 34.
18. *Freeman's Journal*, 4 June 1812, quoting from *Cobbett's Political Register*.
19. Gillen, *Assassination*, p. 35.
20. Parliamentary Debates, vol. 23, p. 178; Hodgson, *A Full and Authentic Report*, p. 36.
21. *The Times*, 15 May 1812.
22. Parliamentary Debates, vol. 23, p. 186. See Gillen, *Assassination*, p. 29.
23. Parliamentary Debates, vol. 23, p. 192; Gillen, *Assassination*, p. 29.
24. Hodgson, *A Full and Authentic Report*, p. 43.
25. *The Times*, 15 May 1812.
26. Parliamentary Debates, vol. 23, pp. 243–7; *The Times*, 14 May 1812.
27. *The Times*, 15 May 1812.
28. *Freeman's Journal*, 18 May 1812.
29. *The Times*, 15 May 1812; *Courier*, 14, 15 May 1812.
30. Parliamentary Debates, vol. 23, p. 223; *The Times*, 16 May 1812.
31. Parliamentary Debates, vol. 23, p. 229. The Duke of Buckingham was assassinated by John Felton in 1628. For more on this assassination, see D. Hanrahan, *Charles II and the Duke of Buckingham: The Merry Monarch and the Aristocratic Rogue* (Stroud: Sutton, 2006), ch. 1.
32. *Freeman's Journal*, 20 May 1812.

Chapter 16

1. *Courier*, 13 May 1812.
2. *Sun*, 14 May 1812.
3. Hodgson, *A Full and Authentic Report*, pp. 37, 38.
4. Ibid., p. 37.
5. Ibid., p. 38.
6. *Freeman's Journal*, 18 May 1812.
7. Ibid.

Chapter 17

1. Hodgson, *A Full and Authentic Report*, p. 47.
2. *The Times*, 16 May 1812.
3. Ibid.
4. Ibid.; see also Hodgson, *A Full and Authentic Report*, p. 48; *Liverpool Mercury*, 22 May 1812.

5. *The Times*, 16 May 1812.
6. Ibid.
7. Hodgson, *A Full and Authentic Report*, pp. 49, 50.
8. *The Times*, 16 May 1812.
9. Hodgson, *A Full and Authentic Report*, pp. 51, 52.
10. Ibid., p. 52.
11. Ibid.
12. This list of names is taken from the report of the trial given in *The Whole Proceedings . . . in the Old Bailey*. There is some confusion regarding the names of jury members. There are a number of differences in the lists given in *The Times*, 16 May 1812, and Hodgson, *A Full and Authentic Report*, p. 54.
13. The Attorney General's opening statement can be found in Hodgson, *A Full and Authentic Report*, pp. 54–60.

Chapter 18

1. Gillen, *Assassination*, p. 95, says that Florence Nightingale was his grandchild.
2. Unless otherwise stated, the evidence of witnesses is taken from *The Whole Proceedings . . . in the Old Bailey*.
3. From Hodgson, *A Full and Authentic Report*, p. 66.
4. Ibid.
5. Ibid.
6. Ibid., p. 67.
7. Gillen, *Assassination*, p. 95; Williams, *The Life and Administration*, p. 252.

Chapter 19

1. This was changed in 1837.
2. *The Whole Proceedings . . . in the Old Bailey*.
3. Ibid.
4. Unless otherwise stated, the version of Bellingham's statement at the trial given here comes from *The Whole Proceedings . . . in the Old Bailey*. There are other versions that, although they differ in some of the words quoted, convey for the most part the same meaning, e.g. Hodgson, *A Full and Authentic Report*, pp. 68–85; *The Times*, 16 May 1812; *Freeman's Journal*, 19, 20 May 1812; Williams, *Life and Administration*, p. 235. Some changes have been made to punctuation in order to aid understanding.
5. *The Times*, 16 May 1812.

Chapter 20

1. Unless otherwise stated, quotations from the witnesses' statements and the cross-examination of witnesses are from *The Whole Proceedings . . . in the Old Bailey*.
2. A variety of names are given for this woman in the press and other contemporary sources, e.g. 'Anne Fidgins' in *The Times*, 16 May 1812, and *Freeman's Journal*, 19 May 1812. I have used the name given in *The Whole Proceedings . . . in the Old Bailey*.
3. Summing-up on behalf of the defence did not begin until 1836.
4. The full list given by Hodgson, *A Full and Authentic Report*, p. 92, is Lord Leveson Gower, Sir Stephen Shairp; Mr Ross and Mr Rick who were secretaries to Lord Gower in St Petersburg; Marquis Douglas, Mr Stuart Minister at St Petersburgh; Marquis Wellesley, Culling Smith, Mr Butler, and Mr Litchfield from the Council Office; Mr Harrison and Mr Hill from the Treasury; Mr Ryder, Mr Beckett, and Mr Breiscke from the Home Department; Colonel McMahon, Mr Read from the Public Office, Bow Street; and Mr Windle, Solicitor.

Chapter 21

1. Justice Manfield's summing-up statement is taken from *The Whole Proceedings . . . in the Old Bailey*.
2. Ibid.
3. Hodgson, *A Full and Authentic Report*, p. 90.
4. Ibid.
5. *The Whole Proceedings . . . in the Old Bailey*; Hodgson, *A Full and Authentic Report*, pp. 90, 91.
6. It lasted eight hours according to the *Gentleman's Magazine* (May 1812), p. 483.
7. Hodgson, *A Full and Authentic Report*, p. 91.
8. *European Magazine*, vol. 61 (May 1812), p. 390.
9. BL Add. MS 48216.
10. Ibid.
11. *The Times*, 16 May 1812.

Chapter 22

1. *Freeman's Journal*, 22 May 1812.
2. *The Times*, 19 May 1812.
3. Ibid.
4. Ibid.
5. Hodgson, *A Full and Authentic Report*, p. 45; Gillen, *Assassination*, p. 114.

6. *Freeman's Journal*, 20 May 1812; Williams, *The Life and Administration*, p. 234.
7. Hodgson, *A Full and Authentic Report*, p. 45; *Freeman's Journal*, 20 May 1812.
8. *The Times*, 19 May 1812.
9. See S. Halliday, *Newgate: London's Prototype of Hell* (Stroud: Sutton, 2006), p. 134, for Dr Forde's opposition to the death penalty.
10. *Freeman's Journal*, 22 May 1812.
11. *The Times*, 19 May 1812.
12. *Freeman's Journal*, 22 May 1812.
13. Ibid.
14. *Morning Chronicle*, 19 May 1812; *Sun*, 18 May 1812.
15. Wilson, *Substance*.
16. Wilberforce states in his diaries that Stephen 'went and devoted himself to trying to bring him [Bellingham] to repentance'; Gillen, *Assassination*, p. 117, believes it was Mr Stephen.
17. Wilson, *Substance*, p. 1.
18. Ibid., p. 2.
19. Ibid., p. 3.
20. Ibid., p. 5.
21. Ibid.
22. Ibid.
23. Ibid., p. 6.
24. Ibid.
25. Ibid.
26. Ibid., p. 10.
27. Ibid.
28. Ibid., p. 11.
29. Ibid.
30. Ibid., p. 12.
31. Ibid., pp. 12–13.
32. Ibid., p. 13.
33. Ibid., p. 14.
34. Ibid., pp. 15–16.
35. Ibid., pp. 17–18.
36. Ibid., p. 18.
37. Ibid., p. 21.
38. Ibid.
39. Ibid., p. 26.
40. Ibid., pp. 30–1.
41. Hodgson, *A Full and Authentic Report*, p. 93.
42. Ibid., pp. 93, 94; *Freeman's Journal*, 23 May 1812.

Chapter 23

1. Gillen, *Assassination*, p. 122, quoting from TNA: HMC, Dropmore MSS, vol. 10, p. 251, Grey to Grenville.
2. Gillen, *Assassination*, p. 122, quoting from Duke of Buckingham, *Court of England during the Regency* (London: Hurst & Blackett, 1856), vol. 1, p. 299.
3. *Freeman's Journal*, 22 May 1812.
4. Lord Byron, *A Self-Portrait*, ed. Peter Quennell (2 vols; London: John Murray, 1950), vol. 1, p. 138.
5. Halliday, *Newgate*, p. 130.
6. *The Times*, 16 May 1812.
7. Ibid., 18 May 1812.
8. Ibid.
9. Ibid., 19 May 1812.
10. Ibid., 18 May 1812.
11. *Freeman's Journal*, 20 May 1812.
12. BL Add MS 48216, Mary Stevens's statement; see Chapter Fourteen.
13. *Liverpool Mercury*, 28 May 1812.
14. Wilson, *Substance*, p. 34.
15. *Gentleman's Magazine* (August 1812), p. 106.
16. See Gillen, *Assassination*, p. 48.
17. *The Times*, 19 May 1812.
18. *Cobbett's Political Register*, vol. 21, no. 21, 23 May 1812.
19. Hodgson, *A Full and Authentic Report*, p. 94.
20. Ibid.
21. *The Times*, 18 May 1812.
22. Hodgson, *A Full and Authentic Report*, p. 94.
23. *Morning Chronicle*, 21 May 1812.
24. Ibid.
25. Ibid.
26. *The Times*, 19 May 1812; Hodgson, *A Full and Authentic Report*, p. 95; *Gentleman's Magazine* (May 1812), pp. 663, 664.
27. Hodgson, *A Full and Authentic Report*, p. 96.
28. *Freeman's Journal*, 22 May 1812.
29. *The Times*, 19 May 1812; *Freeman's Journal*, 22 May 1812.
30. *The Times*, 19 May 1812.
31. Ibid.
32. *Morning Chronicle*, 21 May 1812; see also *Gentleman's Magazine* (May 1812), p. 665.
33. *Freeman's Journal*, 27 May 1812.

Chapter 24

1. Parliamentary Debates, vol. 23, pp. 240–3; *Freeman's Journal*, 27 May 1812; Williams, *Life and Administration*, pp. 254–8.
2. Parliamentary Debates, vol. 23, p. 173.
3. For the letters see TNA: PRO 30/29/6/11.
4. TNA: PRO 30/29/6/11, *'Bellingham'* by G. Peacock;
5. *Freeman's Journal*, 4 June 1812.
6. *Cobbett's Political Register*, vol. 21, no. 22, 30 May 1812; see also *Freeman's Journal*, 4 June 1812.
7. *Cobbett's Political Register*, vol. 21, no. 22, 30 May 1812; see also *Freeman's Journal*, 4 June 1812.
8. *Cobbett's Political Register*, vol. 21, no. 22, 30 May 1812; see also *Freeman's Journal*, 4 June 1812.
9. *Cobbett's Political Register*, vol. 21, no. 22, 30 May 1812; see also *Freeman's Journal*, 4 June 1812.
10. *Freeman's Journal*, 13 June 1812.
11. TNA: PRO 30/29/6/11.
12. Gillen, *Assassination*, p. 143.
13. Ibid.
14. *Freeman's Journal*, 29 May 1812
15. *Dublin Journal*, 2 June 1812.
16. TNA: PRO 30/29/6/11.
17. See Chapter Twenty-one.
18. TNA: PRO 30/29/6/11.
19. *Liverpool Mercury*, 13 November 1812.
20. TNA: PRO 30/29/6/11; Gillen, *Assassination*, p. 162. Gillen wonders whether the Henry Stevens who married a granddaughter of old James Nevill of Wigan and died prosperous in London in 1875 was one of their children. She writes: 'it is pleasant to realize that he could successfully survive so unhappy a background.'
21. Gray, *Spencer Perceval*, p. 464.
22. BL Add. MS 49188, Arden to the Bishop of Bristol, 30 July 1812.
23. *Northamptonshire Daily Record*, 14 May 1900.
24. *Freeman's Journal*, 13 June 1812.
25. *Oxford Dictionary of National Biography*; Walpole, *Life*, vol. 2, pp. 329–32; Treherne, *The Right Honourable Spencer Perceval*, pp. 204–7; Gillen, *Assassination*, pp. 153, 155.
26. For Williams's account of his dream, see Walpole, *Life*, vol. 2, pp. 330–2; Treherne, *The Right Honourable Spencer Perceval*, pp. 204–7.
27. *Freeman's Journal*, 5 June 1812; see also Walpole, *Life*, vol. 2, p. 329, quoting from Rokeby, *Diary*, 5 June, vol. 2, p. 386.

28. Treherne, *The Right Honourable Spencer Perceval*, pp. 199–203, 243–50.

Chapter 25

1. W.C. Townsend, *Modern State Trials* (2 vols; London: Longman, 1850), vol. 1, p. 318.
2. Gillen, *Assassination*, p. 112.
3. *Freeman's Journal*, 21 May 1812.
4. Ibid.
5. S. Warren, *Miscellanie, Critical, Imaginative and Juridical* (2 vols; Edinburgh and London: William Blackwood, 1855), vol. 2, p. 148
6. *Freeman's Journal*, 21 May 1812.
7. *Morning Chronicle*, 21 May 1812.
8. *Freeman's Journal*, 20 May 1812.
9. Romilly, *Memoirs*, vol. 2, p. 257.
10. G. Latham Browne, *Narrative of State Trials in the Nineteenth Century: First Period, 1801–1830* (2 vols; London: Sampson Low, Marston, Searle & Rivington, 1882), vol. 2. p. 62.
11. A. Knapp and W. Baldwin, *The Newgate Calendar* (4 vols; London: 1824–6), vol. 4, pp. 82, 92.
12. Brougham, *Statesman*, vol. 2, p. 19.
13. Cobbett, *Twelve Sermons* (London, 1823), p. 154.
14. As quoted in Gillen, *Assassination*, p. 52.
15. Ibid., p. 107.
16. J.A. Lovat-Fraser, 'The Trial of Bellingham', *Juridical Review* (1917), p. 65.
17. Ibid.
18. I. Ray, *A Treatise on the Medical Jurisprudence of Insanity* (Boston, 1838).
19. R.M. Bousfield and R. Merrett, *Report of the Trial of D. McNaughten for the Wilful Murder . . .* (London, 1843).
20. I am indebted here to the consideration of this question given in Goddard, 'A Case of Injustice?'.
21. By Goddard, in ibid.
22. Judge Mansfield from the trial; see *The Whole Proceedings . . . in the Old Bailey*.
23. Goddard, 'A Case of Injustice', p. 15, argues that he did not.
24. Mansfield from the trial.
25. See Goddard, 'A Case of Injustice'.
26. *The Whole Proceedings . . . in the Old Bailey*.

Chapter 26

1. Thomas Moore, 'Lines on the Death of Mr Perceval'.
2. Gillen, *Assassination*, p. 163; Gray, *Spencer Perceval*, p. 464.
3. Gray, *Spencer Perceval*, pp. 465–6.
4. Hinde, *George Canning*, p. 247, quoting Canning to his mother, 16 May 1812.
5. Hodgson, *A Full and Authentic Report*, p. 6.
6. Wilberforce and Wilberforce, *Life*, vol. 4, p. 26.
7. *Freeman's Journal*, 21 May 1812.
8. Ibid.
9. *Freeman's Journal*, 25 May, 30 June 1812.
10. *Freeman's Journal*, 25 May 1812; see also *A Representation of the Severity, Injustice and Impolicy Directed to a Case Sanctioned by the High Authority of the Late Lord Nelson . . . Exposing the Defamation of that Illustrious Character by the Late Right Hon. . . .* (London: M. Jones, 1812); Gray, *Spencer Perceval*, pp. 125, 126.
11. *A Representation of the Severity, Injustice and Impolicy*; see also *Freeman's Journal*, 25 May 1812; Gray, *Spencer Perceval*, pp. 125, 126.
12. Isabella, Countess of Glencairn, *A Letter to the Rt Hon. Spencer Perceval . . . Containing an Appeal to the British Nation* (Bristol 1812); BL Add MS 38191, fo. 226; BL Add. MS 38247, fo. 136.
13. *The Times*, 20 May 1812.
14. Hodgson, *A Full and Authentic Report*, pp. 6, 7.
15. Gillen, *Assassination*, p. 164, quoting from *Edinburgh Review*.
16. Ibid., quoting from *Monthly Magazine* (1812) pt. 1, p. 485.
17. *Freeman's Journal*, 7 June 1812, quoting from *The Statesman*.
18. *Freeman's Journal*, 4 June 1812.
19. Ibid., 13 June 1812.
20. Williams, *Life and Administration*, p. iv.
21. Dickens, *The Pickwick Papers*, ch. 25.
22. Treherne, *The Right Honourable Spencer Perceval*, p. 114; Walpole, *Life*, vol. 2, pp. 66–8.
23. Treherne, *The Right Honourable Spencer Perceval*, p. 116; Walpole, *Life*, vol. 2, p. 68.
24. Treherne, *The Right Honourable Spencer Perceval*, p. 117; Walpole, *Life*, vol. 2, p. 68.
25. Treherne, *The Right Honourable Spencer Perceval*, p. 177.
26. Walpole, *Life*, vol. 2, p. 113.
27. Gray, *Spencer Perceval*, p. 469; see also the letter from Wellington to Dudley Perceval, 6 June 1835, quoted in Walpole, *Life*, vol. 2, pp. 242–4.

28. Treherne, *The Right Honourable Spencer Perceval*, p. 176.
29. Speech by Benjamin Disraeli in the House of Commons, 1 May 1865.

BIBLIOGRAPHY

Anon., *An Account of the Trial of John Bellingham for the Wilful Murder of the Right Hon. . . .* (Brighton: John Forbes, 1812)

Anon., *An Account of the Trial of John Bellingham, for the Wilful Murder of the Right Hon. . . .* (Leeds: B. Dewhirst, 1812)

Anon., *An Authentic Account of the Horrid Assassination of the Honourable Spencer Perceval* (London, 1812)

Anon., *A Full Report of the Trial of John Bellingham for the Murder of . . . Spencer Perceval . . . Including the Arguments of Counsel and his Own Defence at Length . . . Together with a Copy of Bellingham's Memorial, and of Lord Gower's Statement . . .* (Hull: J. Craggs and J. Simmons, 1812)

Anon., *A Funeral Discourse . . . on the Death of Spencer Perceval* (London, 1812)

Anon., *Inscription for the Monument of the Departed Minister (Spencer Perceval)* (London: 1812)

Anon., *The Trial of J. Bellingham, a Liverpool Merchant, at the Old Bailey, on Friday, May 15, 1812, for the Assassination of . . .* (London: W. Lewis, 1812)

Anon., *Universal Sympathy, or the Martyr'd Statesman; a Poem on the Death of . . . Spencer Perceval* (London, 1812)

Aspinall, A., *The Correspondence of George, Prince of Wales 1770–1812* (8 vols; London: Cassell, 1963–71)

Ashley, M., *A Brief History of British Kings and Queens* (London: Robinson, 2002)

Bartlett, C.J., *Castlereagh* (London: Macmillan, 1966)

Brougham, Lord Henry, *The Life and Times of Henry, Lord Brougham, by himself* (3 vols; New York: Harper Brothers, 1871)

Byron, Lord, *A Self-Portrait*, ed. Peter Quennell (2 vols; London: John Murray, 1950)

Chalmers, George, *An Appeal to the Generosity of the British Nation . . . on Behalf of the Aflicted Widow and Unoffending Offspring of the Unfortunate Mr Bellingham* (London, 1812)

Colchester, Lord, *The Diary and Correspondence of Charles Abbot, Lord Colchester* (3 vols; London: John Murray, 1861)

David, S., *Prince of Pleasure: The Prince of Wales and the Making of the Regency* (London: Little, Brown & Co., 1998)

Davies, N., *Europe: A History* (London: Pimlico, 1997)

—— *The Isles: A History* (London: Macmillan, 1999)

Englefield, D., Seaton, J. and White, I., *Facts about the British Prime Ministers: A Compilation of Biographical and Historical Information* (New York: H.W. Wilson Co., 1995)

Foster, R.E., '"Little P": The Life and Times of Spencer Perceval', *History Review* (December 2005), 13–18

Fraser, A. (shorthand writer), *The Trial of John Bellingham for the Assassination . . .* (London: R. Mercer, 1812)

Gillen M., *Assassination of the Prime Minister* (London: Sidgwick & Jackson, 1972)

Goddard, Kathleen S., 'A Case of Injustice? The Trial of John Bellingham', *American Journal of Legal History*, 46/1 (2004), 1–25

Gower, Lord Granville Leveson, *Gower, Lord Granville Leveson (First Earl Granville): Private Correspondence 1781–1821*, ed. Castalia, Countess Granville (2 vols; London: John Murray, 1916)

Gray, D., *Spencer Perceval: The Evangelical Prime Minister, 1762–1812* (Manchester: Manchester University Press, 1963)

Hague, W., *William Pitt the Younger: A Biography* (London: HarperCollins, 2004)

Halliday, S., *Newgate: London's Prototype of Hell* (Stroud: Sutton, 2006)

Hibbert, C., *George III: A Personal History* (London: Penguin, 1999)

Hinde, W., *George Canning* (London: Collins, 1973)

Hodgson, T., *A Full and Authentic Report of the Trial of John Bellingham, Esq. . . . Also the Arguments of Counsel on Both Sides and Bellingham's Own Defence at Length . . .* (London: Sherwood, Neeley, and Jones, 1812)

Jarrett, D., *Pitt the Younger* (London: Weidenfeld and Nicolson, 1974)

Jay, M., *The Unfortunate Colonel Despard* (London: Bantam Press, 2004)

Jerdan, W., *The Autobiography of William Jerdan* (4 vols; London: Arthur Hall, Virtue & Co., 1852)

Jupp, P., *Lord Grenville 1759–1834* (Oxford: Oxford University Press, 1985)

Knapp, A. and Baldwin, W., *The Newgate Calendar* (4 vols; London: 1824–6)

Latham Browne, G., *Narrative of State Trials in the Nineteenth Century: First Period. 1801–1830* (2 vols; London: Sampson Low, Marston, Searle & Rivington, 1882), vol. 2

Lovat-Fraser, J.A., 'The Trial of Bellingham', *Juridical Review* (1917), 62–8

Peck, Robert, *Trial of John Bellingham* (Hull, 1812)

Perceval, D., *The Church Question in Ireland* (London: Blackwood, 1844)

Porter, R., *Madmen: A Social History of Madhouses, Mad-Doctors & Lunatics* (Stroud: Tempus, 2004)

Reid, L., *Charles James Fox* (London: Longman, 1969)

Reilly, R., *Pitt the Younger 1759–1806* (London: Cassell, 1978)

Romilly, Sir Samuel, *Memoirs* (3 vols; London: John Murray, 1841)

Smith, E.A., *Lord Grey, 1764–1845* (Stroud: Sutton, 1996)

Townsend, W.C., *Modern State Trials* (2 vols; London: Longman, 1850)

Treasure, G., *Who's Who in Late Hanoverian Britain* (London: Shepheard-Walwyn, 1997)

Treherne, P., *The Right Honourable Spencer Perceval* (London: T. Fisher Unwin, 1909)

Walpole, S., *The Life of the Right Hon. Spencer Perceval* (2 vols; London, 1874, 1912)

Warren, S., *Miscellanie, Critical, Imaginative and Juridical* (2 vols; Edinburgh and London: William Blackwood, 1855)

Wilberforce, R. and Wilberforce, S., *The Life of William Wilberforce* (5 vols; London: John Murray, 1838)

Williams, C.V., *The Life and Administration of the Right Honourable Spencer Perceval* (London, 1812)

Williams, Orlo Cyprian, *The Topography of the Old House of Commons* (London, 1953)

Wilson, D., *The Substance of a Conversation with J. Bellingham, the Assassin of the Late Right Hon. S. Perceval, the Day Previous to his Execution . . .* (London: John Hatchard, 1812)

Index